CW00801453

Praise for *Gandhi's Tru*
Fundamentalism and 1 vuc......

"A splendid effort to bring wisdom and sanity to a world mired in religious fundamentalism and hyper-nationalism. The book throbs with creative and critical reinterpretations of Gandhi's Truth from the margins, directed to universal well-being."

—Felix Wilfred, Emeritus Professor,
University of Madras, Chennai, India

"Readers will not only learn new insights about Gandhi but will reconsider how we should approach truth. Clarke and Pickard bring together essays that illustrate the genius and strength of Gandhi's pursuit of truth. What really sets this book apart is their insightful critique of Gandhi, making his message more relevant for today."

—F. Douglas Powe Jr., Director of the Lewis Center for Church
Leadership, and James C. Logan Professor of Evangelism,
Wesley Theological Seminary, Washington, DC, USA

"Gandhi's ideas have informed and infuriated, inspired and irritated nationalists, social justice practitioners, scholars of religion and society, and those working on issues related to peace and human dignity. Without succumbing to hagiography, the authors of *Gandhi's Truth in an Age of Fundamentalism and Nationalism* offer us much to interactively reflect upon and prudently put into practice in these messy and hazardous times. Ideas do travel, and ideas do return home, but they return transformed, and the contributors are to be commended for exploring Gandhi's ideas from their own locations with bold frankness, knowledgeable thoughtfulness, and forward-looking engagement."

—Jayakiran Sebastian, Dean and H. George Anderson Professor of
Mission and Cultures, United Lutheran Seminary,
Gettysburg and Philadelphia, USA

Gandhi's Truths in an Age of Fundamentalism and Nationalism

GANDHI'S TRUTHS

in an Age of
FUNDAMENTALISM
and
NATIONALISM

Editors
**Sathianathan Clarke and
Stephen Pickard**

Fortress Press
Minneapolis

GANDHI'S TRUTHS IN AN AGE OF FUNDAMENTALISM AND NATIONALISM

Scripture quotations are from New Revised Standard Version Bible, copyright © 1989 National Council of the Churches of Christ in the United States of America. Used by permission. All rights reserved worldwide.

Cover image: Silhouette Of Mahatma Gandhi Statue Against Sky. Getty Images, Srividya Vanamamalai / EyeEm, Creative #: 65473999
Cover design: L. Owens

Print ISBN: 978-1-5064-6998-0
eBook ISBN: 978-1-5064-6999-7

Contents

Acknowledgments

This volume of essays had its origin in a consultation in Canberra to mark the 150th anniversary of the birth of Mahatma Gandhi in 2019. The consultation was jointly hosted by the *Australian Centre for Christianity* and the *Public and Contextual Theology Research Centre* at Charles Sturt University. We are very grateful to both centers of the university for hosting and supporting this event and especially the staff of the centers, Hazel Francis, Sarah Stitt, and Lauren Bartley. In particular, we wish to acknowledge the address delivered by His Excellency Dr. A. M. Gondane, High Commissioner, High Commission of India, Canberra. We are extremely grateful to Professor Satendra Nandan for his contributions at the consultation in public lecture, poetry, and the release of his book *Gandhianjali*. We thank those scholars who attended the consultation and gave papers that have become chapters for this present volume: Sathianathan Clarke, Peter Hooton, William W. Emilsen, Stephen Pickard, and Peter Walker. Four scholars who were not at the consultation subsequently wrote chapters for this volume: C. Anthony Hunt, Suka Joshua, Anderson H. M. Jeremiah, and Josiah Ulysses Young III. These scholars took Gandhi from the Canberra context into the United States, India, and the United Kingdom. To other participants at the consultation, we offer our grateful thanks. Thanks are also due to Fortress Press for publishing these essays and especially to Jesudas Athyal, acquiring editor, and Elvis Ramirez, production manager. As ever, we offer our thanks and gratitude to our spouses, Prema and Jennifer, for their constant support and encouragement.

Sathianathan Clarke, Washington, DC (USA)
Stephen Pickard, Canberra (Australia)

Brief Biographical Information on Editors and Authors

Editors

Sᴀᴛʜɪᴀɴᴀᴛʜᴀɴ Cʟᴀʀᴋᴇ is the Bishop Sundo Kim Chair in World Christianity and professor of theology, culture, and mission at Wesley Theological Seminary. He has taught previously at United Theological College in Bangalore, India, and as visiting faculty at Harvard University Divinity School. Clarke is the author of *Competing Fundamentalisms: Violent Extremism in Christianity, Islam, and Hinduism* (2017) and *Dalits and Christianity* (1998) and is coeditor of *The Oxford Handbook of Anglican Studies* (OUP, 2016), *Dalit Theology in the Twenty-First Century* (2010), and *Religious Conversion in India: Modes, Motivations, and Meanings* (2007).

Sᴛᴇᴘʜᴇɴ Pɪᴄᴋᴀʀᴅ is executive director of the Australian Centre for Christianity and Culture and professor of theology at Charles Sturt University in Australia. He is also currently an assistant bishop in the Canberra-Goulburn Diocese in Australia. He was Head of Charles Sturt University's School of Theology from 1998 to 2006. Since then, he has served as an Anglican bishop in the Archdiocese of Adelaide, visiting fellow at Ripon College Cuddesdon, acting CEO Anglicare Canberra and Goulburn, and a priest in a Canberra parish. He is the author of several books, including *Seeking the Church: An Introduction to Ecclesiology* (2012) and *In-between God: Theology, Community, and Discipleship* (2011).

Authors

WILLIAM W. EMILSEN is an associate professor in church history and world religions at Charles Sturt University and a principal researcher at its Public and Contextual Research Centre. He has recently written *Fighting Spirit: A History of Christianity at Warruwi, Goulburn Island* (2016) and the biography of a leading Indigenous leader, *Charles Harris: A Struggle for Justice* (2019). He has had a long-term interest in the life and thought of Mahatma Gandhi and Australian Aboriginal history. He was the inaugural president of the Uniting Church National Church History Society (2017–19) and was the recipient of the 2015 Australian Religious History Fellowship awarded by the State Library of New South Wales. He lives in Leura in the Blue Mountains near Sydney with his wife, Carolyn.

PETER HOOTON is responsible for the Research Secretariat, which undertakes work in public theology at the Australian Centre for Christianity and Culture on Charles Sturt University's Canberra campus. He is a former career diplomat with experience in Africa, the Middle East, South and Southeast Asia, and the South Pacific. He is now a research fellow with the university's Public and Contextual Theology Research Centre and author of *Bonhoeffer's Religionless Christianity in Its Christological Context* (2020).

C. ANTHONY HUNT is an ordained elder in the United Methodist Church and currently serves as the senior pastor of Epworth Chapel UMC in Baltimore, Maryland. He is professor of Systematic, Moral and Practical Theology, and Dunning Permanent Distinguished Lecturer at St. Mary's Ecumenical Institute, and also teaches on the partner/adjunct faculties at Wesley Theological Seminary in Washington, DC, and United Theological Seminary in Dayton, Ohio. He is the author of fourteen books, including volume 4 of *Holding on to Hope: Essays, Sermons, and Prayers on Religion and Race* (2021), *I've Seen the Promised Land: Martin Luther King, Jr. and the 21st Century Quest for the Beloved Community* (2020), *Come Go with Me: Howard Thurman and a Gospel of Radical*

Inclusivity (2019), and *Blessed Are the Peacemakers: A Theological Analysis of the Thought of Howard Thurman and Martin Luther King, Jr.* (2006).

ANDERSON H. M. JEREMIAH is associate professor of religion and politics at Lancaster University and is an Anglican theologian. Anderson's research primarily centers on the study of contemporary Christianity and the sociocultural implications of the shift of Christianity to the Global South. He has authored numerous articles and a book titled *Community and Worldview among Paraiyars of South India: "Lived" Religion* (2012). His areas of academic expertise include Christian theology in Asia, postcolonial approaches to theology, Anglican communion, Dalit studies, contextual theologies, history of Christianity, modern missionary movements, inculturation and faith, biblical hermeneutics, economics and liberation theology, encounters between Christianity and other religions, interfaith understanding, religious fundamentalism and politics, religious pluralism, and politics and society in India.

SUKA JOSHUA is associate professor of English and former chaplain at Lady Doak College in Madurai, India. She studied at American College at Madurai and Madras Christian College, earning her PhD from Madurai Kamaraj University. She recently received a MA in theology at Wesley Theological Seminary in Washington, DC. As chaplain at Lady Doak, where 20 percent of the students are Christian, she supported students of all castes and religions with unbiased tolerance and inclusiveness.

PETER WALKER lectures in theology and history within Charles Sturt University and is principal of United Theological College in Sydney. He is an ordained minister of the Uniting Church in Australia and has studied history, philosophy, and theology at the University of New South Wales, McGill University, and Charles Sturt University. Peter has been president of the Australian Capital Territory Council of Churches and assistant director of the Charles Sturt University Centre for Public and Contextual Theology and is currently assistant editor of the International Journal of Public Theology.

JOSIAH ULYSSES YOUNG III is professor of systematic theology at Wesley Theological Seminary and the author of numerous books and articles. Young specializes in Pan-African theology, which is a synthesis of Black theology, African theology, traditional African religion, and Africana religion generally. He also specializes in European political theology, notably that of Dietrich Bonhoeffer and Jürgen Moltmann. His forthcoming book is *Black Lives Matter: A Contemporary Afro-American Theology*, to be published by Lexington Books.

CHAPTER 1

Introduction

Sathianathan Clarke and Stephen Pickard

Our world is struggling with Covid-19. It arrived like a global invasion in 2020. The virus took the uncommon pathway of an interspecies mutation as it made its visitation upon our worldwide human family.[1] The age-old virus of fear and hatred, however, did not need the help of other species. Such violence has a long history of violation against religious, ethnic, and cultural others. Religion unfortunately plays an ambivalent role in dealing with feared and despised others. It sears even as it heals, ruptures even as it sutures, severs even as it reconciles, and kills even as it brings life. It is ironic. Religions profess to bring peace on earth and goodwill among men and women. Yet they are often identified more with violence than with peace through our twenty-first century. Of course, there are many economic, social, cultural, political, and psychological triggers for the spread of violence in the world today. Religion, however, is also responsible for justifying violation and nurturing violence. "This does not mean," according to Mark Juergensmeyer, "that religion causes violence, nor does it mean that religious violence cannot, in some cases, be justified by other means. But it does mean that religion often provides the framework, mores and symbols that make possible bloodshed—even catastrophic acts of terrorism."[2] So even if religion is not the only source fueling violence on the world

---

1 Originating in bats (most likely from the horseshoe bat) from the city of Wuhan in China, the virus made it through another host species to latch onto human beings in a devastating way. Alice Latinne et al., "Origin and Cross-species Transmission of Bat Coronaviruses in China," *Nature Communications* 11 (2020), https://doi.org/10.1038/s41467-020 -17687-3.

2 Mark Juergensmeyer, *Terror in the Mind of God: The Global Rise of Religious Violence* (Berkeley: University of California Press, 2003), xi.

stage, some of the assault on peace stems from extreme religious agents. Violent this-worldly tactics are justified to shape transcendent ideals.

Religious fundamentalisms of various stripes have had a field day in the twenty-first century. The shrinking world is imagined to be a sprawling theater of sacred drama. Such fundamentalisms, which we take to be religions driven to their extremes (religious extremism), are spreading effectively in some regions of the world. These religious ideologies draw creatively from brawny, inflexible, and imperial scriptural and theological storehouses to inspire movements in the public square that violently alter the world for their respective gods. The origin of the expression *fundamentalism* is narrow and parochial. It emerges from early-twentieth-century American Protestant Christianity.[3] In that historical context, it was used to describe a high view of biblical authority based in literalism and the inerrancy of Scripture, partly in reaction to the wave of modern science, rational philosophy, and antireligious secularism escalating during the last century. However, even at that time, religious fundamentalism was deeply invested in politics. It exhibited a collective will in the United States to construct a strongly Christian nation. Over the last twenty-five years, though, the term is employed more widely across the world, used both in relation to other branches of Christianity and in relation to non-Christian religions. Other religions joined Christianity in leaving behind the "world-renouncing" form of inward religion and embracing the "world-conquering" form of muscular religion turned outward.[4] While the former way of being religious retreats quietly into its own alternate domain, the

---

3 Martin E. Marty attests that the term *fundamentalism*, which originated in the United States, "cannot be found in dictionaries before the 1920s." Martin E. Marty, *When Faiths Collide* (Malden, MA: Blackwell, 2005), 7. For a comprehensive account of the origins and development of fundamentalism in the United States, see Sathianathan Clarke, *Competing Fundamentalisms: Violent Extremism in Christianity, Islam, and Hinduism* (Louisville, KY: Westminster John Knox, 2017), 35–62.

4 These terms are explored in Gabriel A. Almond, Emmanuel Sivan, and R. Scott Appleby, "Examining the Cases," in *Fundamentalisms Comprehended*, ed. Martin E. Marty and R. Scott Appleby (Chicago: University of Chicago Press, 1995), 445–82. Islam is perhaps an exception insofar as it has always had a persistent orientation to the public domain.

latter "world-conquering" form of religion is especially prone to violent actions against those considered nonbelievers.

Violence associated with religious extremism is not a modern phenomenon. The history of religions is littered with instances of intrareligious and interreligious violence. Raimon Panikkar, who knows multiple religions well, says, "Religion includes what is best in human beings. . . . But religion has also produced what is worst, what is most wicked. Religion has not only been an opiate but a poison as well."[5]

Perhaps what is most disturbing in our time is the way in which fundamentalist religions and nation-states collude with one another in the interest of serving high-minded ideologies of power. Religious fundamentalisms strategically and systematically in league with other economic, political, and cultural forces are in the business of seeking to carve out strong nation-states. Nation-states seek to capture extremist religious sensibilities for the purpose of enlisting them in the ascendancy of ideological nationalism. Indeed, it seems that religious fundamentalism and ideologically driven nationalism are deeply entwined in a self-serving manner. Thus Christian, Hindu, Jewish, Buddhist, and Muslim fundamentalisms need legitimate public platforms to translate hallowed belief into mundane practices. Upholding and cultivating strong belief in a comprehensive worldview is only one of the theological ingredients that go into the configuration of violent religious fundamentalisms. Cognitive assent within headstrong believers must also be accompanied by stringent mechanisms to shape everyday living in the real world. This is why the nation-state is needed for religious fundamentalists. On the one hand, religious nationalism craftily employs religio-cultural mantras and rituals to publicly endorse and reinforce common belief. On the other hand, the collusion between such religious fundamentalism and the nation-state greedy for power and control comes to its fulfillment when the nation-state secures the divine imprimatur for the enforcement of macrobeliefs as everyday micropractices of all persons. This often occurs by the use

5 Raimon Panikkar, *The Experience of God: Icons of the Mystery* (Minneapolis: Fortress, 2006), 111.

of violation and violence meted out against other religious and secular communities.

Propagators of absolutist sacred truths collaborate with stealthy promoters of fixed practices in the nation-state. Strong nation-states in the twenty-first century tap into religions across the world. As a 2017 Pew Research study states, "More than 80 countries favor a specific religion, either as an official, government-endorsed religion or by affording one religion preferential treatment over other faiths."[6] Differing compacts between the religion of the majority and a stable nation-state operate in the Christian United States and Zambia, Muslim Afghanistan and Malaysia, Buddhist Bhutan and Sri Lanka, and Hindu India and Nepal. While the protection and promotion of religion by the national state is mostly written into the constitution by countries where Islam[7] and Christianity[8] are majority religions, this volume focuses on majority-Hindu India and the majority-Christian United States. Both these countries claim to keep religion and state separate. However, increasingly, Hinduism and Christianity play a crucial role in influencing politics and inspiring citizens to carve out a Hindu (Hindutva) or Judeo-Christian (redeemer nation) sociopolitical order that violates the rights of those of other religious traditions.

Numerous scholars have analyzed the pact between strong nationalism and Hindu and Christian fundamentalism over the last 150 years.[9] Without getting into the historical interlock of fundamentalist Hinduism (Hindutva) in India and fundamentalist Christianity (white evangelicals) in the United States, we merely point to the remarkable,

---

6 "Many Countries Favor Specific Religions, Officially or Unofficially," Pew Research Center, October 3, 2017, https://www.pewforum.org/2017/10/03/many-countries-favor -specific-religions-officially-or-unofficially/.

7 "Islam is the world's most common official religion. Among the 43 countries with a state religion, 27 (63%) name Sunni Islam, Shia Islam or just Islam in general as their official faith." "Many Countries."

8 "Christianity is the second most common official religion around the world. Thirteen countries (30% of countries with an official religion) declare Christianity, in general, or a particular Christian denomination to be their official state religion." "Many Countries."

9 For a review of literature on Christian and Hindu fundamentalism over the last 150 years, see Clarke, *Competing Fundamentalisms.*

even if alarming, hold they have on contemporary national politics. In the case of India, Prime Minister Narendra Modi has spearheaded a political resurgence of Hindutva (Hindu nationalism) over the last couple of decades. With a sweeping majority won in the parliament in the 2019 election, his brand of Hindu nationalism equates being Indian with being Hindu (79.8 percent of the total population in the 2011 census). In the words of Anthony J. Parel, "Hindutva feeds on Islamophobia, and to a lesser extent on Christianophobia. Its long-term goal is the hinduization of the whole of India. Its short-term goal is the intimidation of the minorities, especially Muslims and Christians— their persons, properties and institutions—and places of worship are under constant threat from Hindu fundamentalists."[10] With regard to the United States, we draw attention to the confidence expressed by 63 percent of white evangelicals about the success with which Christian beliefs have transformed American national policies during the last four years. According to a Pew Research Center survey, "Heading into the 2020 election season . . . white evangelicals largely see Trump as fighting for their beliefs and advancing their interests, and they feel their side generally has been winning recently on political matters important to them."[11]

Firmly embedded within the fields of religion, theology, history, and literature, the authors of this volume concede that fundamentalist religions do envisage and work toward state capture. Even if steeped in resources that can heal the world, religions have recast the capacity and credence of their own agency to affect our age adversely. On the one hand, they have channelized religious faith, which bubbled within enflamed hearts, to spill over calculatedly into the social and political world. Some of this has led to overt destructive actions of passionate believers against their neighbors. On the other hand, religions have

10 Anthony J. Parel, introduction to *Religious Fundamentalism in the Contemporary World: Critical Social and Political Issues*, ed. Santosh C. Saha (Lanham, MD: Lexington, 2004), 1.
11 "White Evangelicals See Trump Fighting for Their Beliefs, though Many Have Mixed Feelings about His Personal Conduct," Pew Research Center, March 12, 2020, https:// www.pewforum.org/2020/03/12/white-evangelicals-see-trump-as-fighting-for-their -beliefs-though-many-have-mixed-feelings-about-his-personal-conduct/.

reimagined their role in relation to the power-wielding nation-states, including when their constitutions have had a history of being secular. Such shrewd capture of the nation-states has led to the concerted, even if hidden, injurious actions of majority religions against religious minorities. It is no wonder then that in our volatile historical age, religious fundamentalism and strong nationalism have emerged as dominant contemporary movements that fire up spectacular violence and stealthy violation both locally and nationally.

The apparent self-serving nexus between religious fundamentalism and nationalist ideology is indicative of a systemic collusion that remains for the most part hidden to both parties. While the focus of this volume is religious fundamentalism, precisely because fundamentalism strives for embodiment in practices and cultural habits, it is most true to its own identity when it achieves political form. Conversely, it remains perennially restless to the extent that it falls short of this political goal. One consequence of this inbuilt drive for political power is that to discuss religious fundamentalism necessarily requires engagement with the nation-state and nationalist ideologies. Herein lies a real difficulty which concerns the fate of nation-states in the modern period (i.e., from the seventeenth century). The loss of a unitary sense of the state and previous compacts between state and religion has meant that in our own time, the governments of nation-states invest considerable energy in promoting the idea of social cohesion. The popular appeal to this concept betrays a deep anxiety about the impact of pluralism and the loss of a sense of societal unity. We no longer appear to know what holds us together. What are the options for the nation-state to secure a stronger and more secure sense of nationhood? In particular, what strategy might it adopt when it comes to the matter of religion? Here the nation-state will either (a) attempt to capture religious forces to assist in the repair of the fragmented social compact or (b) seek to negate the public significance of religious life. What options are available for religions, in particular the fundamentalist stream? For religious fundamentalism, secularist pressures and the emergence of a burgeoning and often radical pluralism mean that religious extremism seizes the opportunity to expand and enter into a struggle for political power. The stage is set for a systemic collusion between nationalist ideology and religious fundamentalism whereby each feeds the other's desires in a mutually self-serving manner. Not surprisingly, violence is never far away.

Interestingly, even if not surprisingly, both religious fundamentalism and strong nationalism are vested in matters of truth. Together, they generate, catalog, and circulate a fixed registry of Truth that creatively and efficiently alters life for all communities living in their religiously imagined nation-state. Religious fundamentalism and strong nationalism are in the truth business. Truth works effectively to induce, unite, valorize, and commission convinced ideologues to become passionate activists. Resources to construe Truth are gleaned from all facets of human life, yet such conceptions of veracity are incubated and cultivated within the imaginary of religion. Religious truths, though, become most effective when they are enacted in the realm of politics. Conversely, the political domain receives its most significant endorsement when it receives a divine imprimatur.

Against this backdrop, the contributors to this edited volume look back in order to move forward by reflecting upon the truth-force (satyagraha) that grounded and guided Mohandas Karamchand Gandhi (1869–1948). Inspired by the occasion of several ceremonious commemorations of Gandhi's 150th birth anniversary (2019), we reexamine the truths of his philosophy and nonviolent strategy to resist the hegemony of religious and political fundamentalisms. Pankaj Mishra reminds us of Gandhi's investment in Truth, which sometimes contained "blunders," mostly remained "restless," and always strove to be "mutually satisfactory." "Far from being a paragon of virtue," he says, "the Mahatma remained until his death a restless work in progress. Prone to committing what he called 'Himalayan blunders,' he did not lose his capacity to learn from them, and to enlist his opponents in his search for a mutually satisfactory truth."[12] Embracing Truth and being

---

12 Pankaj Mishra, "Gandhi for the Post-truth Age," *New Yorker*, October 22, 2018, https://www.newyorker.com/magazine/2018/10/22/gandhi-for-the-post-truth-age.

embraced by Truth was, for Gandhi, the only way to achieve complete freedom (*poorna Swaraj*). The goal of freedom, which Gandhi conceptualized as profoundly personal, expansively communitarian, and organically ecological, emanates from a firm grasp of truth.

This edited volume examines and interprets Gandhi's religious and political ideas of truth in his journey toward freedom for our times. Embedded in the political currents, especially those raging in India and the United States, the authors carefully excavate and creatively employ Gandhi's thought and practice to help reimagine a religiously plural and broadly inclusive nationalism that is rooted in a universal yet many-sided vision of religious truth. It weaves together African American, white Australian, and Indian perspectives to engage Gandhian thought and practice to contest violent truth registries and regimes in our contemporary world. Rather than glorify the Mahatma (great soul), this book revisits Gandhi's ideas of truth-force (satyagraha) in the face of fake news, nonviolence (ahimsa) in the face of religious extremism, and freedom (Swaraj) in the face of strong nationalisms.

The edited volume contains nine essays written from four continents: Asia, Australia, Europe, and North America. Each of these contexts is different, and traces of the context of each of these regions will be apparent in the essays. Also, the communities or individuals that accompany the authors as they seek to live out a common commitment to truth and freedom are various. Such perspicuous sojourners are, as it were, an accompanying "cloud of witnesses." First, there are Dalits, who seek wholeness from millennia of being crushed and broken in India. Then there are African Americans, who strive for "Black Lives [to] Matter" in the United States. There are also religious minorities, who suffer violation of their rights across the world. Finally, there are activist faith leaders such as Nicholas of Cusa, Bonhoeffer, Martin Luther King Jr., and Howard Thurman. The essays in this volume are bound by a conviction that Gandhi's truths are acutely relevant in contemporary contexts where strong religious nationalisms threaten to violate the rights of minority religions and those who practice another religious way of life. Gandhi had clues for how we might both be grounded in a more spacious theology of religion and organize resistance to achieve freedom (Swaraj) for all people. Let us give you a sense of what is covered by the essayists in this book.

William W. Emilsen (chapter 2) argues that truth rather than nonviolence was Gandhi's primary concern and that the discovery of nonviolence was part of his lifelong experimentation with truth. Emilsen explores four aspects of Gandhi's understanding of truth and truthfulness: their origins in India's religious traditions, the practical and national implications of Gandhi's great reversal of the traditional theistic formulation "God is Truth" to "Truth is God," Gandhi's distinction between "absolute truth" and "relative truth," and the high value Gandhi placed on the virtue of truthfulness in three forms—thought, speech and action—in both private and public life. This provides Emilsen with a basis to examine Gandhi's critique of state terrorism exercised by the Indian government under British rule before independence and the violent methods employed by Indian revolutionaries like Madan Lal Dhingra (1883–1909) and Bhagat Singh (1907–31) and their political supporters. Emilsen shows that Gandhi's practices of truthfulness and nonviolence are a direct challenge to contemporary terrorism and violent forms of nationalism.

Sathianathan Clarke (chapter 3) examines Gandhi's vision to dismantle violent religious fundamentalism in four key areas. First, Gandhi weakened the colonial posture of religions by insisting that Truth transcends all religious proclamations of truth. Second, Gandhi sacrificed violent deities of all religions on the altar of ahimsa (nonviolence), the indispensable consort of religious Truth. Third, he relativized the absolutism of scripture (revelation from outside) by experiments with Truth (experience from within). And finally, Gandhi disassembled the robust bonds between religion, blood, and land (Hindutva) to promote an interreligious abode of Truth for a free India (Hind) lit by freedom (Swaraj) for all. Clarke notes that Gandhi sought the solution for structural problems by harvesting the heart—"soft power" when compared to "hard power" of the Dalit Ambedkar, who focused on the coercive power of the system as such. Clarke reminds us that truth, nonviolence, love, and freedom must also incorporate justice. He concludes that Gandhi's vision of truth must learn from the Hebrew prophets as well as the Dalit champion Ambedkar.

Anderson H. M. Jeremiah (chapter 4) further interrogates the Gandhi-Ambedkar engagement in terms of Gandhi's illiberal religionism and Ambedkar's liberal nationalism. The author notes that Gandhi's political thought has a global reach, while Ambedkar's liberal nationalism is often maligned and narrowly defined. Gandhi offered a pan-Indian vision to refocus Hinduism in order to simplify it and enable it to become a force that mobilizes and facilitates change. Ambedkar sought to transform the lives of Dalits and fought for a separate electorate for Dalits to exercise their rights within democracy. Both reformers worked for freedom and effectively shaped modern Indian democracy and the emancipation of Dalits. Jeremiah concludes that to certain extent, they each became a corrective to the other.

Suka Joshua (chapter 5) draws attention to Gandhi's deployment of nonviolent language for resistance and liberation. Joshua argues that Gandhi's deft maneuvering of words, dexterous and fearless handling of crisis, and dedicated giving of service form the dominating patterns in this framework. The author shows how the power of spoken words, performative action, and communicative silence functioned for Gandhi to cultivate the culture of nonviolence that is essential for the attainment of peace within and peace in the world. The Gandhi-Ambedkar encounter—their "war of words" and the use of restraint and silence—sharpened the contrast between Gandhi's focus on the internal change of the heart and Ambedkar's pragmatism rooted in structural change. Importantly, Joshua inquires about Gandhi's relevance and asks, Is there still hope for us to reimagine a religiously plural and inclusive nationalism?

In the context of the current Black Lives Matter movement, Josiah Ulysses Young III (chapter 6) examines the legacy of Gandhi in relation to Martin Luther King Jr.'s nonviolent civil rights leadership and the way of Jesus Christ. Young draws attention to King's not uncontroversial statement that "Christ showed us the way, and Gandhi showed it could work." Young argues that King's assertion reflects his personalist metaphysics and its relation to Gandhi's embodiment of satyagraha and ahimsa. The author points out, in addition, that King's assertion is wed to his radical praxis—his human rights activism that led to his denunciations of white supremacy, the war in Vietnam, and global poverty. The essay concludes with a question about the future of nonviolence and the legacies of King, Gandhi, and Jesus: Are those in power, and those who will them to power, equipped to realize the wisdom of King's either-or, Gandhi's humane spirituality, or Jesus's self-immolating cross? Time will tell.

Peter Hooton (chapter 7) reminds us of the hoped-for visit to Gandhi by the German theologian and martyr Dietrich Bonhoeffer (1906–45). Bonhoeffer wanted the German church, in its opposition to Hitler, to recover the teachings of Jesus in the Sermon on the Mount, the purpose being to explore new ways of countering religion's subordination to the totalitarian aims of the state. Bonhoeffer believed Gandhi might be able to help him in this endeavor. Hooton ponders what might have resulted from such a visit. He asks, Might Bonhoeffer have warmed to the Mahatma's injunction to "melt Hitler's heart" with acts of nonviolent resistance, or would he then perhaps have been even more likely to conclude that the surging tide of Nazism and a Raj on the ebb presented very different challenges, demanding very different solutions? Hooton concludes that Bonhoeffer would have never been converted by Gandhi. He was already firmly on the path that would lead to his murder in a German concentration camp in April 1945, just three weeks prior to Hitler's suicide and a little under three years before Gandhi's own violent death at the hands of a Hindu extremist in New Delhi.

Stephen Pickard (chapter 8) focuses on Gandhi's humble pursuit of truth and nonviolence as a strategy and way of life orientated toward the common good and a renewed sociality. The author argues that Gandhi's engagement with these fundamental themes within the context of an emergent Indian nationalism provides some important markers for contemporary society regarding notions of the common good, social wisdom, and leadership. Pickard argues that Gandhi offers a deeper and more critical wisdom that has the power to bind, heal, and make for the flourishing of a people. In an age of self-interest, Gandhi offers a radical self in the service of others for a greater common good. In this context, the author examines John Henry Newman's famous nineteenth-century hymn "Lead Kindly Light," one source for Gandhi's remarkable energy and resilience. Gandhi believed this hymn contained the "quintessence of all philosophy."[13] It offers a clue to the spiritual energies required for the pursuit of truth, peace, and the renewal of social and political landscapes in our contemporary world.

Peter Walker (chapter 9) examines the concept of swadeshi (self-sufficiency) and applies it to a discussion of conversion and the self-sufficiency of religions. In doing this, Walker draws on the insights of Nicholas of Cusa's concept of the "dialogue of perspectives." The author notes that while Nicholas of Cusa (1401–64) and Mohandas Gandhi (1869–1948) stand a world apart, a common feature of their distant lives was the desire to reconcile differences into unity. This is especially evident in their ideas about relations among the religions. Cusa's pioneering work on interreligious dialogue *On the Peace of Faith* and his mystical masterwork *On the Vision of God* center upon his signature concept that the knowledge of God comes only at the coincidence of opposites. This *coincidence* establishes the value of different religious perspectives when seeking the presence of the Infinite. In Gandhi's ideas about religious conversion, Walker observes that we encounter an intriguingly complementary proposal. Gandhi argued for the spirit of swadeshi in matters of religion. Originally, swadeshi was a popular strategy to reduce India's dependence on British products and promote domestic production—Indian self-sufficiency. Gandhi extended this notion to the religious "market" by promoting the self-sufficiency of each religion and arguing against proselytizing for conversion. If one's ancestral religion is found to be defective, it is to be reformed rather than abandoned. Gandhi believed that each religion contains both truth and error, each may learn from the other, and none may claim superiority. Walker opines that had Gandhi and Nicholas

---

13 William Emilsen, "Gandhi and 'Lead, Kindly Light,'" in *This Immense Panorama: Studies in Honour of Eric J. Sharpe*, ed. Carole M. Cusack and Peter Oldmeadow, Sydney Studies in Religion 2 (Sydney: School of Studies in Religion, University of Sydney, 1999), 230.

ever had an opportunity to speak with each other, they might both have agreed that the process of spiritual reform and refinement, the process of conversion, is enriched by interreligious dialogue.

C. Anthony Hunt (chapter 10) brings the essays of this volume to a conclusion with an important discussion of the significance of Gandhi for Howard Thurman's philosophy of nonviolence as an active force of resistance. Thurman was among the leading African American Christian religious figures attracted to the thinking and praxis of Gandhi. Thurman's contact with Gandhi would codify his thinking with regard to nonviolence while also serving as an impetus for his ongoing search for the realization of what Thurman deemed to be "common ground" in the striving for authentic community. Gandhi's success with social and political reform in India was solid evidence for nonviolence, a praxis of resistance and just peacemaking, and served as a model for the likes of not only Thurman but African American religious leaders like Benjamin Mays, William Stuart Nelson, Mordecai Johnson, Edward Carroll, and Martin Luther King Jr. The chapter explores the ways in which Howard Thurman's engagement with Gandhi served to reinforce, confirm, and provide deeper insights into the efficacy of nonviolence, as expressed in Gandhian satyagraha and ahimsa and the Christian love-ethic, in resistance to racial and social oppression and in the ongoing search for common ground and the quest for peace in the churches and society today.

The essays in this book lift Gandhi's truths high. After all, the objective of this book was to sift Gandhi's philosophy for its relevance for our world of religious nationalism. There are tinges of critical reflection, especially from the viewpoint of Dalits. However, many critical voices have not been included. It is important, as we conclude this introduction, to name a two of them, since Gandhi's truth may have covered over, crowded out, or even violated these other embodied "experiments with Truth."

There is a growing body of Dalit literature that is critical of Gandhi for undercutting the political and economic self-determination of Dalit and Adivasi communities. Since some of this has been dealt with in a few of the essays in this volume, let us merely highlight the main points of this critique. On the one hand, Gandhi patronizingly usurped their representation by assuming that he was their leader in negotiating the interests of Dalits and Adivasis in the nation yet to be born. On the other hand, Gandhi refused to advocate for the dismantling of systems of privilege deeply grounded in Hinduism, which hindered concrete avenues of freedom for Dalits and Adivasis in a caste-duty-determined (varna dharma) ideology.

Another strident critique comes from Indian feminists who unveil Gandhi's ambivalent patriarchy. Since this is not addressed in this book, we need to register their weighty criticism of Gandhi's truths. From one standpoint, Gandhi advocated for equality between men and women from very early in his public life. Thus he was against child marriage, fought the burden of dowry in marriage, and advocated for the education of girls. Moreover, Gandhi inducted women into various forms of public protests at every level from the beginning. Thus Gandhi's movements were not sexually segregated; he encouraged women's leadership, and men were encouraged to undertake roles traditionally done by women. However, a feminist standpoint draws attention to the fact that just as Gandhi worked out of a commitment to retaining the system of caste to undercut the agency of Dalits and Adviasis, he also exhibited patriarchal vestedness in reimagining the freedom hoped for by women. Three justifiable criticisms are leveled against Gandhi. First, Gandhi bought into an essentialist trap that was unfreeing of women. They were viewed as objects in relation to the subjectivity of men. They then were cherished for their purity. As Tanika Sarkar notes, "Gandhi was particularly harsh about unchaste women, demanding more moral purity from women as he believed that they were naturally superior to men: their lapses, therefore, were an offence against their nature . . . there was, thus, great violence in his approach toward 'blemished' women."[14]

---

14 Tanika Sarkar, "Gandhi and Social Relations," in *The Cambridge Companion to Gandhi*, ed. Judith Brown and Anthony Parel (Cambridge: Cambridge University Press, 2012), 186.

Second, Gandhi did not take into consideration the economic development of women. Freedom through economic empowerment was not on his radar when it came to women. So while he encouraged them to join his political moment, Gandhi thought of women's development as secondary to their role within the patriarchal family. This is surely because he thought of them as primarily tied to the home and the family. As Madhu Kishwar rightly concludes, "One of the limitations of Gandhi's thinking, then, was that . . . he failed to put an economic content into his conception of emancipation. Gandhi failed to realize that, among other things, oppression is not an abstract moral condition, but a social and economic experience related to production relations. He tried changing women's position without either transforming their relations to the outer world of production or the inner world of family, sexuality and reproduction."[15]

Third, and finally, there is outrage at Gandhi's eccentric experiments using women as objects to test the triumph of his vow of celibacy. The bizarre nature of these experiments was a form of *yajna* (ritual sacrifice). In 1946 and 1947, Gandhi publicly and deliberately experimented with the practice of sleeping naked with his eighteen/nineteen-year-old grandniece Manu Gandhi to test his mastery over his sexual passion. Perhaps under the delusion that he was transforming sexual body power into spiritual soul power to alter world events in the context of Hindu-Muslim riots, Gandhi, according to his grandson Rajmohan Gandhi, "looked within himself for a weakness to explain the misfortunes around him. He thought that perfecting his celibacy, including by testing himself, would enhance his power over events."[16]

The aforementioned critiques require a frank acknowledgment of the limitations and flaws associated with Gandhi's experiments in Truth. Nonetheless, these essays still reclaim insights from his life and work to heal the wounds from religious garrisons that affect the

---

15 Madhu Kishwar, "Gandhi on Women," in *Debating Gandhi: A Reader*, ed. A. Raghuramaraju (New Delhi: Oxford University Press, 2006), 295.
16 David Courtright, *Gandhi and Beyond: Nonviolence in an Age of Terrorism* (New York: Routledge, 2006), 179.

world violently. In an overflow of religious fundamentalism onto the public square, interreligious solutions that matter cannot remain either within the soft hearts or inside the weighty heads of religious believers. Gandhi bursts these comfortable religious bubbles for the sake of serving the life of the whole world. The world, which is so loved by God, is in need of the resistant and engaging Truth founded in love to bring about freedom in our violent world. Banding together resistant co-religionists engaged in interreligious movements is the only way for peacemakers and justice seekers in a world of religious nationalism. Gandhi invites us into an interreligious vision wherein Truth (Sat), nonviolence (ahimsa), and active collective resistance (satyagraha) can be stitched creatively to march together toward freedom (Swaraj). The freedom sought will be one that looks beyond religious fundamentalism and strong nationalism toward societies that embody open, respectful, and even passionate engagements for the sake of the common good.

Bibliography

Almond, Gabriel A., Emmanuel Sivan, and R. Scott Appleby. "Examining the Cases." In *Fundamentalisms Comprehended*, edited by Martin E. Marty and R. Scott Appleby, 445–482. Chicago: University of Chicago Press, 1995.

Clarke, Sathianathan. *Competing Fundamentalisms: Violent Extremism in Christianity, Islam, and Hinduism*. Louisville, KY: Westminster John Knox, 2017.

Courtright, David. *Gandhi and Beyond: Nonviolence in an Age of Terrorism*. New York: Routledge, 2006.

Emilsen, William. "Gandhi and 'Lead, Kindly Light.'" In *This Immense Panorama: Studies in Honour of Eric J. Sharpe*, edited by Carole M. Cusack and Peter Old-meadow, Sydney Studies in Religion 2, 227–237. Sydney: School of Studies in Religion, University of Sydney, 1999.

Juergensmeyer, Mark. *Terror in the Mind of God: The Global Rise of Religious Violence*. Berkeley: University of California Press, 2003.

Kishwar, Madhu. "Gandhi on Women." In *Debating Gandhi: A Reader*, edited by A. Raghuramaraju, 269–324. New Delhi: Oxford University Press, 2006.

Latinne, Alice, et al. "Origin and Cross-species Transmission of Bat Coronaviruses in China." *Nature Communications* 11 (2020). https://doi.org/10.1038/s41467-020-17687-3.

Marty, Martin E. *When Faiths Collide*. Malden, MA: Blackwell, 2005.

Mishra, Pankaj. "Gandhi for the Post-truth Age." *New Yorker*, October 22, 2018. https://www.newyorker.com/magazine/2018/10/22/gandhi-for-the-post-truth -age.

Panikkar, Raimon. *The Experience of God: Icons of the Mystery.* Minneapolis: Fortress, 2006.

Parel, Anthony J. Introduction to *Religious Fundamentalism in the Contemporary World: Critical Social and Political Issues*, edited by Santosh C. Saha, 1–8. Lanham, MD: Lexington, 2004.

Pew Research Center. "Many Countries Favor Specific Religions, Officially or Unofficially." October 3, 2017. https://www.pewforum.org/2017/10/03/many-countries -favor-specific-religions-officially-or-unofficially/.

———. "White Evangelicals See Trump Fighting for Their Beliefs, though Many Have Mixed Feelings about His Personal Conduct." March 12, 2020. https://www .pewforum.org/2020/03/12/white-evangelicals-see-trump-as-fighting-for-their -beliefs-though-many-have-mixed-feelings-about-his-personal-conduct/.

Sarkar, Tanika. "Gandhi and Social Relations." In *The Cambridge Companion to Gandhi*, edited by Judith Brown and Anthony Parel, 173–196. Cambridge, UK: Cambridge University Press, 2012.

CHAPTER 2

Gandhi on Truth, Truthfulness, and Terrorism

William W. Emilsen

Abstract: In this article, I argue that truth rather than nonviolence was Gandhi's primary concern and that the discovery of nonviolence was part of his lifelong experimentation with truth. I then explore four aspects of Gandhi's understanding of truth and truthfulness: their origins in India's religious traditions, the practical and national implications of Gandhi's great reversal of the traditional theistic formulation "God is Truth" to "Truth is God," Gandhi's distinction between "absolute truth" and "relative truth," and the high value Gandhi placed on the virtue of truthfulness in three forms—thought, speech and action—in both private and public life. In light of these explorations, I examine Gandhi's critique of state terrorism exercised by the Indian government under British rule before independence and the violent methods employed by Indian revolutionaries like Madan Lal Dhingra (1883–1909) and Bhagat Singh (1907–31) and their political supporters. Finally, I comment upon three key elements in Gandhi's practices of truthfulness and nonviolence that clearly challenge contemporary terrorism and violent forms of nationalism: violence is inimical to truth even when it is for a good cause, adherence to truth implies a willingness to address the issues behind terrorism, and finally, there are dangers inherent in absolutizing truth.

Throughout the twentieth century, Mohandas Karamchand Gandhi (1869–1948) was widely revered for his practice and theory of nonviolence. Virtually all the tributes presented to Gandhi on his seventieth birthday in Sarvepalli Radhakrishnan's celebratory volume *Mahatma Gandhi: Essays and Reflections on His Life and Work* refer to Gandhi's "working gospel" of nonviolence and what it might mean for a world seemingly doomed to self-destruction.[1] Since then, there has been no

---

1 Savarpelli Radhakrishnan, ed., *Mahatma Gandhi: Essays and Reflections on His Life and Work; Presented to Him on His Seventieth Birthday, October 2nd, 1939* (London: Allen & Unwin, 1940).

evidence to suggest that interest in Gandhi's ideas on nonviolence has abated. If anything, the dropping of the first atomic bomb on Japan in 1945, the race riots in the United States in the 1960s, the nuclear threat in the 1980s, Al Qaeda's attacks on US embassies in Africa in the 1990s, and the attacks on New York and Washington on September 11, 2001, followed by the United States declaring a "War on Terror" and the subsequent emergence of the Islamic State of Iraq and Syria (ISIS), have intensified popular and scholarly interest in Gandhi's teachings on nonviolence.

With Gandhi almost universally lauded as "an apostle of nonviolence,"[2] it may come as a surprise to many people that nonviolence was not his primary concern. Certainly, nonviolent action was pivotal to Gandhi, but it came to him after years of experimenting with truth. Truth was his primary concern. Truth, he said, was "the sovereign principle" that included all other principles.[3] In his autobiography, subtitled *The Story of My Experiments with Truth*, Gandhi states that he came across the method of nonviolence as part of his endless experimentation with truth.[4] Although truth and nonviolence (ahimsa) were sometimes identified with each other, often paired, and closely intertwined, ahimsa, for Gandhi, was the means, whereas truth was always his goal or end. In 1922, he wrote from Sabarmati prison, "As I proceed in my quest for Truth, it grows upon me that Truth comprehends everything. I often feel that ahimsa is in Truth, not *vice versa*. What is perceived by a pure heart at a particular moment is Truth to it for that moment. By clinging to it, one can attain pure Truth . . . we have to live a life of ahimsa in the midst of a world full of *himsa* [e.g., violence, coercion, duress], and we can do so only if we cling to Truth."[5]

2 Judith M. Brown, "Gandhi and Human Rights: In Search of True Humanity," in *Gandhi's Experiments with Truth: Essential Writings by and about Mahatma Gandhi*, ed. Richard L. Johnson (Lanham, MD: Lexington, 2006), 237.
3 *Gandhi's Autobiography: The Story of My Experiments with Truth* (Washington, DC: Public Affairs, 1948), 6.
4 Johnson, *Gandhi's Experiments*, xi.
5 Gandhi to Jamnalal Bajaj, March 16, 1922, in *The Complete Works of Mahatma Gandhi*, by M. K. Gandhi (Delhi: Ministry of Information and Broadcasting, Government of India, 1969–94), 23:97.

The path for seekers of truth was for the brave, Gandhi insisted. Although he preferred violence to cowardice and, at times, was even prepared to sacrifice ahimsa for truth when political compromise was inevitable, Gandhi never willingly compromised on truth. The technique of nonviolent resistance—satyagraha (variously translated as "truth-force," "clinging to truth," or "holding on to the truth")—may have been his most celebrated experiment with truth, but it was certainly not his only one. Gandhi's many experiments, some monumental failures or "Himalayan miscalculations,"[6] covered diverse areas and continued throughout his life.[7] They included experiments with diet, hygiene, alternative medicine, farming, sanitation, community building, interreligious harmony, social and economic welfare (*Sarvodaya*), and nationalism. Regardless of the sphere of experimentation Gandhi engaged in—moral, spiritual, economic, or political—he believed that, sooner or later, anyone committed to truth would eventually discover the importance of nonviolence. Truth was the foundational idea in Gandhi's thinking, the spiritual bedrock of his political and social engagement. Truth for him was the substance of all morality, the ultimate source of authority and of appeal, the raison d'être of human existence. Truth was Gandhi's "polar star," his "treasure beyond price."[8] Truth effectively became Gandhi's religion and his God.[9] Indeed, he proclaimed that "Truth is the very foundation of religion"[10] or, more boldly, that there is no religion greater than truth.[11] On numerous occasions, Gandhi variously described himself as "a humble searcher after Truth," "a votary of Truth," or "a worshipper of Truth." In an often-quoted passage, he wrote, "I am but a seeker after Truth. I claim to have

---

6 See, for example, *Gandhi's Autobiography*, 6, 575–77.

7 Gandhi, "Two Requests," *Harijan*, March 3, 1946, in *Complete Works*, 83:180.

8 Gandhi to Narandas Gandhi, July 18/22, 1930, in *Complete Works*, 44:42.

9 Raghavan Iyer, ed., *The Moral and Political Writings of Mahatma Gandhi*, vol. 2, *Truth and Non-violence* (Oxford: Clarendon, 1986), 155.

10 Gandhi, "Truth the Only Way," March 12, 1933, in *Complete Works*, 54:67.

11 L. Gopal Prasad, *Religion, Morality and Politics according to Mahatma Gandhi* (New Delhi: Classical, 1991), 84.

found a way to it. I claim to be making a ceaseless effort to find it. But I admit that I have not yet found it."[12]

Devotion to truth gave Gandhi the deepest satisfaction. He insisted that the only life worth living is one that is single-mindedly dedicated to truth. Gandhi's life was devoted to the quest of truth. He called his quest his "true bhakti," a devotion that could very well lead to suffering and death.[13] In order to underscore his unshakeable faith in truth, Gandhi, with some hyperbole, asserted that he was prepared to leap from "the top of the Himalayas for its sake."[14]

Gandhi was not a philosopher in an academic sense, or even a systematic thinker. In all likelihood, he would have refuted Hossien Gara's assertion that he is "an outstanding figure of . . . contemporary Indian Philosophy."[15] Gandhi felt no need to systematize his own thought, or to create a new religion. He did not approve of what came to be called "Gandhism."[16] He eschewed scholarship for the sake of scholarship and had little time for philosophical niceties. Rather, he saw himself as an honest, lifelong experimenter, a doer, a man of action, a *karmayogi*. He professed, "Action is my domain, and what I understand, according to my lights, to be my duty, and what comes my way, I do. All my action is actuated by the spirit of service."[17]

Yet it would be a mistake just to think of Gandhi as an activist and not at all as a thinker. He studied Hindu philosophical works throughout his life, particularly during times of incarceration. He was a prolific writer, and scattered throughout the hundred volumes of his collected works, his ideas on practically every conceivable subject are expressed in a clear, thoughtful, and unambiguous manner. The consequence of

---

12 Gandhi, "Introspection," *Young India*, November 17, 1921, in *Complete Works*, 21:457.

13 Gandhi to Narandas Gandhi, 41.

14 Gandhi, "What Is Truth?," *Navjivan*, November 20, 1921, in *Complete Works*, 21:474.

15 Hossien Nemat Zadeh Gara, "Truth and Non-violence: Core Principles of Gandhi," in *Gandhi in Twenty-First Century*, ed. Ashu Pasricha and Jai Narain Sharma (New Delhi: Deep & Deep, 2011), 143.

16 Gandhi, "Speech at Gandhi Seva Sangh Meeting–III," March 3, 1936, in *Complete Works*, 62:223–23. The basic idea of Gandhism was that for India to be truly free, it must remain faithful to its cultural heritage.

17 Gandhi, "Two Requests," 180.

this, however, is that any attempt to systematize Gandhi's ideas on truth and truthfulness from his numerous sayings scattered among six decades of letters and speeches is, as observed the Indian politician and author Ranganath Diwakar (1894–1990), like trying "to churn butter from milk."[18]

A related difficulty in discerning Gandhi's teachings on truth and truthfulness is that he did not attach much importance to consistency in argument. Those who look for consistency in Gandhi's writings are soon "flabbergasted," laments political scientist and Gandhi scholar Kusum Lata Chadda.[19] His inconsistencies, which exasperated both supporters and opponents alike, have led some to question whether or not there was a firm center to the man.[20] Gandhi, however, was unconcerned with such criticism. "Consistency is a hobgoblin," he declared, channeling the American essayist, philosopher, and poet Ralph Waldo Emerson (1803–82). "My aim is not to be consistent with my previous statements on a given question, but to be consistent with the truth as it may present itself to me at a given moment."[21] Indeed, Gandhi believed that inconsistency might even be thought of as a virtue; he regarded changing his mind or seeming to contradict an earlier position or statement as a sign of growth, evidence of his relentless search for truth and truthfulness.[22]

Gandhi may have appeared to be an unsystematic thinker, but his underlying metaphysical concept of truth is a key to understanding the practical dimensions of his thought. His ideas, especially those, as we shall see, relating to terrorism and violent forms of nationalism, are most meaningful and understandable when viewed through the lens of truth. Gandhi's insistence on truth is the golden thread that weaves

---

18 Ranganath Diwakar, preface to *The Core of Gandhi's Philosophy*, by Unto Tähtinen (New Delhi: Abhinav, 1979), 8.

19 Kusum Lata Chadda, *Reading Gandhi* (New Delhi: Kanishka, 2008), 152.

20 Erik H. Erikson, *Gandhi's Truth: On the Origins of Militant Nonviolence* (London: Faber & Faber, 1979), 396.

21 Quoted in Johnson, *Gandhi's Experiments*, 152.

22 S. Kumat Saxena, *Ever unto God: Essays on Gandhi and Religion* (New Delhi: Indian Council of Philosophical Research, 1988), 2.

his thought into an integrated whole. Truth mattered to him more than anything. The English writer and philosopher Aldous Huxley (1825–95) quipped that Gandhi would have found hell with honest men more bearable than paradise full of angelic shams.[23] And the Indian philosopher Raghavan Iyer (1930–95), in a more serious vein, noted, "No political thinker with the possible exception of Plato, has insisted as Gandhi did on Truth as absolute value."[24] Similarly, the religious studies scholar Glyn Richards (1923–2015), author of *The Philosophy of Gandhi* (1982), emphasized that Gandhi's underlying concept of truth both gives coherence to his basic ideas and provides a key to understanding his practice.[25]

Gandhi's conception of truth and truthfulness was deeply rooted in India's religious traditions. On several occasions, he acknowledged his indebtedness to ancestral religion. Gandhi maintained that he had not introduced new principles and doctrines; he had simply applied the "eternal principles" of truth and nonviolence inherent in Hinduism in new ways to contemporary problems. "Truth and nonviolence," he insisted, were "nothing new; they have been in existence from the beginning of creation."[26]

Despite Gandhi's tendency toward eclecticism, and accusations of heterodoxy by some high-caste Hindus, it was in Hinduism that he primarily lived, moved, and had his being.[27] He firmly believed in transmigration, or rebirth, which is one of the hallmarks of Indian religions. He often claimed to be a *sanatani*, a Hindu with roots in ancient traditions, because he believed in the sacred texts and the traditional values

---

23 Newman H. Rosenthal, *The Uncompromising Truth: Mahatma Gandhi 1869–1948* (London: Nelson, 1969), 138.
24 Iyer, *Truth and Non-violence*, 224.
25 Glyn Richards, *The Philosophy of Gandhi: A Study of His Basic Ideas* (London: Curzon, 1982), 1.
26 Gandhi, "Talk with Manu Gandhi," April 18, 1947, in *Complete Works* 87:304.
27 Although the term *Hinduism* has been identified by Geoffrey Oddie and others as "an ill-defined, somewhat amorphous concept," there was a lively debate among higher castes and the educated about Gandhi's religious identity. See Geoffrey A. Oddie, "Introduction: Hinduism in India," in *Hinduism in India: Modern and Contemporary Movements*, ed. Will Sweetman and Aditya Malik (New Delhi: Sage, 2016), ix.

and concepts of Hinduism. The book that became Gandhi's strongest bond with Hinduism as well as the greatest influence on him was the ancient Hindu text the Bhagavad Gita. He described it as "the book par excellence for the knowledge of Truth."[28] Though Gandhi drew inspiration from other religions, such as Jainism and Christianity, he was thoroughly Hindu in character. Most Indians saw him as a devout Hindu, a great Hindu, a mahatma (great soul). Jawaharlal Nehru (1889–1964), who became the first prime minister of India, spoke for many when he said that Gandhi was "a Hindu to the depths of his innermost being."[29] The American journalist and early biographer of Gandhi Vincent Sheean (1899–1975) also observed that centuries of Hinduism had produced Gandhi and that he was "profoundly Hindu."[30]

Gandhi sometimes wrote of truth as an impersonal absolute, an unseen power or unifying force pervading all things, the changeless essence of life beyond all name and form. In 1905, for example, while still in South Africa, he wrote an article about the "Oriental Ideal of Truth" in his recently established newspaper, *Indian Opinion*. In this article, Gandhi refuted Lord Curzon's claim (Curzon was viceroy of India from 1899–1905) that truth was largely a Western conception, whereas in the East, craftiness and diplomatic wile were esteemed. The article is important because it provides clear and early evidence that Gandhi was sufficiently familiar with a whole range of texts on truth and truthfulness from various Hindu scriptures, the Indian epics, the Indian saint Kabir, as well as Buddhist and Sikh sources, which he used to refute what he called Curzon's "baseless and offensive imputations."[31] There, as well, Gandhi defined truth in ontological and metaphysical terms: "Truth is That which Is, and Untruth is That which Is Not." And he supported this definition of truth with a saying from Bhishma, the hero of the epic *Mahabharata*: "Truth is eternal Brahman. . . . Everything rests on Truth."[32]

28 Ved Mehta, *Mahatma Gandhi and His Apostles* (New York: Viking, 1977), 167.
29 Jawaharlal Nehru, *The Discovery of India* (London: Meridian, 1960), 366.
30 Vincent Sheean, "Last Days," in Radhakrishnan, *Mahatma Gandhi*, 452.
31 Iyer, *Truth and Non-violence*, 150.
32 Gandhi, "Oriental Ideal of Truth," *Indian Opinion*, April 1, 1905, in *Complete Works*, 4:393.

Despite Gandhi's remarks to the contrary, it would be a mistake to think of him as an Advaitin—that is, a believer in some indeterminate, nondescript, impersonal Absolute. Gandhi was a theist. He was born into a Vaishnava family that conceived of God as possessing many auspicious qualities and perfections like pure undefiled consciousness, omnipotence, omniscience, benevolence, love, and all-mercifulness. Gandhi frequently refers to God as Brahma (the personification of Brahman and the creator in the Trimurti).[33] However, the fullest description of God for Gandhi was "God is Truth."[34] He wrote in his autobiography, "There are innumerable definitions of God, because His manifestations are innumerable. They overwhelm me with wonder and awe and for a moment stun me. But I worship God as Truth only. I have not yet found Him, but I am seeking after Him."[35]

Arthur Llewellyn Basham (1914–86), author of the classic *The Wonder That Was India* (1954), traces the source of Gandhi's emphasis on truth back to his nurse who taught him as a child to call on the name of God in the form of Rama.[36] One of the commonest mantras of Indian Vaishnavism, explains Basham, is "The name of Rama is true" or "The name of Rama is Truth." The implication of the phrase to the believer is that God is Truth and that God carries out his promises without swerving and expects his followers to do likewise.[37] Throughout his life, Gandhi was impelled by this intense theistic faith that he had learned as a child. He lived and died believing in Rama. "My Rama," said Gandhi, "is the eternal, the unborn, the one without a second. Him alone I worship."[38]

---

33 The triad of the three gods Brahma, Vishnu, and Shiva.
34 Suman Khanna, *Gandhi and the Good Life* (New Delhi: Gandhi Peace Foundation, 1985), 20.
35 *Gandhi's Autobiography*, 6.
36 A. L. Basham, "Traditional Influences on the Thought of Mahatma Gandhi," in *Essays on Gandhian Politics: The Rowlatt Satyagraha of 1919*, ed. R. Kumar (Oxford: Clarendon, 1971), 19–20.
37 Basham, 24.
38 Gandhi, "Speech at Prayer Meeting, New Delhi," April 4, 1946, in *Complete Works*, 83:364.

Gandhi profoundly believed in God, and for almost three-quarters of his life, he identified God with truth. For him, "God is Truth" was the deepest expression of God. By the mid-1920s, however, Gandhi began to reverse the traditional theistic formulation "God is Truth." First, he talked as if God and truth were convertible terms. Then he argued that "it is more correct to say that Truth is God than to say that God is Truth."[39] Then finally, in December 1931 when Gandhi was asked by a group of conscientious objectors in Lausanne, Switzerland, why he regarded God as Truth, he replied that he had now, after fifty years of continuous and relentless searching, moved from saying "God is Truth" to saying "Truth is God."[40]

Gandhi's reversal of the proposition "God is Truth" bristles with philosophical difficulties, which have been dealt with by others.[41] My concern here is with the main reasons for the reversal. Raghavan Iyer identifies at least four. First, the reversal of the traditional theistic formulation was for Gandhi an attempt to be as inclusive as possible. As a national political figure with an inclusive nationalist vision, he had to work with Muslims, Parsis, Christians, Buddhists, Jains, Theosophists, and other religious minorities who held understandings of God different from his and, as well, with people who for various reasons had no belief in God at all or seriously doubted God's existence. He discovered that truth still had an enormous appeal to them all, regardless of their views about God. Gandhi was fond of telling the story of his meeting the famous English atheist and political activist Charles Bradlaugh (1833–91) when he was a student in London: "I recall the name of Charles Bradlaugh—a great Englishman who lived 50 years ago. He delighted to call himself an atheist. But knowing as I do something of his life, I never considered him an atheist. I would call him a godfearing man although he would reject the claim, and I know his face would redden. I would say: No Mr. Bradlaugh, you are a truth-fearing man, not a

---

39 Gandhi, "Hind Swaraj (Indian Home Rule) and Related Writings," in Johnson, Gandhi's Experiments, 149.
40 Gandhi, "Speech at Meeting in Lausanne," December 8, 1931, in Complete Works, 48:404.
41 Richards, Philosophy of Gandhi, 1–15.

god-fearing man, and I would disarm his criticisms by saying 'Truth is God' as I have disarmed criticisms of many a young man."[42]

The proposition "Truth is God" enabled Gandhi to embrace theists, atheists, and agnostics. Certainly, the notion of "seeing truth" was a lot less problematic, especially for secularists, than that of "seeing God" or "glimpsing God." Jawaharla Nehru agreed with Gandhi. He recognized Gandhi's "dominating passion"[43] for truth and wrote, "So long as Gandhi was talking about God, I did not fully know what he meant. But now when he says that truth is God, I understand him better."[44] Second, Gandhi believed that it was more precise to say "Truth is God" than to say "God is Truth." Truth was not merely an incidental quality; it was the very essence of what we name or know as God. Third, the proposition "Truth is God" dispensed with thinking about God as a person such as a ruler, king, or lord. Such anthropomorphic images of divinity, Gandhi believed, may generate fear, acting as a deterrent from sin and an impulse toward virtue, but good deeds, he considered, ought not to be done either out of fear or out of the expectation of any reward but out of love for the virtue itself. Finally, the proposition "Truth is God" placed the emphasis on truth rather than other concepts usually associated with divinity, such as "love," "life," "goodness," "peace," "justice," "beauty," and "hope." Gandhi's experiments with truth had led him to the conclusion that when one says "God is Truth," it could also mean "God is love," or "God is light," or "God is good." However, when one says "Truth is God," it is more definitive. In Gandhi's understanding, the pursuit of goodness, beauty, and love was contained in the pursuit of truth.[45]

Closely associated with Gandhi's reversal of the proposition "God is Truth" was the important distinction he made between "absolute truth" and "relative truth." For Gandhi, absolute truth alone is God. He

---

42 Gandhi, "Speech at Meeting in Lausanne," 404–5.
43 Jawaharlal Nehru, *Mahatma Gandhi* (Kolkata: Signet, 1949), 162.
44 Quoted in T. K. Mahadevan, ed., *Truth and Nonviolence: Report of the UNESCO Symposium on Truth and Nonviolence in Gandhi's Humanism, Paris, 14–17 October 1969* (New Delhi: Gandhi Peace Foundation, 1970), 58.
45 Iyer, *Truth and Non-violence*, 186.

confessed that while absolute truth is beyond our reach while we are in the body, it should be regarded as an ideal to constantly pursue and meditate upon.[46] This Gandhi did by introducing the idea of relative truth, which served as a guide on the way toward absolute truth.[47] Unlike absolute truth, we can know relative truth and follow it to the best of our abilities. Gandhi stated, "But as long as I have not realized this Absolute Truth, so long must I hold by the relative truth as I have conceived it. That relative truth must, meanwhile, be my beacon, my shield and buckler."[48] Humans, according to Gandhi, can at best only approximate absolute truth through their understanding of relative, imperfect, and historically and culturally conditioned truths.[49] Or, put theologically by Gandhi, "The more truthful we are, the nearer we are to God."[50]

The word *satya* means not only "truth" but also "truthfulness," and Gandhi, in common with most Indian thinkers, placed the utmost emphasis upon the virtue of truthfulness in private and public life. In his cottage in Sevagram in the state of Maharashtra, Gandhi kept before him the following quotation from the prominent English social thinker John Ruskin (1819–1900): "The essence of lying is in deception, not in words; a lie may be told by silence, by equivocation, by the accent on a syllable, by a glance of the eye attaching a peculiar significance to a sentence; and all those kinds of lies are worse and baser by many degrees than a lie plainly worded."[51]

As well, from the formation of Satyagraha Ashram in Ahmedabad, Gujarat, in 1915, Gandhi listed truth as "the first and the foremost" of the five ashram's *yamas*, or vows or disciplines—the other four being *brahmacharya* (sexual restraint), nonviolence, poverty, and nonpossession.[52] These five vows were expanded for practical reasons to eleven,

---

46 Iyer, 176.
47 Johnson, *Gandhi's Experiments*, 319.
48 *Gandhi's Autobiography*, 6.
49 Johnson, *Gandhi's Experiments*, 319.
50 Saxena, *Ever unto God*, 15.
51 Shriman Narayan, *Gandhi: The Man and His Thought* (New Delhi: Publication Division, Government of India, 1968), 3.
52 Gandhi, "Speech on 'Ashram Vows' at Y.M.C.A., Madras," February 16, 1916, in *Complete Works*, 13:227–28.

put into song form by the Indian social reformer Vinayak Narahari
(Vinoba) Bhave (1895–1982), and recited during the daily prayers in
Gandhi's ashrams. All eleven vows—truth, nonviolence, nonsteal-
ing, brahmacharya, nonpossession, bread or body labor, control of
palate, fearlessness on all occasions, equal regard for all religions,
swadeshi, and removal of untouchability—Gandhi believed, could
be derived from truth.[53]

Gandhi admitted no exception to truthfulness. In his ashrams,
everyone was encouraged to examine themselves daily from the
point of view of truthfulness or Gandhi's "pragmatic insistence that
truth could be applied."[54] This examen was not unlike the Jesuit
devotional exercise involving reflection on and moral evaluation of
one's thoughts and conduct. It entailed asking questions such as, Did
I deceive anybody knowingly? Did I try to win someone's respect or
esteem by pretending to have certain virtues that in fact I did not
possess? Did I exaggerate in my speech? Did I hide my misdeeds
from persons to whom I should have confessed them? Did I answer
honestly?[55]

Truthfulness, for Gandhi, meant truthfulness in three forms—in
thought, speech, and action. Truthfulness in the sphere of thought
meant devotion to facts and an eagerness to discover the truth of
any matter before arriving at a decision. Careful observation, sifting
of evidence, and the dispassionate use of reason were the methods
that he used for the discovery of truth. In any conflict between reason and authority, whether personal or scriptural and however high,
Gandhi would always follow reason. Gandhi had a strong rational
streak. Yet there was a mystical one as well. Whenever Gandhi felt
puzzled, he would retire into himself and, through a process of self-
analysis and self-purification, try to clear his mind in order to listen
to the clear "voice within," which he, at various times, identified with
God or conscience. "Truth," he would say, "is by nature self-evident.

---

53 Gandhi, "How Did I Begin It?," *Harijan*, June 8, 1947, in *Complete Works*, 88:59.
54 Margaret Chatterjee, *Gandhi's Religious Thought* (London: Macmillan, 1983), 70.
55 Gandhi, *"Hind Swaraj,"* 151.

As soon as you remove the cobwebs of ignorance that surround it, it shines clear."[56]

Truthfulness in speech Gandhi regarded as the natural outcome of truthfulness in thought. To think one thing and speak another was untruth. What we say about others (and their views) has to be true. There is no place for fraud, lying, or deceit. "Lying," he said, "is the mother of violence."[57] Truthfulness, however, did not mean speaking the truth (however beneficial) in a harsh, rude, or violent manner. The truth had to be spoken in a pleasant way. Truth-telling and love were inseparable in Gandhi's mind. Satyagraha, or Gandhi's strategy for nonviolent resistance, sought to be always gentle; it never deliberately resorted to violence, and it never set out to wound. If one could not speak the truth in a gentle manner, then it was better not to speak at all. Speaking the truth with gentleness and humility, Gandhi admitted, was no easy task; he often compared it to "walking on a razor's edge"[58] or "balancing oneself on the edge of a sword."[59] At various times, he described truth-telling as an art that had to be perfected through constant effort and practice in the everyday decisions of life.[60]

Gandhi's view of truthfulness went beyond thought and speech to include action. The actual pursuit of truth in Gandhi's understanding involved a fusion or a harmonizing of thought, speech, and action. Constructive thought, truthful speech, and timely action were inseparable. One of the abiding attractions of Gandhi is that he spoke what he thought and did what he said. For example, having committed himself to serve the people of India, especially the poor, he dressed like the poor, ate like the poor, and lived as they lived. Truthfulness was not something to be recognized in theory and ignored in practice. His emphasis was on doing the truth (including active opposition

---

56 Dhirendra Mohan Datta, *The Philosophy of Mahatma Gandhi* (Madison: University of Wisconsin Press, 1953), 94–95.

57 Gandhi, "On Satyagraha," in *Nonviolence in Theory and Practice*, ed. R. L. Holmes (Belmont, CA: Wadsworth, 1990), 56.

58 Gandhi to Narayan M. Khare, February 10, 1932, in *Complete Works*, 49:80.

59 Gandhi to Narandas Gandhi, July 28/31, 1930, in *Complete Works*, 44:57.

60 Saxena, *Ever unto God*, 15–16.

to untruth) in all of one's involvements with people and the whole of creation.[61]

Gandhi always stressed the harmonious link among thought, words, and action as an important criterion of truth.[62] It was for this reason that he argued that the quest for truth cannot be prosecuted in a cave. It must be tested in the laboratory of life.[63] Going against quietist elements within Hinduism, Gandhi did not look upon involvement in public affairs with contempt; rather, he asserted that it was only through public service that a vision of God was possible.[64] Harmony was the main reason Gandhi opposed the separation of the public and the private and the compartmentalization of the political, social, economic, and religious spheres of life. For Gandhi, religion was the foundation of all his action. Every activity, especially his political leadership, was governed by his religious convictions. Pointedly, he wrote, "To see the universal and all-pervading Spirit of Truth face to face one must be able to love the meanest of creation as oneself. And a man who aspires after that cannot afford to keep out of any field of life. That is why my devotion to Truth has drawn me into the field of politics."[65]

How did Gandhi's resolute commitment to truth and truthfulness shape his response to contemporary terrorism and extreme forms of religious nationalism? Certainly, terrorism was no stranger to Gandhi. It was a religiopolitical issue for him just as much as it is for world leaders today. Gandhi's writings are laced with explicit references refuting terrorism and those variously described as "terrorists," "extremists," "anarchists," "revolutionaries," "votaries of violence," and the "party of violence." Three brief examples are indicative: In a letter written in February 1919 to the prominent Parsi politician and a founding member of the Indian National Congress Dinshaw Wacha (1844–1936), Gandhi forcefully argued that satyagraha or truth-force is "the only way . . . to

---

61 Narayan, *Gandhi*, viii.
62 Gandhi to Narayan M. Khare, February 10, 1932, in *Complete Works*, 49:80.
63 Johnson, *Gandhi's Experiments*, 319.
64 Johnson, 69.
65 Arne Naess, *Gandhi and the Nuclear Age* (Totowa, NJ: Bedminster, 1965), 40.

stop terrorism."[66] Then in article titled "My Friend, the Revolutionary," published in *Young India* in April 1925, Gandhi stated, "I do not regard killing or assassination or terrorism as good in any circumstances whatsoever."[67] Similarly, in December 1931 at a Round Table Conference in London with Prime Minister Ramsay MacDonald present, Gandhi twice unequivocally rejected terrorism, including those "who directly or indirectly would encourage terrorism."[68] Gandhi did not regard killing or assassination or terrorism as good under any circumstance. Terrorism, in Gandhi's opinion, would never bring freedom to India; it would only lead to disaster.

For over four decades, Gandhi was vigorously engaged in prolonged debates with Indians who endorsed terrorism and valorized terrorists for political ends. Repeatedly, he had to refute the violent methods employed by nationalist revolutionaries like Madan Lal Dhingra (1883–1909) and the immensely popular Bhagat Singh (1907–31) and their mentors and political supporters. On occasion, he even had to chastise some in the Indian National Congress who considered bombings and political assassinations acceptable as a means of achieving Swaraj. In 1934, when Gandhi was asked how he would tackle the "terrorist problem" in Bengal, he responded, "I am a determined opponent of the cult of violence. Not a day passes when I do not do or think something about this question which is one of life and death to me."[69] Gandhi struggled to reconcile his own nonviolent principles with political power and, according to Steger, did not recognize the "traces of conceptual violence" in his own nationalist vision.[70] Only a year or two before he was assassinated by a fundamentalist Hindu, he wrote, "I have discussed this question of violence threadbare with so many

---

66 Gandhi to Sir Dinshaw Wacha, February 25, 1919, in *Complete Works*, 15:107.

67 Gandhi, "My Friend, the Revolutionary," *Young India*, April 9, 1925, in *Complete Works*, 26:489.

68 Gandhi, "Speech at Plenary Session of Round Table Conference," December 1, 1931, in *Complete Works*, 48:359.

69 Gandhi, "Interview to the Press," August 2, 1934, in *Complete Works*, 58:287.

70 Manfred B. Steger, *Gandhi's Dilemma: Nonviolent Principles and Nationalist Power* (New York: St. Martin's, 2000), 186.

terrorists and anarchists. It is terrible whether the Arab does it or the Jew. It is a bad outlook for the world if this spirit of violence takes hold of the mass mind."[71]

Gandhi was also obliged to confront imperial as well as anti-imperial terrorism. In early April 1919, after the Imperial Legislative Council in Delhi passed the Anarchical and Revolutionary Crimes Act, popularly known as the "Rowlatt Act" or "Black Act," which enabled the government to imprison any person suspected of terrorism for two years without a trial, Gandhi, increasingly, began to charge the British with acting in the "spirit of terrorism."[72] Less than two weeks afterward, Gandhi's accusations of terrorism were validated when over 1,650 unarmed Indian civilians were wounded and 379 were killed at the infamous Jallianwala Bagh massacre in Amritsar on the orders of General Reginald Dyer (1864–1927). Durba Ghosh rightly argues that it was at this time that Gandhi began to use the language of terrorism to describe the actions of the state.[73]

The substance of Gandhi's stand against political terrorism was first formulated in a small book called *Hind Swaraj, or Indian Home Rule*, written in November 1909 on his return voyage from London to South Africa. In it, Gandhi felt the necessity to respond to the ideology of political terrorism adopted by expatriate Indians much influenced by various revolutionary movements in Europe at the time. Gandhi was disturbed that they were broadly supportive of Madan Lal Dhingra's assassination of the British India Office official Sir William H. Curzon-Wyllie only ten days before Gandhi arrived in London.[74] A decade later, Gandhi recalled the circumstances surrounding the writing of *Hind Swaraj*: "In answer to the Indian school of violence, and its prototype in

---

71 Gandhi, "Discussion with Ian Stephens," [on or after December 1, 1945], in *Complete Works*, 82:151.

72 Gandhi, "Telegram to S. Kasturi Ranga Iyengar"; "Telegram to Swami Shraddhanand"; "Letter to the Press on Delhi Tragedy," April 3, 1919, in *Complete Works*, 15:172, 175–76.

73 Durba Ghosh, "Gandhi and the Terrorists: Revolutionary Challenges from Bengal and Engagements with Non-violent Political Protest," *South Asia: Journal of South Asian Studies* 39, no. 3 (2016): 567.

74 Ghosh, 563.

South Africa, I came in contact with every known Indian anarchist in London. Their bravery impressed me, but I feel that their zeal was misguided. I felt that violence was no remedy for India's ills, and that her civilization required the use of a different and higher weapon for self-protection."[75]

Gandhi continued to regard *Hind Swaraj* as a true expression of his nationalism. In it, he sought to develop an original version of Indian nationalism that was distinct from the nationalism of the Moderates, who regarded English rule as providential, and the Extremists, who were hostile to the British and often believed that violence was necessary to chase the British out of India.

Hind Swaraj is written in the form of an imaginary dialogue between an editor (Gandhi's mouthpiece) and a reader (representing a variety of viewpoints, including those Indian expatriates he had met in London who accepted violence and terrorism as a legitimate means in the struggle for political independence). In it, Gandhi argues that terrorism is "morally objectionable and politically self-defeating."[76] He has his reader state, "We shall assassinate a few Englishmen and strike terror; then, a few men who will have been armed will fight openly. . . . We will undertake guerrilla warfare, and defeat the English." The editor replies, "It is a cowardly thought, that of killing others. Whom do you suppose to free by assassination? The millions of India do not desire it. Those who are intoxicated by the wretched modern civilization think these things."[77]

Gandhi's high view of truth impacted on his attitude to terrorism in three important ways. First, it caused him to draw an important distinction between "terrorists" and "terrorism." While on the one hand, he was adamantly opposed to acts of violence and political positions that justified terrorism even for a good cause, on the other hand, he was remarkably lenient toward terrorists and extreme nationalists because

---

75 Gandhi, "'Hind Swaraj' or the 'Indian Home Rule,'" *Young India*, January 26, 1921, in *Complete Works*, 19:277.

76 Ronald J. Terchek, "Gandhi: Nonviolence and Violence," *Journal of Power and Ethics: An Interdisciplinary Review* 2, no. 3 (2001): 235.

77 Gandhi, *Hind Swaraj or Indian Home Rule* (Ahmedabad: Navajivan, 1938), 69.

he believed that they may be motivated by fragments of truth. Some in "the party of violence," Gandhi admitted, were "earnest spirits, possessing a high degree of morality, great intellectual ability and lofty self-sacrifice."[78] He acknowledged their sincerity and admired their courage and religious devotion. He had some sympathy with their anarchic patriotism. He also recognized that they shared the same political goal as he did: Swaraj, or independence for India from colonial rule. Gandhi took their cause seriously but rejected their violent methods and exclusive emphasis on Hindu solidarity. Dhingra, for example, may have been a patriot, but his love, in Gandhi's eyes, was blind and his thinking clouded by those who believed that violence was the solution to British colonialism.[79] Bhagat Singh, too, may have been a man of great daring and unblemished character, but his murderous deeds were considered by Gandhi to be deluded and reprehensible. Gandhi's attitude toward terrorists, explains the American socialist Mark Juergensmeyer, "was more of pity than of revenge."[80] Some terrorists may have been misguided, in Gandhi's view, but they were not monsters, and often their cause, if not their methods, illuminated aspects of truth in unexpected ways.

Second, Gandhi's receptiveness to the partial truths that may motivate terrorists and extreme nationalists meant that he took seriously the underlying social, political, and economic conditions behind terrorism. To focus on an act of terrorism without addressing its underlying causes, in Gandhi's view, was futile and counterproductive. It would be like focusing solely on teenage suicide bombers without any effort to understand the desperate and humiliating conditions that motivated them to commit such violent acts in the first place. Without seeking to justify terrorism in any way, Gandhi challenged opponents of terrorism to first examine the root causes of violence before compounding violence with more violence. For example, he advised British officials to find out what the terrorists meant by freedom. Perhaps then they

78 Gandhi to Lord Ampthill, October 30, 1909, in *Complete Works*, 9:509.
79 Ghosh, "Gandhi and the Terrorists," 564.
80 Mark Juergensmeyer, "Gandhi vs. Terrorism," *Daedalus* 136, no. 1 (Winter 2007): 34.

might understand that the absence of freedom was "the root cause" of the disease of terrorism.[81]

Finally, despite the fact that Gandhi's thought revolved around the notion of truth, he repeatedly warned against those who claimed to know the truth in any absolute sense. Despite his unparalleled commitment to truth, its fragmentary nature, nonetheless, demanded openness, humility, and mutual respect toward those with differing understandings. Thus Gandhi firmly resisted those who claimed a monopoly on truth and repeatedly reminded others of the human inability to fully know the truth. Not even a votary of truth should regard their own views as being alone truthful. One of the great mistakes terrorists make, in Gandhi's view, is to take a relative truth and turn it into an absolute one. The Gandhi scholar and peace activist Douglas Allen catches well the danger of absolutist claims: "One of the most arrogant and dangerous human moves is to make what is relative into an absolute. This is the move of those inflicting terrorism, whether emanating from Al Qaeda, IS and other militant Islamists, or from militants in Washington and the military-industrial complex, who act as if they possess the absolute truth, and all others are absolutely evil."[82] "We cannot know certainty in this world," wrote Gandhi. "All that appears and happens about and around is uncertain, transient. Only God that is Truth is certain. We are blessed if we catch a glimpse of that certainty."[83]

The source of Gandhi's opposition to terrorism was grounded in his vision of Swaraj. In Gandhi's Swaraj, there would be no killing, no murder, and no violence; there would be no rulers and no ruled, no colonizer and no colonized. Gandhi's Swaraj was a "kingdom of non-violence." It was neither vindictive nor punitive. There was no room for terrorism in it. Terrorism is like a virus. It causes harm. It usurps

---

81 Gandhi, "If I Were Viceroy," *Young India*, November 27, 1924, in *Complete Works*, 25:366.

82 Douglas Allen, "Terrorism and Violence: Gandhi after 9/11 in the USA and 26/11 in India," in *Gandhi after 9/11: Creative Nonviolence and Sustainability* (New Delhi: Oxford University Press, 2019), available at Oxford Scholarship Online, April 2019, accessed March 1, 2020, doi: 10.1093/oso/9780199491490.003.0007.

83 R. K. Prabhu and U. R. Rao, eds., *The Mind of Mahatma Gandhi* (Ahmedabad: Navajivan, 1967), 43–44.

freedom. It retards Swaraj. It destroys and kills. The only means to resist terrorism, according to Gandhi, is satyagraha—to strive to be wholly truthful and wholly nonviolent in thought, word, and deed. Gandhi's vision of national independence or Swaraj involved Gandhi in a lifelong search for truth.[84] Though he was not sanguine about the extreme difficulty of realizing it, he, nonetheless, called on leaders in the interim to embody truth and truthfulness and to pursue it fearlessly in the struggle against religious terrorism and violent nationalism.

Bibliography

Allen, Douglas. *Gandhi after 9/11: Creative Nonviolence and Sustainability*. New Delhi: Oxford University Press, 2019.

Chadda, Kusum Lata. *Reading Gandhi*. New Delhi: Kanishka, 2008.

Chatterjee, Margaret. *Gandhi's Religious Thought*. London: Macmillan, 1983.

Datta, Dhirendra Mohan. *The Philosophy of Mahatma Gandhi*. Madison: University of Wisconsin Press, 1953.

Erikson, Erik H. *Gandhi's Truth: On the Origins of Militant Nonviolence*. London: Faber & Faber, 1979.

Gandhi, M. K. *The Complete Works of Mahatma Gandhi*. Delhi: Publication Division Ministry of Information and Broadcasting, Government of India, 1969–1994.

———. *Gandhi's Autobiography: The Story of My Experiments with Truth*. Washington, DC: Public Affairs, 1948.

———. *Hind Swaraj, or Indian Home Rule*. Ahmedabad: Navajivan, 1938.

Ghosh, Durba. "Gandhi and the Terrorists: Revolutionary Challenges from Bengal and Engagements with Non-violent Political Protest." *South Asia: Journal of South Asian Studies* 39, no. 3 (2016): 560–576.

Holmes, R. L., ed. *Nonviolence in Theory and Practice*. Belmont, CA: Wadsworth, 1990.

Iyer, Raghavan, ed. *The Moral and Political Writings of Mahatma Gandhi*. Vol. 2, *Truth and Non-violence*. Oxford: Clarendon, 1986.

Johnson, Richard L., ed. *Gandhi's Experiments with Truth: Essential Writings by and about Mahatma Gandhi*. Lanham, MD: Lexington Books, 2006.

Juergensmeyer, Mark. "Gandhi vs. Terrorism." *Daedalus* 136, no. 1 (Winter 2007): 30–39.

Khanna, Suman. *Gandhi and the Good Life*. New Delhi: Gandhi Peace Foundation, 1985.

Kumar, R., ed. *Essays on Gandhian Politics: The Rowlatt Satyagraha of 1919*. Oxford: Clarendon, 1971.

---

84 M. G. Gandhi, "Statement to the Press," September 14, 1933, in *Complete Works*, 55:426.

Kumar

Mahadevan, T. K., ed. *Truth and Nonviolence: Report of the UNESCO Symposium on Truth and Nonviolence in Gandhi's Humanism, Paris, 14–17 October 1969.* New Delhi: Gandhi Peace Foundation, 1970.

Mehta, Ved. *Mahatma Gandhi and His Apostles.* New York: Viking, 1977.

Naess, Arne. *Gandhi and the Nuclear Age.* Totowa, NJ: Bedminster, 1965.

Narayan, Shriman. *Gandhi: The Man and His Thought.* New Delhi: Publication Division, Government of India, 1968.

Nehru, Jawaharlal. *The Discovery of India.* London: Meridian, 1960.

———. *Mahatma Gandhi.* Kolkata: Signet, 1949.

Pasricha, Ashu, and Jai Narain Sharma, eds. *Gandhi in Twenty-First Century.* New Delhi: Deep & Deep, 2011.

Prabhu, R. K., and U. R. Rao, eds. *The Mind of Mahatma Gandhi.* Ahmedabad: Navajivan, 1967.

Prasad, L. Gopal. *Religion, Morality and Politics according to Mahatma Gandhi.* New Delhi: Classical, 1991.

Radhakrishnan, Savarpelli, ed. *Mahatma Gandhi: Essays and Reflections on His Life and Work; Presented to Him on His Seventieth Birthday, October 2nd, 1939.* London: Allen & Unwin, 1940.

Richards, Glyn. *The Philosophy of Gandhi: A Study of His Basic Ideas.* London: Curzon, 1982.

Rosenthal, Newman H. *The Uncompromising Truth: Mahatma Gandhi 1869–1948.* London: Nelson, 1969.

Saxena, S. Kumat. *Ever unto God: Essays on Gandhi and Religion.* New Delhi: Indian Council of Philosophical Research, 1988.

Steger, Manfred B. *Gandhi's Dilemma: Nonviolent Principles and Nationalist Power.* New York: St. Martin's Press, 2000.

Sweetman, Will, and Aditya Malik, eds. *Hinduism in India: Modern and Contemporary Movements.* New Delhi: Sage, 2016.

Tähtinen, Unto. *The Core of Gandhi's Philosophy.* New Delhi: Abhinav, 1979.

Terchek, Ronald J. "Gandhi: Nonviolence and Violence." *Journal of Power and Ethics: An Interdisciplinary Review* 2, no. 3 (2001): 213–242.

CHAPTER 3

Gandhian Truths of Yesterday, for Today, and Always

A Vision to Dismantle Violent Religious Fundamentalisms

Sathianathan Clarke

Abstract: This essay mines Gandhi's wisdom to dismantle a contentious fortress of unitary religious truths in search of a hegemonic nation-state and reassemble a hospitable dwelling place for Truth that engenders interreligious flourishing. I expound on four pillars that support Gandhi's Truth, which dismantle religion's legitimation of violence under the cover of fundamentalisms. First, he weakened the colonial posture of religions by insisting that Truth transcends all religious proclamations of truth. Second, Gandhi sacrificed violent deities of all religions on the altar of ahimsa (nonviolence), the indispensable consort of religious Truth. Third, he relativized the absolutism of scripture (revelation from outside) by experiments with Truth (experience from within). And finally, Gandhi disassembled the robust bonds among religion, blood, and land (Hindutva) to promote an interreligious abode of Truth for a free India (Hind) lit by freedom (Swaraj) for all. Gandhi's spacious yet enduring conception of religious truth thus undercuts religious fundamentalists' ploy to legitimize violation and violence via the operations of strong nation-states.

> It is a curious paradox that though Gandhi's attitude to religion holds the key to understanding his life and thought, its nuances and significance have often been missed by his admirers and critics.
> —B. R. Nanda, *In Search of Gandhi: Essays and Reflections*

> True knowledge of religion breaks down the barriers between faith and faith. Cultivation of tolerance for other faiths will impart to us a truer understanding of our own.
> —M. K. Gandhi, *From Yeravda Mandir*

Religious fundamentalism and strong nation-states have long been natural bedfellows. Hardheaded religious ideologues are always in search of sociopolitical turf on which to actualize their theologies. After all, powerful ideas need fertile land and hardworking laborers to transform ardent beliefs into fecund practices. One sees this working relationship in operation in two contemporary contexts I am familiar with as an immigrant from India who is a naturalized citizen of the United States of America. The capture of political power by religious fundamentalists in India and the United States is on full display in Narendra Modi's Hindu nation and Donald Trump's Christian kingdom. Both illustrate nicely why nation-states become crucial for strong religions. Religious nationalism is a sociopolitical and historico-geographical space in which hallowed beliefs transform into mundane practices. Upholding and cultivating unwavering belief in a comprehensive and complete, divinely revealed worldview is only one of the theological ingredients that go into the configuration of violent religious fundamentalisms. Cognitive assent within headstrong believers must be accompanied by strong mechanisms to affect life in the real world. This is why the nation-state is sorely needed for religious fundamentalists. Religious nationalism is a political reality fueled by a religious ideal. On the one hand, the nation-state craftily employs religious mantras and rituals to publicly endorse and reinforce common belief. On the other hand, the nation-state effectively oversees the process wherein divinely manifest macrobeliefs are enforced as everyday micropractices of all persons, often by the use of violation and violence meted out against other religious and secular communities.

Gandhi, I argue in this essay, has insights that might dismantle a contentious fortress of unitary religious truths in search of a hegemonic nation-state and reassemble a hospitable dwelling place of truth for interreligious flourishing. Gandhi's spacious yet enduring conception of religious truth undercuts religious fundamentalists' ploy to construct Hindu and Christian religious nations. These religious fundamentalists fabricate a rigid theology arising out of an absolutist worldview rooted in revealed scripture, which in turn demands specific ethical ways of living in the world. As an alternative to the constructed idea of truth that promotes a sacred takeover of the national space, this paper examines four pillars that support Gandhi's understanding of truth, which disassembles religion's legitimation of violation and violence under the cover of religious fundamentalism. But before I get to the formidable props that Gandhi takes apart to present his theory of truth, let me comment on Gandhi's genius in engendering a discourse about truth that threatened the external imperial fabrications of the British Empire and the internal hegemonic concoctions of Hindu nationalism.

Truth as Domain for Gandhi's Discourse: Experiments in Interreligious Political Theology

As a forerunner of postcolonialism, Gandhi realized that colonialism was something to be overcome in the natives' consciousness.[1] He knew that emancipating the colonized mind was needed to free the captured body. Unless colonialism as a mentality, which gradually pervades and then firmly reigns like a deity from within, was identified and exorcised, India's colonized peoples would always be an enslaved community.[2] Truth (satya) was a domain like economics and politics that prescribed a working relationship between the natives and the colonizers. The truth spun by colonizers as a universal garment to fit the British and Indians into the complex relationships of colonialism was devised to seep deep into the colonized psyche. Gandhi knew that he had to strip down such a scaffolding of colonial truth that held sway over his people even as he circulated a countermodel of truth that would energize colonized Indians toward complete freedom (*purna Swaraj*).

Some of Western colonization was entangled in the major thrust of world mission, which asserted that Christianity is the *only* way to the

---

1 Gandhi's ideas preceded the influential anticolonial thinkers that became catalysts for postcolonialism. I am thinking of the following well-known postcolonial authors: Frantz Fanon, Albert Memmi, and Aimé Césaire.

2 Gandhi's great-granddaughter has written about postcolonialism's debt to Fanon and Gandhi in her early book, Leela Gandhi, *Postcolonial Theory: A Critical Introduction* (New York: Columbia University Press, 1998).

life-giving treasure chest that contains truth for all of humanity. The International Missionary Council confidently came to Tambaram (on the outskirts of Madras/Chennai), India in 1938. While Gandhi was visiting village after village, strengthening the Indian independence movement by building bridges between Hindus and Muslims and caste and Dalit communities, these mission theologians and strategists from across the world were putting their weight behind Hendrik Kraemer's definitive Christian theology regarding other world religions. The triumphant neoorthodox theology advocated in the colonized subcontinent, which was the birthplace of numerous religions, was univocal: there is no salvation in other religions outside of the redemptive work of Jesus Christ.[3] Gandhi's iconic spinning wheel (*charkha*) was more than a symbol of native resistance against buying British-made textiles made from exported cotton grown in India. It might also be construed as generating local threads of truth that could be woven into Truth for all human beings, including Christians.

Even while contending with Christian absolutism, which dominated the Western mission mindset of the time, Gandhi was also up against another unitary native vision of truth spreading in India. Vinayak Damodar Savarkar (1883–1966) developed the rationale for Hindu nationalism in the 1920s. Under the label *Hindutva* (Hinduness), Savarkar developed a vision of historical and geographical truth, around a much more militant and much less religiously inclusive India. He harnessed the narrow and exclusivist elements of Hinduism to foster religious hegemony and political militancy in India.[4] Savarkar was not merely "untroubled by the violence," but his writings "are steeped in

---

3 The International Missionary Council took place between December 12 and 29, 1938. For an excellent summary of the 1938 council proceeding in the context of the other councils, see Jan van Lin, *Shaking the Fundamentals: Religious Plurality and Ecumenical Movement* (Lieder, NL: Brill Rodopi, 2002).

4 For a convincing essay on how the "militant chauvinism" and "authoritarian fundamentalism" of Savarkar's Hindutva is the antithesis of Gandhi's Hinduism, see Rudolf C. Heredia, "Gandhi's Hinduism and Savarkar's Hindutva," *Economic and Political Weekly* 44, no. 29 (July 18, 2009): 62–67.

a desire for revenge against those who have humiliated Hindus."[5] His pitch to coreligionists was straightforward: "I want all Hindus to get themselves re-animated and re-born into a martial race."[6] Commenting upon the Hindu fundamentalist mythology spun around Savarkar, who is referred to with the prefix *Veer* (fearless) by his admirers, Chetan Bhatt surmises, "The overarching theme in his hagiographies are undoubtedly those of uncompromising Hindu militancy, violence, masculine strength and daring, both against British colonial rule and against Indian Muslims."[7]

Gandhi's discourse on truth rooted in nonviolence was, thus, directed toward external and internal hegemonic visions circulating in India. This might partly explain why he consciously claimed the term *satyagraha* (truth-force) to define his nonviolent movement for freedom for his compatriots. Such a discourse on truth coupled with nonviolence was designed to overcome the British's violent colonial rule and to eject militant aspirations for Hindutva rule in India. Truth-force thus, for Gandhi, was the political working out of "reality as it is" (satya) in the interreligious public square of free India. Interreligious nationalism was Gandhi's alternate vision in the face of a religiously Hindu nation.

Gandhi's Truths Displace Four Props That Legitimize Absolutist Fundamentalist Religion

In the rest of the essay, I inquire into what Gandhi might teach us in India and the United States about religious truth. Both contexts hold rigid and muscular conceptions of truth that fund violations against the right to believe and practice differently. These milieus are also guilty of fueling violence against religious minorities who do not conform

---

5 "Savarkar, Modi's Mentor: The Man Who Thought Gandhi a Sissy," *Economist*, December 20, 2014, http://www.economist.com/news/christmas-specials/21636599-controversial-mentor-hindu-right-man-who-thought-gandhi-sissy.

6 "Savarkar, Modi's Mentor."

7 Chetan Bhatt, *Hindu Nationalism: Origins, Ideologies and Modern Myths* (Oxford: Berg, 2001), 79.

to the absolutist religious worldviews of the majority populations. All religions that wish to turn their backs on violence and embrace peace in this world need to revisit these postulates of Gandhi's Truth. So how does Gandhi's notion of Truth, which he pens with a capital *T*, undercut imperial and muscular ones bolstered by fundamentalist Christianity and Hinduism circulating in these strong nation-states?

Pillar 1: Gandhi Undermined the Colonial Posture of Religions by Insisting That Truth Transcends All Religious Proclamations of Truth

Gandhi's thinking on truth emerged in the face of missionizing Christianity's absolutism spearheaded by the West and Hindutva's native absolutism directed against so-called alien religions in the Indian subcontinent. Yet he did not take the easy route of simply relativizing truth, which he consistently equated with God (the Ultimate). Instead, he maintained a firm grip on ultimate truth while claiming that it is particular, dialogical, and public. Truth, thus, for Gandhi, was ultimate yet available in the particular as it unfolded through nonviolent mediation in the interreligious public square. An interreligious theology of truth, for him, had to be inclusive to fund a public ethic for the well-being of the whole community.

In his conception of truth, Gandhi creatively comingled a crafty recovery of antiexclusive Western traditions with a concerted reinterpretation of inclusive native sources. He was thus against all imperial notions of truth. Gandhi asserted that there was ultimacy to truth. However, such ultimacy was not projected as simply universalizing parochial pronouncements of individual religions. Rather, what was ultimately true involved mediating between truths embedded within various religions. In a forest of lush spiritual resources available to God's whole human family, Gandhi reimagined the relationship between various religions. One way Gandhi reframed the mediation between religions against the historical clash between imperial postures of Islam and Christianity in India was proposing new root metaphors for reflecting on the relationships between religions. Religions, in Gandhi's way of thinking, no longer needed to be conceived of as *aggressive organizations*.

Islam and Christianity were often interpreted in Hindu India as "warring creeds." But in Gandhi's imaginary, religions could be reconfigured as *harmonious organisms*. Using organic rather than mechanistic images for reimagining the interrelatedness of religions, Gandhi described them through master metaphors of a garden endowed with myriad blossoming plants or a tree with many thriving branches. As he put it, "For me, the different religions are beautiful flowers from the same garden, or they are branches of the same majestic tree."[8]

The ambivalence one notices in Gandhi's insistence on the partial but ultimate truth of religious professions became his rationale for engaging in interreligious conversation in the public domain. Just as there is a God behind the various symbols for god, so also is there a "true and perfect religion" from which all religions draw their particular manifestations of ultimate truth. Religions, for Gandhi, become complexly tainted through the cultural and historical materializations of perfect religion. The sure way to testify to this perfection involves adopting a respectful interreligious conversation that might unveil the common source (Truth) that spawns and nourishes each of these particular branches. To quote Gandhi, "Even as a tree has a single trunk, but many branches and leaves, so there is one true and perfect Religion, but it becomes many, as it passes through the human medium. The one Religion is beyond all speech. Imperfect men put it into such language as they can command, and their words are interpreted by other men equally imperfect."[9]

Because all religions testify profoundly but partially to truth, they need to be engaged in the public square. Religions exchange truths to pool resources for building up the common good by circulating among one another their particular learnings of the Truth. Gandhi freed up public space and harnessed dialogical interchange to discern ways in which religions not only complement but also supplement one another.

---

8   M. K. Gandhi in *Gandhi on Christianity*, ed. Robert Ellsberg (Maryknoll, NY: Orbis, 1991), 65. Originally from *Harijan*, January 30, 1937.

9   M. K. Gandhi, *My Religion*, comp. and ed. Bharatan Kumarappa (Ahmedabad: Navajivan, 1955), 28, https://www.mkgandhi.org/ebks/my_religion.pdf. Original written by Gandhi in 1945.

Truth emerges from such interreligious exchange but, equally importantly, the imperfections hidden in particular religions are also disclosed. Gandhi, in a letter written from Yeravda prison in 1930, states,

> If we had attained the full vision of Truth, we would no longer be mere seekers, but have become one with God, for Truth is God. But being only seekers, we prosecute our quest, and are conscious of our imperfection. And if we are imperfect ourselves, religion as conceived by us must also be imperfect. We have not realized religion in its perfection, even as we have not realized God. . . . All faiths constitute a revelation of Truth, but all are imperfect, and liable to error. Reverence for other faiths need not blind us to their faults. We must be keenly alive to the defects of our faith also, yet not leave it on that account, but try to overcome those defects. Looking at all religions with an equal eye, we would not only not hesitate, but would think it our duty, to blend into our faith every acceptable feature of other faiths.[10]

Gandhi decolonized the imperial postures of exclusivist religions that assert absolute truth without interrogation in the public square. He did this by appealing to the Truth that lies behind all religious truth encapsulated in the scriptures and traditions of particular religions. Human beings' shared sightings of valuable fragments of such Truth are what represent the perfection of satya (Truth that leaks into the truths of religion). However, for Gandhi, Truth was inextricably entwined with another universal principle, which became the basis for understanding how he transfigured the second prop of religious fundamentalism's robust theological edifice.

Pillar 2: Gandhi Sacrificed Violent Deities of All Religions on the Altar of Ahimsa (Nonviolence), the Indispensable Consort of Religious Truth

In surmising Gandhi's religion in relation to his politics, Akeel Bilgrami shares a fundamental finding: "The methodological proposal, then, seems to be this: two underlying commitments (to 'truth' and 'nonviolence') are found in all religious books and they provide the

---

10 M. K. Gandhi, *From Yeravda Mandir*, trans. and ed. Valji Govindji Desai, 3rd ed. (Ahmedabad: Navajivan Mudranalaya, 2001), 26, https://www.mkgandhi.org/yeravda/yeravda.htm. First edition published in 1932.

criteria for a test for how to detect the spirit that informs their own detailed narratives and normative injunctions."[11] Having dealt with religious truth thus far, the above-mentioned quote nicely segues into nonviolence, which, for Gandhi, dismantled the second strong prop of fundamentalist religions.

Gandhi's clever constructivism is evident in the way in which he subtly sacrificed fierce representations of god in various religions on the altar of ahimsa. Perhaps his method's cunning reveals his training as a shrewd lawyer by colonial Britain. Gandhi's versatile strategy elevated nonviolence to become fused with truth. God is revealed in a twofold manifestation. Nonviolence joins truth to become one side of the universal coin against which all religious symbols, including gods and goddesses, must be valued and negotiated. "Ahimsa and Truth are so intertwined that it is practically impossible to disentangle and separate them," stated Gandhi, before going on to say, "They are like the two sides of a coin, or rather of a smooth unstamped metallic disc."[12] Nonviolence, for Gandhi, was the omnipresent and perceptible accompaniment to the somewhat abstract manifestations of truth. Differently worded, Truth must pass the taste and smell test of nonviolence, for ahimsa alone is the accompanying sign of truth available among us. The logic is imaginative—Truth is made indistinguishable from God and then made discernable as God by nonviolence. For Gandhi, God is a two-faced gift for all of humankind: "Ahimsa is my God, and Truth is my God. When I look for Ahimsa, Truth says, 'Find it through me.' When I look for Truth, Ahimsa says, 'Find it out through me.'"[13]

Gandhi argued for the interchangeability of the symbols of Truth and God. In fact, to give precedence to the public span and interreligious scope of truth, Gandhi favored the philosophical formulation "Truth is God" rather than the more theological expression "God is

11 Akeel Bilgrami, "Gandhi's Religion and Its Relation to His Politics," in *The Cambridge Companion to Gandhi*, ed. Judith M. Brown and Anthony Parel (Cambridge: Cambridge University Press, 2011), 94.

12 Gandhi, *From Yeravda Mandir*, 9–10.

13 M. K. Gandhi, *Truth Is God*, comp. K. R. Prabhu (Ahmedabad: Navajivan, 1955), 5, https://www.mkgandhi.org/ebks/truth_is_god.pdf. Originally from *Young India*, June 4, 1925.

Truth." When the phrase is articulated this way, some of God's strong parochial characteristics are transferred to the interreligious and even atheistic public domain of Truth. On the one hand, Truth becomes the spacious universal metasymbol under which all human beings may gather comfortably. Gandhi contended that even atheists would not be offended if they were labeled as "truth-fearing" men and women rather than "God-fearing" ones. As he put it, "But in their passion for discovering truth, the atheists have not hesitated to deny the very existence of God—from their own point of view rightly. And it was because of this reasoning that I saw that rather than say that God is Truth, I should say that Truth is God."[14] On the other hand, for Gandhi, ahimsa was the incarnational sign wherein Truth as God finds habitation both deep within each human being and among us as humankind on Earth. In a bidirectional way, nonviolence's divine dynamic is the resident god within us even as it is the God into whom we empty ourselves. Just like Truth, nonviolence is an active, transforming, and life-giving divine force. "Nonviolence is an active force of the highest order," says Gandhi. Energizing human beings from the inside, "it is soul-force or the power of Godhead within us."[15] Yet for Gandhi, it also transforms us to "become Godlike," since only "to the extent [that] we realize nonviolence . . . [can we] become wholly God."[16] Ingeniously, gods and goddesses were defanged and declawed on the altar of nonviolence for truth's sake.

Sacrifice (*yajna*) was an essential theme in Gandhi's thinking. However, he was continually moving people's imaginations away from violent bloody sacrifice, which was quite prevalent in India in his time. Gandhi found the notion of self-sacrifice to be an appealing alternate way that witnessed powerfully to nonviolent Truth (God). "At one time they sacrificed animals to propitiate angry gods," he said, but then "they taught that sacrifice was meant to be of our baser self, to please

14 Gandhi, 14. Originally from *Young India*, December 31, 1931.
15 Gandhi, 37. Originally from *Harijan*, November 12, 1938.
16 Gandhi, 37.

not angry gods, but the living God within us."[17] One must not fail to note the skillful (one might even say crafty) manner in which Gandhi dealt with the ambivalent nature of divine representations in religions. He neutralized violent deities on the altar of nonviolence for the cause of Truth. Throughout his one hundred volumes, he appears to have turned his lazy eye on God's violent manifestations while preferentially overreading the motif of nonviolence strewn across various religious scriptures and traditions. So for example, he made the nonviolent Jesus, who suffered on the cross for the life of the world, stand out as the exemplar of Christianity, thereby dwarfing all other fiercer manifestations of God, especially as contained in the Old Testament. He did this by exalting the Synoptic Gospels' Jesus as an interpretive key to decipher all other understandings of God in the Bible. Gandhi construed the nonviolent, self-giving suffering of Jesus symbolized by the cross as the redeeming light on all the shadowy hostilities contained in the Christian religion. "We can understand, then," says James W. Douglas, "why Gandhi looked to Jesus as the supreme example of nonviolence: on the cross, suffering love reached its fullest expression, even in the eyes of one who could not affirm Christ as uniquely divine."[18]

One can also notice this tendency to underread violence while overreading nonviolence in Hinduism and Islam's religious traditions. In interpretations of his own religion, Gandhi tended to overlook the violent imagery of his favorite scripture (Bhagavad Gita) while focusing on the spiritual meaning of sacrificing oneself to the obligation of doing one's dharma (moral obligation to the law of the universe). He was careful not to specify from where he drew his actual scriptural warrants while referencing Hinduism. For instance, in 1929, he simply claimed, "The most distinctive and the largest contribution of Hinduism to India's culture is the doctrine of ahimsa. It has given a definite

---

17 Gandhi quoted in B. R. Nanda, *In Search of Gandhi: Essays and Reflections* (New Delhi: Oxford University Press, 2004), 17. Originally from *Harijan*, October 3, 1936.
18 James W. Douglas, "From Gandhi to Christ: God as Suffering Love," in *Gandhi on Christianity*, ed. Robert Ellsberg (Maryknoll, NY: Orbis, 1991), 106.

bias to the country's history for the last three thousand years and over and it has not ceased to be a living force in the lives of India's millions even today."[19] Similarly, when addressing the overall message of nonviolence in Islam, Gandhi appealed to the Koran's overall rationale rather than specific texts. He starts with an inclusive affirmation: "I certainly regard Islam as one of the inspired religions and, therefore, the Holy Koran as an inspired book and Muhammad as one of the prophets."[20] He then goes on to insist more generally that the overall teaching of the Koran advanced nonviolence. "I have come to the conclusion that the teaching of the Koran is essentially in favour of nonviolence," declared Gandhi. He makes the subtle point that while "nonviolence is enjoined as a duty[,] violence is permitted as a necessity" in this divine revelation.[21]

Gandhi diligently extracted and elevated the pearl of nonviolence from the oyster shells of the different religions. Truth and nonviolence, as the two faces of God, were Gandhi's highest principles. At the altar of nonviolence, the violence manifested by gods and goddesses and the aggression legitimized by scriptures and traditions were surrendered for the well-being of all human beings. All deities and their scriptural testimonies submit to the valuation of God as truth and nonviolence. Gandhi's struggle against these other fiery, lesser gods was a righteous fight, since divine entities were employed by "strong religion" to propagate "inhumanity in the world." "It is said," Satendra Nandan recalls, "that Gandhi fought three battles: against himself, against the ills prevalent in Indian society, and against the British Empire." To this, he suggests, one could "add another one: Against God for man's inhumanity in the world." Nandan ends by reminding us that Gandhi's struggle arose from the fact that "he loved all four."[22]

19 M. K. Gandhi, *The Mind of Mahatma Gandhi*, comp. and ed. R. K. Prabu and U. R. Rao (Ahmedabad: Navajivan Mudranalaya, 1960), chap. 17, https://www.mkgandhi.org/momgandhi/chap17.htm. Originally from *Harijan*, March 24, 1929.
20 Gandhi, chap. 17. Originally from *Harijan*, July 13, 1940.
21 Gandhi, chap. 17. Originally from *Harijan*, July 13, 1940.
22 Satendra Nandan, *Gandhianjali* (Fiji: Ivy, 2019), 35.

Maybe there were more than four entities that Gandhi was struggling against in his journey for Truth as God, which was always accompanied by nonviolence. The absolutism of scripture as a fixed and closed source for Truth was another idol of religious fundamentalism that animated his struggle. Scripture as inflexible canon is the third prop of strong religion that Gandhi dismantled. Let us turn to how Gandhi reconfigured the absolutism of sacred scripture.

Pillar 3: Gandhi Relativized the Absolutism of Scripture (Revelation from Outside) by Experiments with Truth (Experience from Within)

Religious fundamentalisms build their steely beliefs and practices on the rock-solid foundation of scriptures revealed "from above or outside" to command human obedience to divine order. Whether as adherence to the "word of God" in Christianity or as compliance with sharia ("the way") in Islam or as submission to the dharma ("moral order of the universe") as revealed by the eternal Vedas, fundamentalists prop up scriptures as a fixed revelation to which the religious faithful must conform fully and finally. Elsewhere, I have undertaken a comprehensive study of the absolute authority and overpowering role of scripture (Word-visions revealed "from beyond") in Christian, Muslim, and Hindu fundamentalism. Let me simply quote a brief summary that highlights the absolutist, imperial, and normative character of such "Word-visions" divinely given for the well-being of the whole world:

> Religious fundamentalisms promote unquestioning belief in their Word-visions. Religions become imperialistic when they accept the Word-vision categorically, seeing it as applicable to all historical situations and obligatory for all human beings irrespective of their own religious persuasions. Fundamentalists assert that this "meaning-package" is normative since it alone encompasses the whole truth, supplementing or supplanting human beings' fragmented insights. This is the logic that legitimizes claims for the incontestable authority of the Word-vision. Word-visions are "fundamental"; they ground and precede all other forms of human knowing. . . . The primordial dimension of this religious metanarrative, steeped in the revelation of scripture, is palpable in the examples of Christian, Muslim, and Hindu fundamentalism.[23]

---

23 Sathianathan Clarke, *Competing Fundamentalisms: Violent Extremism in Christianity, Islam, and Hinduism* (Louisville, KY: John Knox Westminster, 2017), 129–30.

It was the absolutist status and imperialist claim of scripture in religious fundamentalisms that Gandhi destabilized. Gandhi may have consistently referred to himself as a "sanatanist Hindu" (an original or eternal adherent to the Hindu dharma). This did entail taking seriously the orthodoxy required by Hinduism to accept the absolute authority of the Vedas (primary scriptures referred to as *sruthi*, "that which is heard eternally") or the Puranas and Epics (secondary scriptures referred to as *smrithi*, "that which is remembered methodically"). Gandhi, however, explicitly transferred authority for his journey into Truth from scriptural revelations to experience emanating from his ongoing experiments in life. He was thus more a scientist steeped in experiments with truth on the ground than a religious exegete propounding eternal truths encapsulated in the Shastras (religious scriptures). Shiv Visvanathan captures this aspect of Gandhi remarkably well: "Mention the name Gandhi and people would say pacifist, *satyagrahi*, nationalist, anti-colonial . . . Hindu, [and] vegetarian." Yet, he says, "Gandhi went beyond the official or dictionary definition of each word . . . [since] he was a nationalist who fought the nation-state, an anti-colonialist who wished to redeem the British, a Hindu who happily bypassed the *Shastras*." Visvanathan explains the incongruity by adding, "One word is missing in this list . . . the noun 'scientist.'" Gandhi, accordingly, "was one of the great scientists of the *swadeshi* [freedom] era."[24]

As a scientist deeply engaged with an interreligious community yearning for freedom, Gandhi moved away from the art of textual interpretations of scripture and toward the science of experiments with truth enmeshed in life. By shifting religious authority from a fixity on specialized texts to the wonderfully complex textures of everyday experience, Gandhi was involved in a reformation of sorts. First, as earlier noted, Gandhi sought to free truth from its confinement within the temple, mosque, and church to play a liberating role in the interreligious public domain, including determining the political future of colonized peoples. Truth spilled over from scribes and priests in the

---

24 Shiv Visvanathan, "Reinventing Gandhi," in *Debating Gandhi*, ed. A. Raghuramaraju (New Delhi: Oxford University Press, 2006), 199.

sanctuary onto the insurgents and protestors on the streets. Second, Gandhi veered away from the challenge of learning the mostly unfamiliar language of various scriptures (Sanskrit for Hindus, literary Tamil or Hindi for Christians, and Arabic for Muslims) and instead elevated the language of the heart for encountering and realizing the truth. Truth thus did not involve leaning on the absolute directives of scriptural revelation. Instead, it entailed listening to what Gandhi "called, variously, antaryami [indwelling controller], spirit, the dweller within, the inner voice, or the 'small, still voice.'"[25] And finally, Gandhi aligned religious truths with experimentation with the totality of life, which, as communal life, included various religious scriptures. He collated bits and pieces from various sacred scriptures after sifting them through the sieve of experience and sutured them into a living truth for the entire Indian community.

For Gandhi, scientific experimentation undermined strong commitment to scriptural absolutism, which tends to view truth as confined within the revealed scripture of one valid religion. Instead, for the well-being of all, Truth, for Gandhi, was entwined with life experiences in all its richness. The human experiential realm for excavating living truth was a substitute for the scriptural expositions of truth. Experimenting with truth permitted Gandhi to be a scriptural eclectic rather than an exclusivist and a practitioner rather than a cognitivist of that which is real. As Bilgrami puts it, "What this means is that truth for Gandhi is not a cognitive notion at all. It is an experiential notion. It is not a proposition purporting to describe the world of which truth is predicated, it is only our own moral experience which is capable of being true. This was of utmost importance for him."[26]

Let me conclude this section with a couple of qualifications about Gandhi's experimental nature of truth: Gandhi's conception of Truth is not an imitation of Western individualism beholden to the

---

25 Tridip Suhrud, editor's introduction to *An Autobiography, or The Story of My Experiments with Truth: A Critical Edition*, by in M. K. Gandhi, ed. Tripid Suhrud (New Haven, CT: Yale University Press, 2018), 26.

26 Bilgrami, "Gandhi's Religion," 261.

autonomous self or Western existentialism divorced from reason. In fact, one can even say that just as his notion of Truth refused to be contained as objective propositions in the sacred deposits of scripture, it also declined to be usurped by the subjectivity of the autonomous self. Faisal Devji reminds us to keep Truth as the universal subject in all interpretations of Gandhi. In a review of his autobiography, he states, "In its Gujarati original, the title of Gandhi's book, rendered into English as 'The Story of My Experiments with Truth,' reads something like 'Truth's Experiments' (*satya-na prayogo*), in which it is not the Mahatma who is the subject but instead truth. Rejecting the spiritualism that emerged as a reaction against what used to be called 'bourgeois' individualism only to reinforce it, Gandhi's autobiography audaciously seeks to tell the story of truth's experiments with the self it both sustains and destroys."[27]

Gandhi's refusal to pedestalize the autonomous self was one facet of his anticolonial thinking. But this was complemented by his insistence on embracing the faculty of reason for sifting experience on the journey to Truth. Western existentialism and rigid scripturalism were undercut in experiments with truth by invoking reason. "Every formula of every religion, in this age of reason," states Gandhi, "has to submit to the acid test of reason and universal justice if it is to ask for universal assent. . . . Error [thus] can claim no exception even if it can be supported by the scriptures of the world."[28] Even though Gandhi does appeal to reason to mediate between individual experiences of the truth, reason "was not a transcendental or natural faculty, but a socially acquired capacity presupposing and constantly shaped and nurtured by tradition."[29] Bhikhu Parekh captures the transformational

27 Faisal Devji, "Destroyed by Truth," review of *An Autobiography, or The Story of My Experiments with Truth: A Critical Edition*, by M. K. Gandhi, ed. Tripid Suhrud, *Los Angeles Review of Books*, November 7, 2018, https://www.lareviewofbooks.org/article/destroyed-by-truth.

28 M. K. Gandhi, *The Essence of Hinduism*, comp. V. B. Kher (Ahmedabad: Navajivan, 1987), vi. Originally from *Young India*, February 26, 1925.

29 Bhikhu Parekh, *Colonialism, Tradition, and Reform: An Analysis of Gandhi's Political Discourse* (New Delhi: Sage, 1989), 23.

objective in Gandhi, who seeks to honor the Indian tradition while also filtering it through the colander of reason: "The reformer's task was both to elucidate the *historical rationale* of unacceptable practices and to expose their *irrationality*. He required both sympathetic understanding and critical spirit, both patience and indignation."[30]

The complex process of discovering Truth that "both sustains and destroys" the self through experimentation while also tapping into reforming reason might explain how Gandhi formulated his objective of freedom (Swaraj) for the human community. Gandhi reimagined freedom for a colonized people in search of an independent nation-state without concealing the genuine plurality of the communities, envisioning a hospitable abode for all. This leads us to describe the manner in which Gandhi reconfigured the final concrete prop of religious fundamentalism.

Pillar 4: Gandhi Disassembled the Robust Bonds between Religion, Blood, and Land (Hindutva) to Promote an Interreligious Abode of Truth for a Free India (Hind) Lit by Freedom (Swaraj) for All

The claim by fundamentalists that the divine has gifted geographical tracts of land to specific religious communities has spawned violation and violence in various regions in the world.

Such a solid relationship among blessed religion, chosen people, and sacred land has led to violence for millennia. Religious communities battle with one another, claiming that God sanctioned the land for God's own elect (Jews, Christians, Muslims) or that the land was sanctified for a religio-cultural people (Hindus, Buddhists, US Christians). Extremist factions in many religions thus aggressively assert dominance of the public space for themselves and their religion. Apart from the hostility that prevails in the "holy land" of the Middle East, one can see the spread of religiously inspired violence in other regions of the world—Hindus, Buddhists, and Christians are establishing their own religious homelands.

---

30 Parekh, 24 (emphasis in original).

Such a compact among religion, blood, and land has seeped into the imaginings of the nation-state in the United States and India. Christian fundamentalism has had its ebbs and flows in the United States over the last one hundred years. In a contrived logic, somewhat at odds with the plain-sense teachings of the historical Jesus, becoming great and being Christian were conflated in order to pursue Christian fundamentalism's national calling (chosen nation) to bring to fruition the well-being of the world (redeemer nation).[31] Christian fundamentalism has seen a national resurgence in the last decades, playing a particularly active role in Donald Trump's election to the presidency in 2016. In Trump's vision for America, the desire to capture the nation-state for white Christians and dominate the world has become a dream partially realized in actuality. The United States has long held that its blessed land was given by divine providence to white Christians to set up a nation under God. The interweaving of religion (Christianity), blood (the white race), and land (nation under God) forms the basis of white Christian America. In the words of Robert P. Jones, "The historical record of lived Christianity in America reveals that Christian theology and institutions have been central cultural tent poles holding up the very idea of white supremacy."[32] He describes in his recent book how such a racially and religiously based foundation for the nation-state has led to discrimination in its policies and practices against Black, brown, and Muslim communities over centuries.

India also has emerged as the land for Hindus in this century. Narendra Modi's India is a Hindu nation. Brought to power with a thumping victory in the 2019 national election, his Hindu-based Bharatiya Janata Party has gone about religionizing politics with gusto and dexterity. The reclamation of the site of the Ram temple in Ayodhya by Hindu fundamentalists, who demolished a medieval mosque there in

---

31 For a comprehensive study on the way in which these "myths" (chosen nation, innocent nation, and millennial nation) are woven together in Christian America, see Richard Hughes, *Christian America and the Kingdom of God* (Champaign: University of Illinois Press, 2010).

32 Robert P. Jones, *White Too Long: The Legacy of White Supremacy in American Christianity* (New York: Simon & Schuster, 2020), 6.

1992, is the hub around which the drama of politics and religion has played out. The temple of Ram, as the restored symbol of Hindu rule in the land of India, is a theme that is touted in political culture. In a widely celebrated event that captured the attention of the whole nation, Modi laid the foundation stone for the Hindu temple on August 5, 2020. Hindus heralded the stage-managed and well-publicized event as a victory across the country while it stirred fear among Muslims and Christians. The words of Asaduddin Owaisi, president of the All India Majlis-e-Ittehad-ul-Muslimeen (All India Council for Unity of Muslims), who also is a member of parliament, are worth quoting: "India is a secular country. The Prime Minister has violated the oath of office and tenet of secularism by attending the ceremony in his official capacity. He laid the foundation for 'Hindu Rashtra.' This is the day of the defeat of democracy and secularism, and success of 'Hindutva.'"[33]

But let me get back to Gandhi. I have already addressed the rationale of Hindu fundamentalism that Gandhi was pitted against. Hindutva, first articulated in 1923 by V. D. Savarkar, carefully braided the strands of blood, land, and religion into a cogent religio-cultural national narrative. As a biological community with common blood, Hindus were invited to glory in their common religious culture and devote themselves to flourish in their sacred land. Savarkar puts this together convincingly: "We Hindus are bound together not only by the ties of love we bear to a common fatherland and by the common blood that courses through our veins and keeps our hearts throbbing and our affections warm, but also by the ties of common homage we pay to our great civilization—our Hindu culture. . . . We are one because we are a nation, a race and own a common Sanskriti (civilization)."[34] Gandhi's countervision for a nation-in-waiting claimed India's land and rivers as a home of freedom for communities that were interracial, interreligious, and intercultural. *Hind Swaraj* (home rule / freedom)

---

33 *Telengana Today*, August 6, 2020, https://news.rediff.com/commentary/2020/aug/05/pm
-violated-oath-of-office-by-bhoomi-pujan-owaisi/0243766b206ba6cc15ea794cf90db81a.

34 Vinayak Damodar Savarkar, *Hindutva: Who Is a Hindu?*, 2nd ed. (Bombay: Veer Savarkar Prakashan, 1969), 91–92.

was Gandhi's alternative vision to Hindutva. Interestingly, Gandhi thought of Swaraj as "the gospel" for India that links the love of self with the self-sacrificing love for neighbor. Speaking to village workers in Nagpur in 1935, he said, "I am afraid I must repeat the gospel to you and remind you that when you demand swaraj, you do not want swaraj yourself alone, but for your neighbor too."[35]

The concept of Swaraj went through several makeovers through Gandhi's long years of struggle. It was first popularized by Gandhi's *Hind Swaraj*, which he wrote in Gujarati while traveling from London to South Africa onboard the SS *Kildonan Castle* between November 13 and November 22, 1909. Though it was originally banned as sedition propaganda by the British, Gandhi translated it into English in 1910. The British only lifted the ban in 1938, but it had already made its way into the hands of nationalists across India. After Gandhi's early publication, the term *Swaraj* evolved into a much more spacious, positive, and rich goal than its literal meaning of home- or self-rule for India. It increasingly took on connotations that included the idea of freedom and liberation. So by the end of Gandhi's life, *Swaraj* knit together the motif of independence from alien British colonial rule and the idea of living in freedom in a land ruled by its own commitment to Truth and nonviolence. Such a vision of Swaraj, which Gandhi also labeled *purna Swaraj* (complete freedom or liberation), was in contrast to the homogenous vision of Hindutva. Freedom, for Gandhi, was not "based on religion, race or language"[36] as it was for alien Europeans or native believers in Hindutva. Accordingly, "the nation for him was not a *homogenous organic community*, but a *pluralistic political community*."[37]

---

35 Raghavan Iyer, ed., *The Essential Writings of Mahatma Gandhi* (New Delhi: Oxford University Press, 1998).

36 Anthony Parel, "Gandhi and the State," in Brown and Parel, *Cambridge Companion to Gandhi*, 160.

37 Parel, 160 (emphasis in original).

Conclusion

Religion does play a role in communal life. It can either galvanize a takeover to homogenize community life (religious nationalism) or nurture the community toward a life of pluralistic freedom (interreligious nation). Gandhi's vision for emancipation was both religious and political. Rooted in Truth and nonviolence, which Gandhi interpreted as the two faces of God, he imaginatively constructed a political theology for India that has much relevance for interreligious relations in the contemporary world. As an alternative to the external colonial prototype of the British and the internal imperial archetype of Hindutva, Gandhi's religiopolitical vision was inclusive, pluralistic, dialogical, experiential, and liberational. Drawing from the words of Shiv Visvanathan, we might agree that Gandhi's imaginative model was "universalistic but localized" and "self-reflective and critical," moving "beyond liberation to emancipation" by postulating "categories that would avoid the rebrutalization of our societies, seeking to redeem both British and Indian society."[38]

Through his long life and voluminous writings, Gandhi offered many images through which to think about religions in his desire to stress their complementarity. At a time in which it was politically expedient to lift high the competing, even conflictual, relationship between Christianity, Islam, and Hinduism, Gandhi drew upon organic metaphors from the field of horticulture. Gandhi's decision to shift the field from which he mined a rethinking of the relationships between religions is noteworthy. No longer was he comfortable extracting from the field of military studies, which employs war, crusade, and battle as images with which to understand the relations between religions. Rather, Gandhi tapped into the field of horticulture, in which gardens, trees, leaves, and flowers grow in their complementary beauty.

A couple of critical comments may be appropriate as I conclude this essay. The first points to a philosophical inconsistency between

---

38 Shiv Visvanathan, foreword to U. R. Ananthamurthy, *Hindutva or Hind Swaraj* (Noida, India: Harper Perennial, 2018), xviii.

the images Gandhi offered us, especially if we want to account for genuine plurality among religions. Let me zero in on two of these images to make my point. In one instance, Gandhi talked about religions as being numerous leaves growing out of one tree. He says, "Just as a tree had a million leaves, similarly though God was one, there were as many religions as there were men and women though they were rooted in one God."[39] In another place, Gandhi moved from the image of religions being "a million leaves" from the same tree to religions being the many flowers, presumably from many flowing plants, within the same garden. "For me the different religions are beautiful flowers from the same garden," he stated, and so "they are equally true, though being received and interpreted through human instruments equally imperfect."[40] While the first quote suggests that the variations among religions are merely differences in form expressing the same substance, the second is much more suggestive that there may be real differences between religions as flowers from a garden with numerous types of plants.

Though the idea that various religions are just different forms emanating from the same substance is closer to Gandhi's nondualistic (Advaita) worldview, one wonders if the garden image with diverse flowers also celebrates and advances the distinctive divergences among religions. Stephen Prothero is right when he says, "One of the most common misconceptions about the world's religions is that they plumb the same depths, ask the same questions. They do not. Only religions that see God as all good ask how a good God can allow millions to die in tsunamis. Only religions that believe in souls ask whether your soul exists before you are born and what happens to it after you die. And only religions that think you have one soul ask after the 'soul' in the singular."[41] Perhaps teasing out and creatively stretching the image of religions as "beautiful" yet delightfully different "flower[ing

39 M. K. Gandhi, *The Selected Works of Mahatma Gandhi*, vol. 5, *The Voice of Truth*, ed. Shriman Narayan, trans. Valji Govindji Desai, (Ahmedabad: Navajivan, 1968), sec. 5, https://www.mkgandhi.org/voiceoftruth/unityofallreligions.htm. Originally from *Harijan*, March 16, 1947.

40 Gandhi, sec. 5. Originally from *Harijan*, January 30, 1937.

41 Stephen Prothero, *God Is Not One* (New York: HarperOne, 2010), 24.

plants] from the same garden" may be the way to inject plurality into a philosophical framework to ground interreligious nations. This alone can account for actual diversity, since religions interpret the universal human predicament in the world in varying ways and then offer blessed solutions to their adherents to overcome the particular human problem identified by their religious wisdom.

There is another problem with Gandhi's attractive organic image of the garden with its trees, flowers, and leaves: it failed to take seriously the structural elements that determine the fecundity of majestic trees, beautiful flowers, and lush leaves. The kind of soil, how water is distributed, and how much fertilizer is given to each plant or tree decide and regulate the garden's political economy. In addition, one cannot expect to effect the flourishing of the garden without the difficult task of dealing with this dimension of religious power systems. Gandhi valued the soft elements of power generated by the heart. Thus he was drawn to images that describe religion through this subtle world of persuasive power. Take another example. According to Gandhi, "A rose does not need to preach. It simply spreads its fragrance." This is precisely why he goes on to say, "The fragrance of religious and spiritual life is much finer and subtler than of the rose."[42] Roses, though, cannot bring forth their fragrance apart from the reality of the political economy (soil, water, and fertilizer) of the garden. They are dependent on hard power that decides on matters of soil quality, availability of water, and amount of fertilizer. This was the crux of the iconic Dalit leader B. R. Ambedkar's (1891–1956) criticism. Gandhi, he said, sought the solution for structural problems by harvesting the heart. Thus internal transformation through persuasive power was key in his philosophy. Ambedkar, as a Dalit representing the outcaste communities of India, knew that the coercive power of the system was another beast altogether. He targeted those who wielded hard power within the system, who often had their heart vested in control of land, water, and wealth.[43] So

---

42 Gandhi, *Voice of Truth*, sec. 5. Originally from *Harijan*, March 29, 1935.
43 This insight is carefully worked out by D. R. Nagaraj, *The Flaming Feet and Other Essays* (Kolkata: Seagull, 2011).

from the viewpoint of emancipation for the downtrodden, Ambedkar advocated for political, economic, and legal solutions to aid his people. Perhaps we need both soft and hard power to come together in a journey toward Truth and nonviolence for Swaraj's objective. Truth, nonviolence, love, and freedom must also incorporate justice. Gandhi's vision of Truth must learn from the Hebrew prophets, as well as the Dalit champion Ambedkar.

Bibliography

Bhatt, Chetan. *Hindu Nationalism: Origins, Ideologies and Modern Myths.* Oxford: Berg, 2001.

Bilgrami, Akeel. "Gandhi's Religion and Its Relation to His Politics." In *The Cambridge Companion to Gandhi*, edited by Judith M. Brown and Anthony Parel, 93–116. Cambridge: Cambridge University Press, 2011.

Clarke, Sathianathan. *Competing Fundamentalisms: Violent Extremism in Christianity, Islam, and Hinduism.* Louisville, KY: John Knox Westminster, 2017.

Devji, Faisal. "Destroyed by Truth." Review of *An Autobiography, or The Story of My Experiments with Truth: A Critical Edition*, by M. K. Gandhi, ed. Tripid Suhrud. *Los Angeles Review of Books*, November 7, 2018. https://www.lareviewofbooks .org/article/destroyed-by-truth.

Douglas, James W. "From Gandhi to Christ: God as Suffering Love." In *Gandhi on Christianity*, edited by Robert Ellsberg, 101–108. Maryknoll, NY: Orbis, 1991.

Economist. "Savarkar, Modi's Mentor: The Man Who Thought Gandhi a Sissy." December 20, 2014. http://www.economist.com/news/christmas-specials/21636599 -controversial-mentor-hindu-right-man-who-thought-gandhi-sissy.

Ellsberg, Robert ed. *Gandhi on Christianity.* Maryknoll, NY: Orbis, 1991.

Gandhi, Leela. *Postcolonial Theory: A Critical introduction.* New York: Columbia University Press, 1998.

Gandhi, M. K. *The Essence of Hinduism.* Compiled by V. B. Kher. Ahmedabad: Navajivan, 1987.

———. *From Yeravda Mandir.* Translated and edited by Valji Govindji Desai. 3rd ed. Ahmedabad: Navajivan Mudranalaya, 2001. https://www.mkgandhi.org/ yeravda/yeravda.htm.

———. *The Mind of Mahatma Gandhi.* Compiled and edited by R. K. Prabu and U. R. Rao. Ahmedabad: Navajivan Mudranalaya, 1960.

———. *My Religion.* Compiled and edited by Bharatan Kumarappa. Ahmedabad: Navajivan, 1955.

———. *The Selected Works of Mahatma Gandhi.* Edited by Shriman Narayan. Translated by Valji Govindji Desai. Vol. 5, *The Voice of Truth.* Ahmedabad: Navajivan, 1968. https://www.mkgandhi.org/voiceoftruth/unityofallreligions.htm.

———. *Truth Is God*. Compiled by K. R. Prabhu. Ahmedabad: Navajivan, 1955.

Heredia, Rudolf C. "Gandhi's Hinduism and Savarkar's Hindutva." *Economic and Political Weekly* 44, no. 29 (July 18, 2009): 62–67.

Hughes, Richard. *Christian America and the Kingdom of God*. Champaign: University of Illinois Press, 2010.

Iyer, Raghavan ed., *The Essential Writings of Mahatma Gandhi* (New Delhi: Oxford University Press, 1998).

Jones, Robert P. *White Too Long: The Legacy of White Supremacy in American Christianity*. New York: Simon & Schuster, 2020.

Lin, Jan van. *Shaking the Fundamentals: Religious Plurality and Ecumenical Movement*. Lieder, NL: Brill Rodopi, 2002.

Nagaraj, D. R. *The Flaming Feet and Other Essays*. Kolkata: Seagull, 2011.

Nanda, B. R. *In Search of Gandhi: Essays and Reflections*. New Delhi: Oxford University Press, 2004.

Nandan, Satendra. *Gandhianjali*. Fiji: Ivy, 2019.

Parekh, Bhikhu. *Colonialism, Tradition, and Reform: An Analysis of Gandhi's Political Discourse*. New Delhi: Sage, 1989.

Parel, Anthony. "Gandhi and the State." In *The Cambridge Companion to Gandhi*, edited by Judith M. Brown and Anthony Parel, 154–172. Cambridge: Cambridge University Press, 2011.

Prothero, Stephen. *God Is Not One*. New York: HarperOne, 2010.

Savarkar, Vinayak Damodar. *Hindutva: Who Is a Hindu?* 2nd ed. Bombay: Veer Savarkar Prakashan, 1969.

Suhrud, Tridip. Editor's introduction to *An Autobiography, or The Story of My Experiments with Truth: A Critical Edition*, by M. K. Gandhi, edited by Tripid Suhrud, 1–36. New Haven, CT: Yale University Press, 2020.

Telengana Today, August 6, 2020. https://news.rediff.com/commentary/2020/aug/05/pm-violated-oath-of-office-by-bhoomi-pujan-owaisi/0243766b206ba6cc15ea794cf90db81a.

Visvanathan, Shiv. Foreword to *Hindutva or Hind Swaraj*, by U. R. Ananthamurthy, v–xxii. Noida, India: Harper Perennial, 2018.

———. "Reinventing Gandhi." In *Debating Gandhi*, edited by A. Raghuramaraju, 195–222. New Delhi: Oxford University Press, 2006.

CHAPTER 4

Mediating Truths

GANDHI'S ILLIBERAL RELIGIONISM AND AMBEDKAR'S LIBERAL NATIONALISM

Anderson H. M. Jeremiah

Abstract: Mahatma Gandhi's political thought has a global reach, while B. R. Ambedkar's liberal nationalism is often maligned and narrowly defined. This chapter is a critical conversation around this perceived disparity. Gandhi, through a pan-Indian vision, helped to refocus Hinduism and simplify it, so that it became a force that mobilizes and facilitates change, especially in the context of India seeking freedom from colonial rule. Ambedkar, on the other hand, driven by a fundamental desire to transform the lives of Dalits, viewed Gandhi and his religion as illiberal and sought social liberation and emancipation through constitutional social liberalism. Gandhi effectively shared his message of Swaraj (freedom) through satyagraha. Ambedkar, also in the pursuit of freedom, fought for a separate electorate for Dalits to exercise their rights within democracy. Gandhi and Ambedkar, as contemporaries, pursued truths that effectively shaped modern Indian democracy and the emancipation of Dalits. This chapter's contention is that to a certain extent, they both became a corrective to each other.

Gandhi was my childhood hero. He was a glorified saint who abstained from immoral Western culture and preserved his chastity and remained pure. My schoolteachers exhorted us to follow in the footsteps of Gandhi to be better human beings. Gandhi alone showed humanity the virtue of nonviolence, and through his pursuit of Truth, he single-handedly brought down the mighty British Empire. We heard about Gandhi every day; not a single day passed by without reflecting on Gandhi's mighty achievements. So honestly, I didn't have an option but to immortalize Gandhi and consider him as my hero too. Even though I vaguely remember walking past a statue of a suited man standing with a book in his hand right next to Gandhi's statue in our local bus station in the 1990s, I never bothered to ask who that man was. All through my school days, neither in the classroom nor outside did I hear the name of B. R. Ambedkar. It was always Mahatma (great soul) Gandhi. Babasaheb (revered father) Ambedkar didn't make the cut. At least not until I was doing my postgraduate studies. Sadly, I didn't give Ambedkar a chance to be my childhood hero! My experience is not an isolated one. Many Indian youth in the past few decades have heard only about the achievements of Gandhi and not about those of Ambedkar, despite his significant contributions to the development of constitutional democracy in India. With this brief personal note, what I wish to offer in this chapter is a critical conversation around a wisely constructed and broadly marketed public perception of Gandhi's political thought and the much maligned and narrowly defined liberal nationalism of Ambedkar.

Tryst with Truth

Gandhi and Ambedkar both claimed that they were pursuing truth for the emancipation of humanity, albeit differently. Gandhi wanted to transform his inherited religion of Hinduism because for him, every aspect of life flowed from that deep commitment to the divine. For obvious reasons, Hinduism over centuries of accumulation and absorption evolved into a convoluted philosophical worldview with complex layers of socioritualistic practices. "Under Hinduism's sacred canopy," says Stephen Prothero, "sit a dizzying variety of religious beliefs and behaviours practiced in the wildly complex and contradictory subcontinent of India."[1] Perhaps Hinduism's undefinable and unruly variety lent itself to Gandhi, who set about to reform it as a scaffolding to build a national movement for independence from the British Empire. Gandhi wanted to refocus Hinduism and simplify it so that it became

---

1 Stephen Prothero, *God Is Not One: Eight Rival Religions That Run the World* (New York: HarperOne, 2011), 135.

a force that mobilizes and facilitates change, especially in the context of India seeking freedom from colonial rule.

For Gandhi, Hinduism was the vehicle through which political freedom could be achieved. Reasons for Gandhi's choice of overtly embracing Hinduism for constructing his overall philosophy for fortifying India's freedom movement are multiplex. It was a combination of his socialization into Hindu religiosity by his mother, cultural familiarity with the social customs of a Hindu way of life, filial piety that came from high regard for his clan, and pragmatism, since at least two-thirds of the subcontinent was Hindu. Whatever the reasons, Gandhi set about "reimagining" Hinduism as the religion of love, peace, and nonviolence. These are universal values, reckoned Gandhi, and one can find much of these if one only searches Hinduism's lavish sources. Gandhi perceptively used select knowledge of Vedic scriptures, along with various parts of the Puranas (with special attention to the Bhagavad Gita). He deployed these effectively to get his message across, which contributed considerably to the making of the Mahatma.

Gandhi's reimagined Hinduism was not free of structures and values but, on the contrary, meticulously shaped by the adherence to *varnashrama dharma*, a strict code of practice that governed social and ritual relationship among Hindus and prescribed duties that governed various chronological stages in an individual's life. This involves doing one's moral duty (dharma) throughout one's lifetime in accordance with the caste within which one is born (varna) and the stage of life (ashrama) one finds oneself in as one grows from childhood to old age. Although Gandhi sought to give a new meaning and purpose to varnashrama dharma, it still remained a vehicle of social division and segregation. The different caste communities would be interdependent, Gandhi envisioned, but unrestricted social mobility to subvert the caste system was not in the cards. To understand the nuance in Gandhi's thinking, one needs to know the distinction between varna and jati in the varnashrama system.

Varna is the larger frame of Hindu society. It refers to the broad and somewhat less straitjacketed fourfold caste categorization that allowed for some movement of occupation, including a more ambiguous ascription of purity and pollution as articulated in *Manusmriti*.[2] Jati, on the other hand, refers to distinctive subcastes in the Hindu social system. There are thousands of such tightknit and closed clans throughout India that loosely sit within the fourfold varna categories. Two characteristics of jati are what make it nonegalitarian and open to abuse. The jati social arrangement prescribes exclusive occupations for its members (usually males, with jobs such as cobbler or priest or scavenger), and it ascribed ritual purity or pollution to each of these occupations. Of course, Dalits[3] were outcastes and thus outside of varna, often forced to do the occupations that were most polluting. Gandhi, we can say, was unwilling to dismantle varna, which he thought was foundational to Hinduism, but was open to weakening jati, which he argued was a corruption of Hinduism. Tanika Sarkar makes this point well. For Gandhi, she argues, varna "was supposedly the rational and liberal core of the [Hindu] faith. It contained no contempt for any caste or labour forms but, at the same time, enjoined hereditary labour divisions."[4] Whereas jati, in Gandhi's judgment, "was extraneous, complicating the elegant simplicity of the fourfold varna structure" of Hinduism.[5] In his naïve and buoyant optimism, Gandhi believed that his reimagined varna-adopting but jati-rejecting Hinduism would weed out the perversion of untouchability.

Gandhi advocated an imagined Hinduism that was far removed from the lived aspect of a complex, diverse, and often disparate set of religious practices. Gandhi embraced a utopian ideal of Hinduism that functioned nonetheless on a clearly articulated and coherent set of values, with a well-organized structure of social relationship, built around the varnashrama dharma. While it may have sounded virtuous

---

2 *Manusmriti* is the law of Manu as found in the *Rig-Veda* that articulates the fourfold varna system and its social obligations.

3 Dalit is an affirmative term used to refer to former untouchable communities in India and will be used as such. Gandhi used the term *Harijan*, and Ambedkar used the terms *untouchable* and *broken ones* interchangeably.

4 Tanika Sarkar, "Gandhi and Social Relations," in *The Cambridge Companion to Gandhi*, ed. Judith M. Brown and Anthony Parel (Cambridge: Cambridge University Press, 2011), 180.

5 Sarkar, 180.

in theory, Gandhi's revision was of little use to the Dalits. They lived under the crushing weight of varna, since they were forced to do the polluted occupations not undertaken by the four castes in Hindu society, which further ejected them from the interactions of the human system of reciprocal relationship. It is not that what he envisioned was unworthy of praise, but it was far from the reach of millions of people who worshipfully followed him. From a *sanatani* (believer in *sanatana dharma*, eternal religion) background, Gandhi fashioned a Hinduism that was a fine reflection of other major world religions. As a connoisseur of critical religious thinking, Gandhi developed an ability to gather important views from a range of religions and mold his imagined Hinduism. The unintended consequence of the Gandhian version of Hinduism was that it reduced the complex schools of religious philosophy across the Indian subcontinent into a homogenized, narrow set of religious practices resting on a rigid social worldview.

Ambedkar, from a social liberalism perspective, viewed religion suspiciously, especially with his experience of Hinduism from the bottom of the heap. For him, religion must mainly be a matter of principles only. It cannot be a matter of rules. The moment it degenerates into rules, it ceases to be a religion, as it kills responsibility, which is the essence of a true religious act. People and their religion must be judged by social standards based on social ethics. No other standard would have any meaning if religion were held to be a necessary good for the well-being of the people. Ambedkar vehemently attacked the caste system from the point of view of the "broken ones," who were crushed under its unbearable weight. He said that inequality is the soul of Hinduism, and its morality is only social. Responding to Gandhi, Ambedkar wrote in *Harijan*, "The outcaste is a by-product of the caste system. There will be outcastes so long as there are castes. Nothing can emancipate the outcaste except the destruction of the caste system. Nothing can help to save Hinduism . . . except the purging of the Hindu faith of this odious and vicious dogma."[6] So for Ambedkar,

---

6 B. R. Ambedkar quoted in *Journalist Gandhi (Selected Writings of Gandhi)*, comp. Sunil Sharma (Mumbai: Gandhi Book Center, 1994), 51. Originally in *Harijan*, February 11, 1933.

caste was a system of graded sovereignties, which reaffirmed Brahmin hegemonic ideology because each caste oppressed inferior castes and was in turn subject to the Brahmins' contempt. In this context, religion as envisaged by Hindus is nothing but a multitude of commands and prohibitions. Ambedkar felt that it had to dismantled in its entirety. The subtleties of saving varna while rejecting jati were a distraction. Rather, Ambedkar wanted to advocate a religion that taught liberty, equality, and fraternity.

Gandhi and Ambedkar developed their own understandings of Hinduism and its impact on their respective lives. Gandhi borrowed liberally from broad-ranging sources to develop his political philosophy but called it Hinduism—an imagined Hinduism, far from the lived reality of millions. Precisely because of his deft meandering under the rubrics of spiritual journey, it is difficult to pin down his underlying commitments and vision. Ambedkar, on the other hand, was utterly convinced that it is Hinduism that valorizes caste practice in the name of the varna system, which prescribes a graded worldview passed on as Indian cultural nationalism. Therefore, for Gandhi, the satya (truth) is self-evident in the Hinduism he has come to embrace, and for Ambedkar, the truth is achieved when caste is annihilated and an equal society is realized. Both Gandhi and Ambedkar wanted to redeem elements of a fundamental religious essence for the betterment of the respective communities they wanted emancipate.

Gandhi had a pan-Indian vision, whereas Ambedkar was focused on the Dalits. However, their desires converged on the cause of social liberation. Gandhi declared himself as a *sanatani* Hindu, one who believes in the Vedas, Upanishads, and Puranas, as well as the varna dharma. Gandhi sought transformation through ahimsa (nonviolence), satyagraha (nonviolent force of truth and love), and Swaraj (self-rule). In Gandhi's view, that's how we know God who himself represents *Sat* (Truth), *Chit* (Knowledge), and *Ananda* (Bliss).[7] Gandhi hoped that this revitalized and idealized Hinduism would offer a harmonious coexistence of different

7 M. K. Gandhi, *Selected Writings of Mahatma Gandhi*, ed. Ronald Duncan (Glasgow: Fontana, 1972), 41.

varna groups as interdependent constituents. Gandhi's effort to rid his reimagined Hinduism of untouchability should be acknowledged and appreciated. However, Ambedkar was convinced that the ideology of varna and its corresponding dehumanizing hierarchies had deeply infected the very fabric of Hinduism. So for Ambedkar, the only way out of this is to completely abandon it. Thus while Gandhi encouraged the burning of government permits and foreign cloth, Ambedkar and his followers burned the *Manusmriti*, a volume of traditional Hindu law bearing on caste.[8] There is no way to reimagine Hinduism's utility in empowering those who have been dehumanized in the first place.

Interestingly, Ambedkar applied the same critique to Buddhism in the process he employed to develop a different path to Theravada, Mahayana, and Vajrayana Buddhism. He proposed what is known as Navayana Buddhism, which focused specifically on social equity and community empowerment. Following on his critique of "religion," as represented by the varnashrama dharma-based Hinduism advocated by Gandhi, Ambedkar reinterpreted Buddhism with rational morality infused with social relevance. In his magnum opus, *The Buddha and His Dhamma*, Ambedkar articulated a moral social order in the form of Navayana Buddhism, which would be an antidote to the social problems of inequality and exclusion perpetuated by Brahmanical Hinduism upon the Dalits. In this reconstruction of Buddhism, Ambedkar not only offers a new reading of Buddha and his message but challenges the traditional understanding of Buddhism itself. Especially in his essay on Buddha and Karl Marx,[9] it is obvious that Ambedkar, noticeably influenced by Marxism, presents Buddhism not simply as a religion but more as a set of beliefs and practices that facilitates the formation of a new community of equals. Ambedkar was convinced that the purpose of a religion is not just to explain the origin of humanity but to offer a moral social path that has direct impact on the lives of

---

8 Joseph Lelyveld, *Great Soul: Mahatma Gandhi and His Struggle with India* (New York: Vintage, 2011), 210.

9 B. R. Ambedkar, *The Essential Writings of B. R. Ambedkar*, ed. Valerian Rodrigues (New Delhi: Oxford University Press, 2002), 173.

Dalits—hence his rejection of Hinduism and embrace of Buddhism, which gave him the space to articulate his socially liberating vision. Ambedkar's Navayana Buddhism, was an engaged religion, reimagined "from below" to offer a more egalitarian and ethical framework for Indian society.

Gandhi's Illiberal Religionism and Ambedkar's Liberal Nationalism

Was Gandhi a religious mystic and an astute Machiavellian political operator because he envisioned a religious grounding for the formation of a nation-state—that is, reimagined Hinduism? Was Ambedkar a political opportunist and antinational because he rejected Indian cultural nationalism—that is, nonegalitarian Hinduism? Interestingly, Gandhi and Ambedkar both sought social liberation and transformation by using religion as a vehicle to deliver that change. Yet there were differences in their approaches to this common objective.

Gandhi's Illiberal Religionism

Gandhi envisioned an all-consuming way of life in his imagined Hinduism. This path required ultimate sacrifices and fierce abstinence from physical pleasure in order to attain spiritual fulfillment. Public life and political engagement were part of this worldview. As mentioned earlier, for Gandhi, the pursuit of Truth, which is another name for God, involved every aspect of human life. Religion as he had come to understand it is the matrix within which political engagement played out. They are intertwined. For Gandhi, this homegrown Hinduism is diametrically opposed to the colonial powers. He was convinced that it was through the path of satyagraha (holding on to truth nonviolently) that India would achieve her freedom. However, there were serious issues in Gandhi's conceptualization of Hinduism. As an ardent critic of modernity and Western civilization, Gandhi was convinced that India should remain vigilant; otherwise, she would fall prey to the evil of modernity. Being true to his early perceptions, Gandhi thought of modernity and modern civilization as utterly evil. For example, he says, "Medical sciences is the concentrated essence of Black Magic.... Hospitals are the instruments that the devil has been using for his own purposes, in order to keep his hold on his kingdom. They perpetuate vice, misery, and degradation, and real slavery."[10]

Gandhi was certainly influenced by secularist ideas that emerged from postwar Europe, as well as popular Christian viewpoints. However, Gandhi's political theory was built around two fundamental principles: satyagraha (nonviolent force of truth and love) and Swaraj (theory of freedom or self-rule). Gandhi, through the principle of Hind Swaraj, forged a nationalist hegemony that was fundamentally opposed to Western modern secular liberal democracy.[11] Gandhi observed that the secular liberal democracy of Europe is evil. Conversely, Gandhi's imagined Hinduism, as we have seen, was built on the counter-Western and antimodern ideology of varna, which he equivocally endorsed. He even purported this to be a form of Hindu science. Gandhi says,

> I am one of those who do not consider caste to be a harmful institution. In its origin caste was a wholesome custom and promoted national well-being.... I believe that caste has saved Hinduism from disintegration.... Varnashrama is in my opinion, inherent in human nature and Hinduism has simply reduced it to a science. It does attach to birth. A man cannot change his varna by choice. Not to abide by one's varna is to disregard the law of heredity. I am inclined to think that the law of heredity is an eternal law and any attempt to alter that law must lead, as it has before led, to utter confusion. I can see very great use in considering a Brahmin to be always a Brahmin throughout his life.[12]

Even though Gandhi's view on caste and varna evolved over a period of time, he still held an uncompromising view of Hinduism as the backbone of Swaraj. Especially with regards to the economic model

---

10 M. K. Gandhi, *Mahatma Gandhi: The Essential Writings*, ed. Judith M. Brown (Oxford: Oxford University Press, 2008), 74.
11 David Hardiman, *Gandhi in His Time and Ours: The Global Legacy of His Ideas* (London: Hurst, 2003), 22, 72.
12 Gandhi, *Selected Writings*, 167, 178.

that Gandhi advocated as part of Hind Swaraj, a subsistence and self-reliant village economy that was essentially a glorified feudal agrarian model, Gandhi spoke very clearly in support of the landlords and their right to own land. In his view, since it is the landlords who will contribute to the well-being of the entire village economy, their rights and privileges should be protected.[13] This is an economic model shaped within the religious views Gandhi held very dear to his heart.

Gandhi took a positive attitude toward religious pluralism. He deeply respected the religions that had made their home in India. He celebrated the religious resources of Islam, Buddhism, Sikhism, Jainism, and Christianity. In fact, he mined the philosophy of nonviolent love and peace from many of these religions, often using them against militant forms of Christianity and Islam. Yet he personally advocated adherence to Hinduism as the religion of India. Gandhi did say, "Even as a tree has a single trunk, but many branches and leaves, so there is one true and perfect Religion, but it becomes many, as it passes through the human medium."[14] Nonetheless, it seems as though his adherence to Hinduism steered him to a foundational preconception about religions in relation to Hinduism. Other religions are celebrated by Gandhi as valuable "branches and leaves," which are carefully pruned into an eternal Hinduism (sanatana dharma) that remains the "single tree trunk."

Having said that, one must also acknowledge that Gandhi did advocate repentance from Hindus for using religion to inflict untouchability on millions of people in India. In his words, "Even so it is necessary for us Hindus to repent of the wrong we have done, to alter our behaviour towards those whom we have suppressed by a system as devilish as we believe the English system of the government of India to be. We must not throw a few miserable schools at them: We must not adopt the air of superiority towards them. We must treat them as our blood brothers as they are in fact. We must return to them the

---

13 M. K. Gandhi, *Collected Works of Mahatma Gandhi*, ed. Indian Ministry of Information and Broadcasting, vol. 23 (New Delhi: Government of India, 1999), 158.
14 M. K. Gandhi, *My Religion*, comp. and ed. Bharatan Kumarappa (Ahmedabad: Navajivan, 1955), 28. Original written by Gandhi in 1945.

inheritance of which we have robbed them. I regard untouchability as the greatest blot in Hinduism."[15]

Gandhi no doubt did want to facilitate the betterment of Dalits, but in his own way. First, it had to be done while retaining the nonegalitarian system of varnashrama dharma, and second, it was to be done under his leadership and according to his norms because Gandhi was convinced that the Dalits cannot think for themselves.[16] Gandhi did not give agency to the Dalits. He says,

> I abhor with my whole soul the system which has reduced a large number of Hindus to a level less than that of beast. The vexed problem would be solved if the poor Panchama was allowed to mind his own business. Unfortunately, he has no mind or business he can call his own. Has a beast any mind or business but that of his master's? Has a Panchama a place he can call his own? He may not walk on the very roads he cleans and pays for by the sweat of his brow. He may not even dress as the others do.[17]

If one reads carefully between the lines, Gandhi's true colors come out. Gandhi knew *panchamas* (literally, the fifth, which refers to the Dalits outside the fourfold caste system) needed a savior, and he decided he was the one who was going to represent them. Gandhi did not endorse economic equality but rather conceived of some form of mutual cooperation between landlord and tenant. He even promised this to the landed class by saying, "Let me assure you that I shall be no party to dispossessing the propertied classes of their private property without just cause."[18] Commenting on Gandhi's attitude, Ramchandra Guha says, "Gandhi's approach could be patronizing. During his famous fast in Yerwada prison in 1932, he argued that if the suppressed castes 'are ever to rise, it will not be by reservation of seats but will be by the strenuous work of Hindu reformers in their midst.' While putting the onus on the upper castes to reform themselves, this perspective

---

15 Gandhi, *Selected Writings*, 173.
16 Hardiman, *Gandhi in His Time*, 132.
17 M. K. Gandhi, *Mahatma Gandhi: Selected Political Writings*, ed. Dennis Dalton (Cambridge: Hackett, 1996), 119.
18 Gandhi, *Selected Political Writings*, 133.

robbed the Dalits of agency. Why couldn't the suppressed caste rise through organizing themselves for (non-violent) action against injustice and discrimination?"[19]

Gandhi's imagined Hinduism and the hegemonic socioeconomic structures it propped up can be best described as conservative and illiberal religionism. The Brahmanical hegemonic worldview, the backbone of Hinduism, was offered as the macroepistemological framework to privilege superiority and purity. Such a worldview is inherently illiberal and hierarchical. The political and religious ideas of swadeshi (self-reliance) and Swaraj (self-rule) were fundamentally in opposition to Western liberal democracy, which Gandhi considered to be great threat to India.[20] Notwithstanding his efforts to abolish untouchability, as a Hindu patriarch, Gandhi ensured not only the stability but the continuation of a social system that was deeply inequitable. This was mainly because Gandhi's social and political views were couched within this mystical, homegrown, imagined Hinduism.

Ambedkar's Liberal Nationalism

With Gandhi's larger-than-life shadow looming over him, Ambedkar sought to chart his own political path. As a product of Western secular political philosophy, Ambedkar wholeheartedly embraced social liberalism as the path to social emancipation for the masses, particularly the Dalit community that he toiled to lift out of oblivion. Holding a diametrical opposing view from Gandhi, he believed Hinduism to be the source of tyranny and oppression of the *panchamas*. Ambedkar thus systematically argued for the annihilation of the caste system. He says, "What the Depressed Classes want is a religion that will give them equality of social status . . . nothing can be more odious and vile than that admitted social evils should be sought to be justified on the ground of religion. The Depressed Classes may not be able to overthrow inequities to which they are subjected. But they have made

---

19 Ramachandra Guha, *Gandhi: The Years That Changed the World, 1914–1948* (New York: Alfred Knopf, 2018), 914.
20 Gandhi, *Essential Writings*, 82.

up their mind not to tolerate a religion that will lend its support to the continuance of these inequities."[21]

On the back of a detailed analysis of the Vedas and Puranas, Ambedkar launches a fierce critique of Brahminical ideology that is built on the foundation of the caste system. For Ambedkar, the impenetrable caste organization is a product of the Brahminical imagination of the world that lacks reason and morality and is founded on strict obedience to the sacred law, *Manusmriti*. Ambedkar argued that it is the irrational adherence to Brahmanical ideology prescribed by the sacred law that inflicts pain and suffering upon the Dalit communities. The irrational and illiberal religion of Hinduism makes it almost impossible for equality and social justice to be practiced.[22] Ambedkar was convinced that the kind of illiberal religionism Gandhi advocated demands unfettered devotion to its fundamental principles and cannot envision or accept change. While giving a Kale Memorial Lecture in 1939, Ambedkar launched a scathing attack on Gandhi's views:

> To my mind there is no doubt that this Gandhi age is the dark age of India. It is an age in which people instead of looking for their ideals in the future are returning to antiquity. It is an age in which people have ceased to think for themselves and as they have ceased to think they have ceased to read and examine the facts of their lives. The fate of an ignorant democracy which refuses to follow the way shown by learning and experience and chooses to grope in the dark paths of the mystics and the megalomaniacs is a sad thing to contemplate.[23]

Gandhism, as Ambedkar calls it, does not seek to pursue a socially egalitarian society that would include all people. Ambedkar does not hold back his views while critiquing the village economy supported by Gandhi as shortsighted and self-defeating. Gandhism does not ensure economic equality or democratic participation for all, especially

---

21 B. R. Ambedkar, *Babasaheb Ambedkar Writings and Speeches*, vol. 9, ed. Vasant Moon (Bombay: Education Department, Government of Maharashtra, 1979), 111.

22 B. R. Ambedkar, *Annihilation of Caste: The Annotated Critical Edition*, ed. S. Anand (London: Verso, 2016), 303.

23 B. R. Ambedkar, "Federation versus Freedom" (Kale Memorial Lecture, Gokhale Institute of Politics and Economics, Pune, India, 1939).

the Dalits. According to Ambedkar, Gandhi, through his ideal village economy, was simply painting an ideal picture, which is built on the inherent inequalities of the caste system. Therefore, the common man and woman have to continue to toil ceaselessly with no hope of breaking out of misery. Ambedkar argued that following the path of Gandhi would be surrendering to the class structure, where "there is on the one hand, tyranny, vanity, pride, arrogance, greed, selfishness and on the other hand insecurity, poverty, degradation, loss of liberty, self-reliance, independence, dignity, and self-respect."[24] Hence Ambedkar encouraged his supporters to embrace a social liberalism that undercuts the roots of tyrannical religionism, primarily through constitutional and political reform.[25]

Ambedkar wholeheartedly believed in constitutional liberal democracy that ensures equal participation of all citizens. He was convinced that until a separate electorate for Dalits was realized, the social and political exclusion and cultural oppression would continue. Speaking through All India Radio (AIR) on October 3, 1954, Ambedkar rearticulated his political philosophy: "Positively, my social philosophy may be said to be enshrined in three words: Liberty, equality and fraternity." Ambedkar, through his exploration of religious and philosophical deliberations within Buddhism, arrived at these fundamental liberal social values as the core political principles that could alleviate the misery of millions of the Dalit community. Offering an alternative to Gandhi's illiberal religionism, Ambedkar emphasized the social and political virtues of liberty, equality, and fraternity. Instead of religion becoming the foundation for a new India, as envisioned by Gandhi, Ambedkar wanted social justice to be at the heart of nation building. However, he didn't want to underestimate the power of religion and belonging among the masses. Hence Ambedkar grounded his project of reconstructing a new social order with liberal nationalism in the shape of Navayana Buddhism. Ambedkar says, "The purpose of religion is to explain the origin of the world. The purpose of Dhamma is

24 Ambedkar, *Essential Writings*, 160.
25 Ambedkar, *Annihilation of Caste*, 307.

to reconstruct the world."[26] Summarizing Ambedkar's views in forging this new reality, Gail Omvedt observes,

> Ambedkar's revival of Buddhism in India was based on several convictions: that Brahmanism (or Brahmanical Hinduism) was the religious ideology that had not only enslaved untouchables for thousands of years but had the entire Indian society under the grip of stagnation; that some form of religion was needed to provide the bondage, the moral force for governance in any society that a new religion was specifically needed by the ex-untouchables to escape the mental slavery of Brahminic Hinduism; and above all that Buddhism was the appropriate religion for untouchables, for India, and for a new social order because it was a rational religion centred around a morality of liberty, equality and community.[27]

In order to deconstruct the Brahminical worldview that was offered as the macroepistemological framework to privilege superiority and purity by Gandhi's imagined Hinduism, Ambedkar sought to reconstruct a new religious path that would promote liberty, equality, and community. Ambedkar became acutely aware of the fact that social and political liberation will not come to fruition without a religious moral framework. To this end, as explained earlier, Ambedkar envisaged Navayana Buddhism as an educative and organizing paradigm with his slogan "educate, agitate, and organise."[28] Ambedkar forged a new religious path in Navayana Buddhism, which gave him a platform for the pursuit of liberal nationalism and to challenge the Hindu hegemony.

A Mystic and a Dissenter

Gandhi and Ambedkar were towering political figures during the formative period of independent India. Both had their utopian ideals and

---

26 B. R. Ambedkar, *The Buddha and His Dhamma* (Lucknow: Samyak Prakashan, 2019):322.

27 Gail Omvedt, "Liberty, Equality, Community: Dr. Babasaheb Ambedkar's Vision of New Social Order," in *Contemporary Relevance of Ambedkar's Thoughts*, ed. A. Ramaiah (Jaipur: Rawat, 2017), 97.

28 Ambedkar, *Writings and Speeches*, vol. 17, ed. Hari Narake et al. (Bombay: Education Department, Government of Maharashtra, 1979), 276.

were driven by a passion to transform, but in all reality, they also may have succumbed to their own ideals. Ambedkar, as a social liberal, had genuine hope in the state and its constitutional power as the only mechanism to annihilate caste and its enduring legacy of untouchability. However, as a rural romantic and anarchist with deep suspicion for the state, Gandhi believed that spiritual transformation that would eventually lead to social transformation. Commenting on these two great political personalities, Ramchandra Guha observes, "Ambedkar placed more faith in constitutional process, in changes in the law. . . . Gandhi saw more hope in social change, in the self-directed renewal of individuals and communities. Ambedkar emphasized the creation of jobs for untouchables; Gandhi the creation of a sense of spiritual equality between Hindus of all castes. An upper caste reformer, Gandhi was motivated by a sense of guilt, the desire to make reparation for past sins, whereas as one born in an untouchable home, Ambedkar was animated by the drive to achieve a position of social equality and human dignity for his followers."[29]

In this brief analysis, what I sought to do was not simply to critique and condemn Gandhi from a Dalit perspective but to find ways to also acknowledge his fierce criticism of the West's future-oriented rationalist ideals, which he believed would eviscerate peaceful coexistence of diverse communities in an equitable relationship. Responding to the persistent critique from Ambedkar and other Dalit leaders, Gandhi actually began to reconsider his views on the caste system and eventually reluctantly supported the taking apart of the caste system. Having said that, we also need to pay attention to Ambedkar's critique that exposes the gaps in Gandhi's worldview. In a lecture on "Federation versus Freedom," Ambedkar particularly deconstructs Gandhi's resistance to accept the role of Dalits in the federation and their separate electorate because Gandhi wanted them to stay in the Hindu majoritarian fold.[30] On the back of Gandhi's disastrous underrepresentation of concerns from various sections of Indian society in the Round Table

---

29 Guha, *Years That Changed the World*, 444.
30 Ambedkar, "Federation versus Freedom."

Conferences (1930–32), Ambedkar launches a pointed critique of Gandhi. Ambedkar accuses him of dragging the country backward as a mystic who listens to the "inner voice" and not the cries of millions of Dalits. Ambedkar criticizes Gandhi's insincerity in opposing untouchability but supporting varnashrama dharma. Gandhi still remains the Mahatma, a saint, but we shouldn't turn away from the criticisms posed by Ambedkar. How could we glorify ahimsa, satyagraha, and Swaraj that willfully discount the experiences of the Dalits? Can we divorce Gandhi's views from the reality of his unflinching commitment to varna-based discrimination of "graded sovereignties"? Simultaneously, Ambedkar's radical social liberalism bordering on communism also needs to be carefully analyzed, especially his views on sifting workable resources from the nation's vast majority who are Hindus.

This analysis assumes significance in the contemporary Indian political landscape, which is experiencing Hindu nationalism's spirited defense of their own imagined sanatana dharma on one side and the continued categorical denunciation of *Manusmriti* (law of Manu) by Ambedkarite Dalit politicians on the other. The heart of the issue over the past decades appears to be whether to continue along the pathway of the imagined Hinduism of Gandhi rooted in Brahmanical hegemony or to choose another pathway carved out of liberal and egalitarian principles based on the laws of whole people (the Indian Constitution). This preoccupation has been fused with the ideology of Hindutva, which considers *Manusmriti* to be the preeminent and most worshipable scripture after the Vedas. The Hindutva ideologues, following Vinayak Damodar Savarkar, have located *Manusmriti* as the basis of building a Hindu nation, along with its culture, customs, thought, and practice. In other words, *Manusmriti* is Hindu law. Today, ahimsa, satyagraha, and Swaraj have all been infused or rather infected with and flow from this fundamental commitment. Dalit communities, on the other hand, envision another foundation for a liberal, even if religious, nation. Eulogizing Ambedkar as the "father of the Indian constitution," in contrast to Gandhi as the "father of the nation," Dalits represent him as an iconic symbol with an Indian constitution in hand.

As the symbol of the reimagining of the "broken ones," who bear the scars of the Hindu law, they lift up an alternate vision for India's future development, a wholistic Swaraj.

Both Gandhi the mystic and Ambedkar the dissenter have offered invaluable insight into the deliberations of shaping modern Indian democracy and the emancipation of Dalits. To a certain extent, they each became a corrective to the other. As in the words of D. R. Nagaraj, "Both having jumped into action, they cured each other's excesses; they emerged as transformed persons at the end of a very intense encounter."[31] The truth Gandhi and Ambedkar sought occupied the realms of both religion and politics. After a long arduous journey with immense personal cost, Gandhi and Ambedkar realized that their spiritual and political quest couldn't be achieved in isolation. Swaraj without liberty, equality, and fraternity would be vacuous. Herein lie our lessons in the context of competing truth claims.

Bibliography

Alter, Joseph. *Gandhi's Body*. Philadelphia: University of Pennsylvania Press, 2000.

Ambedkar, B. R. *Annihilation of Caste: The Annotated Critical Edition*. Edited by S. Anand. London: Verso, 2016.

———. *Babasaheb Ambedkar Writings and Speeches*. Vol. 9. Edited by Vasant Moon. Bombay: Education Department, Government of Maharashtra, 1979.

———. *Babasaheb Ambedkar Writings and Speeches*. Vol. 17. Edited by Hari Narake, M. L. Kasare, N. G. Kamble, and Ashok Godghate. Bombay: Education Department, Government of Maharashtra, 1979.

———. *The Buddha and His Dhamma*. Lucknow: Samyak Prakashan, 2019.

———. *The Essential Writings of B. R. Ambedkar*. Edited by Valerian Rodrigues. New Delhi: Oxford University Press, 2002.

———. "Federation versus Freedom." Kale Memorial Lecture, Gokhale Institute of Politics and Economics, Pune, India, 1939.

———. *What Congress and Gandhi Have Done to the Untouchables*. 2nd ed. Bombay: Thacker, 1946.

Barua, Ankur. "Revisiting the Gandhi–Ambedkar Debates over 'Caste': The Multiple Resonances of Varṇa." *Journal of Human Values* 25, no. 1 (2019): 25–40.

Brown, Judith M., and Anthony Parel, eds. *The Cambridge Companion to Gandhi*. Cambridge: Cambridge University Press, 2011.

---

31 D. R. Nagaraj, *Flaming Feet and Other Essays* (Kolkata: Seagull, 2011), 2.

Gandhi, M. K. *Collected Works of Mahatma Gandhi.* Edited by Indian Ministry of Information and Broadcasting. Vol. 23. New Delhi: Government of India, 1999.

———. *Journalist Gandhi (Selected Writings of Gandhi).* Compiled by Sunil Sharma. Mumbai: Gandhi Book Center, 1994.

———. *Mahatma Gandhi: Selected Political Writings.* Edited by Dennis Dalton. Cambridge: Hackett, 1996.

———. *My Religion.* Compiled and edited by Bharatan Kumarappa. Ahmedabad: Navajivan, 1955.

———. *Mahatma Gandhi: The Essential Writings.* Edited by Judith M. Brown. Oxford: Oxford University Press, 2008.

———. *Selected Writings of Mahatma Gandhi.* Edited by Ronald Duncan. Glasgow: Fontana, 1972.

Guha, Ramachandra. *Gandhi: The Years That Changed the World, 1914–1948.* New York: Alfred Knopf, 2018.

Hardiman, David. *Gandhi in His Time and Ours: The Global Legacy of His Ideas.* London: Hurst, 2003.

Jaffrelot, Christophe. *Dr. Ambedkar and Untouchability: Analysing and Fighting Caste.* Rev. ed. London: Hurst, 2005.

Lelyveld, Joseph. *Great Soul: Mahatma Gandhi and His Struggle with India.* New York: Vintage, 2011.

Nagaraj, D. R. *The Flaming Feet and Other Essays.* Kolkata: Seagull, 2011.

Omvedt, Gail. "Liberty, Equality, Community: Dr. Babasaheb Ambedkar's Vision of New Social Order." In *Contemporary Relevance of Ambedkar's Thoughts*, edited by A. Ramaiah, 74–103. Jaipur: Rawat, 2017.

Parel, Anthony J. *Pax Gandhiana: The Political Philosophy of Mahatma Gandhi.* Oxford: Oxford University Press, 2016.

Pati, Biswamoy. *Invoking Ambedkar: Contributions, Receptions, Legacies.* New Delhi: Primus, 2014.

Prothero, Stephen. *God Is Not One: Eight Rival Religions That Run the World.* New York: HarperOne, 2011.

Rege, Sharmila, ed., *Against the Madness of Manu: B.R. Ambedkar's Writings on Brahmanical Patriarchy.* New Delhi: Navayana, 2013.

Sarkar, Tanika. "Gandhi and Social Relations." In *The Cambridge Companion to Gandhi*, edited by Judith M. Brown and Anthony Parel, 171–195 Cambridge: Cambridge University Press, 2011.

Singh, Aakash. "Gandhi and Ambedkar: Irreconcilable Differences?" *International Journal of Hindu Studies* 18, no. 3 (2014): 413–449.

Thorat, Sukhadeo, ed. *Ambedkar in Retrospect: Essays on Economics, Politics, and Society.* Jaipur: Rawat, 2007.

Verma, Ajay, and Aakash Singh Rathore. *B. R. Ambedkar.* New Delhi: Oxford University Press, 2011.

Zene, Cosimo, ed. *The Political Philosophies of Antonio Gramsci and B. R. Ambedkar: Itineraries of Dalits and Subalterns.* New York: Routledge, 2013.

CHAPTER 5

Gandhi's Nonviolent Language for Resistance and Liberation

SPOKEN WORDS, PERFORMATIVE ACTION, AND COMMUNICATIVE SILENCE

Suka Joshua

Abstract: This essay draws together the various strands of Gandhian ideologies like Truth, nonviolence, satyagraha, and Swaraj and spins a fabric that is interlaced with people, events, and incidents that helped in the making of the Mahatma. Gandhi's deft maneuvering of words, dexterous and fearless handling of crisis, and dedicated giving of service form the dominating patterns in this framework. The Gandhi-Ambedkar encounter and the "war of words" between these two stalwarts are configured to highlight the paradoxical meaning of silence and to bring together the idealism of Gandhi, rooted in internal change, with the pragmatism of Ambedkar, rooted in structural change. Foregrounding the power of spoken words, performative action, and communicative silence, the essay answers the following questions: Is Gandhi relevant today, and what would it take to function like Gandhi? Is there still hope for us to reimagine a religiously plural and inclusive nationalism?

Gandhi's Language: Power to Light Fire in the Human Mind

Speaking about the power of words, Diane Setterfield duly states, "There is something about words. In expert hands, manipulated deftly, they take you prisoner, wind themselves around your limbs like spider silk, and when you are so enthralled you cannot move, they pierce your skin, enter your blood, and numb your thoughts. Inside you they work like magic."[1]

---

1 Diane Setterfield, *The Thirteenth Tale* (New York: Washington Square, 2007), 4.

Yes, words in Gandhi's hands have the power to light fire in the minds
of people. Gandhi rightly fits into Ralph Waldo Emerson's definition of
eloquence. Eloquence according to Emerson is "the power to translate
a truth into language perfectly intelligible to the person to whom you
speak."[2] Emerson's emphasis is on the "transfer of inmost truth," and
that is what we see in Gandhi's speech and writings. History stands
witness to the fact that the right words at the right time by the right
people who succeeded in transferring their inmost truth have shaped
world events. Gandhi was well aware of this mantra. He had the power
to translate truth into language, and he wielded that tool to silence
the arrogance of his opponents, to mesmerize masses, to win public
support, and above all, to communicate Truth. He mastered the art
of rhetoric. He used it well to persuade people to think the way he
did. Gandhi used this to promote and implement his ideals on the rich
and the poor, the educated and the uneducated. He knew how to use
cadence and context to imbue people with a sense of mission and to
tune into the energy of his audience. It is not hyperbole to state that
he used the "gift of gab" as a tool of manipulation. In Gandhi's hands,
not only speech but also silence and actions were powerful means to
communicate Truth. Various instances from Gandhi's life and career
illustrate his power of persuasion in spoken and unspoken as well as
written and action languages. Through myriad means, Gandhi told the
world what Truth holds in store for him and the world. The fabric of
this essay is woven together with these strands of different themes and
events. It holds together incidents and people associated with the making of the Mahatma. Starting from Gandhi's instinct for language and
the intrinsic worth of words, this chapter foregrounds the significance
of Gandhi's use of silence and discusses the importance for him of the
power of performative action. The chapter concludes with a discussion of the relevance of Gandhi today and the necessary conditions for
someone to function in a Gandhi-like manner.

---

2 Emerson quoted in Johannes Voelz, *Transcendental Resistance: The New Americanists and
   Emerson's Challenge* (Hanover, NH: University Press of New England, 2010), 102.

An Instinct for Language

The credit for molding a young Mohan into a mahatma can be attributed to Gandhi's twenty-one years of sojourn in South Africa between the years 1893 and 1914. When he arrived in Natal in 1893, he did not know much about the "indentured" Indian laborers and their semislavery situation. It was the heyday of European imperialism and English arrogance, and it was "the hostility of European politicians, officials and merchants, and the helplessness of the Indian merchants and laborers that drew young Gandhi into the vortex of the politics of Natal."[3] His very first unpleasant encounter with the magistrate in the court of Durban, the humiliating train incident, and his resistance and reaction to these incidents immediately conjure up an enthralling figure who commands respect and adoration. Behind the brown skin and bony frame was hidden the status, dignity, and assurance that he had inherited from his family and the credentials and impeccable English he earned as a London-trained barrister. In his later day politics, these characteristics gave Gandhi the language he needed to express and explain what Truth meant.

Gandhi knew the inherent and intrinsic worth of languages. For him, learning languages was not only a means to have a better understanding of the world around him but also a means to effect a change for the better. Gandhi's four pillars of Swaraj gave expression to Gandhi's vision of a free and better India. His four pillars bring to mind Franklin Roosevelt's "four essential human freedoms"—the freedom of speech and expression, the freedom of every person to worship God in their own way, freedom from want, and freedom from fear—that are essential for building a healthy nation. None would disagree that command over language enhances freedom of speech and expression, instills confidence, and commands respect. Gandhi knew this well. Accordingly, during his time in law school, he started to learn other languages. He took great efforts to pass the University of London matriculation exam, which meant a great deal of labor, the labor of learning even Latin. He

---

3 R. S. Nanda, *Gandhi and His Critics* (New Delhi: Oxford University Press, 1985), 29.

learned Sanskrit, English, French, Hindi, and Urdu with the sole intention of communicating effectively with his own people and with others. In his autobiography, *The Story of My Experiments with Truth*, he states, "It is now my opinion that in all Indian curricula of higher education there should be a place for Hindi, Sanskrit, Persian, Arabic and English, besides of course the vernacular."[4] Gandhi knew language learning builds up leadership ideologies and ingrains conviction and competence. Gopalkrishna Gandhi rightly said of Gandhi that he "spoke or wrote because he needed to. He wrote because writing was part of the activities that grew around his convictions. . . . His instincts grew into a style."[5] He had on several occasions stunned the British with his impeccable English. It was his mastery over this language that helped him impact the world with his message of truth, love, nonviolence, and universal fraternity. His proficiency combined with conviction empowered him to remain true to his path of truth, never writing in anger or malice but exercising great restraint in the use of his words. His artistic use of language enabled him not only to convey information but to convert people to his own point of view as well. His *London Diary*, the *Indian Opinion*, *Young India*, *Navjivan*, and *Harijan* were some of the powerful literary tools in his spiritual armory that he wielded to win the world, to show Indians the way to courage, self-respect, and political potency.

The dramatic beginning of Herrymon Maurer's book *Great Soul: The Growth of Gandhi*—"Into a world lighted by Truth, fed by it, kept alive by it, but yet ignorant of it, there came a man who sought it, felt it, and declared it"—posits the fact that Gandhi did not simply fight for and bring India's freedom, but through this, he grew in Truth and emanated that Truth.[6] Maurer's ascription of greatness to this great soul is captured in his histrionic rendering: "In a world of oppression and killings Gandhi lived Truth; in a world of frivolities he sought Truth; in a world where the

---

4 Mohandas K. Gandhi, *Autobiography: The Story of My Experiments with Truth* (New York: Dover, 1983), 15.

5 Gopalkrishna Gandhi, "Mahatma Gandhi Wrote to Convey Not to Impress," *National Herald*, September 28, 2019, https://www.nationalheraldindia.com/india/mahatma-gandhi-wrote-to-convey-not-to-impress.

6 Herrymon Maurer, *Great Soul: The Growth of Gandhi* (New York: Country Life, 1948), 9.

strong hurt the weak he fought back with Truth; in a world where men boasted their goodness he hid himself in Truth; in a world where men were in bondage he found freedom in Truth. . . . His aim was that men might like him, grow in Truth."[7] To put it plainly, Gandhi's spoken words, performative actions, and communicative silences were saturated with the message of love, liberation, and truth!

Silence as Concentrated Action

Where others would have used skill, wiliness, and violence, Gandhi used only fasting, prayer, and silence to achieve his goal. For him, silence had become both a physical and spiritual necessity. As a seeker of Truth, silence for him was a powerful tool. The British supremacy had legitimized its domination and Indian subjugation and attributed passivity, weakness, and cowardice as the norms of Indian culture and character. At such a time, Gandhi's courage exhibited in unflinching deeds of satyagraha and nonviolence gave a rude shock to the British power. Gandhi believed in the efficacy of prayerful thought. His silence was not inaction but a preparation for Gandhi-in-action. In Gandhi's words, "When time for action has come, God will give the light and guidance. I therefore watch, wait and pray holding myself in momentary readiness to respond. What appears to be inaction . . . is really action."[8] Gandhi's patient wait for the right words brings to mind the following beautiful lines from Nissim Ezekiel's poem "Poet, Lover, Birdwatcher":

> *To force the pace and never to be still*
> *Is not the way of those who study birds*
> *Or women. The best poets wait for words.*
>
> *. . . .*
>
> *In this the poet finds his moral proved*
> *Who never spoke before his spirit moved.*[9]

---

7 Maurer, 10.

8 Joseph Lelyveld, *Great Soul: Mahatma Gandhi and His Struggle with India* (New Delhi: HarperCollins, 2011), 199.

9 Nissim Ezekiel, "Poet, Lover, Birdwatcher," All Poetry, accessed October 14, 2021, https://allpoetry.com/Poet,-Lover,-Birdwatcher.

The resilience and resolve of the young Gandhi, as brought to our
attention by Joseph Lelyveld in the pages of *Great Soul*, elicits awe
for Gandhi's language of resistance, expressed more in action than
in words. One cannot but marvel at Gandhi's power of perseverance,
his self-denying love, and his strenuous life. The twenty-one years
of sojourn in South Africa turned out to be a crucible in which the
young Mohan's language and bearing were shaped and molded to befit
a mahatma. His refusal to remove his headgear before the magistrate
in the court of Durban, his bold walkout, and his retaliating letter to
the newspaper all at once bring before our minds an "engaging figure,
soft-spoken but not at all reticent."[10] The humiliating train incident at
Pietermaritzburg in South Africa gave him the impetus to initiate the
struggle against racial oppression and to fight for national self-respect.
This incident should have stirred his fury, but "in an alchemy that
was uniquely his own, it turned also into something totally different,
something creative, something redemptive, something that changed
shock and fury into a transformational resolve. . . . He fell a passenger
but rose a patriot; fell a barrister but rose a revolutionary; his sense of
human decency transformed itself into a passion for human justice.
The personal died within him that moment and turned public; 'mine'
became 'thine.'"[11] Adversities and humiliations fortified Gandhi to
fight for his people in South Africa and also intensified his vision
for India. Were it not for these experiences, he could not have fought
the impending Asiatic Law Amendment Ordinance of 1906. Indians
should be grateful for September 11, 1906, the day that marked the
start of Gandhi's resistance campaign, which ultimately became
the satyagraha movement. The magnetism of Gandhi's language of
love and resistance, the charisma of his every move, deed, and demeanor,
enchanted the people to the extent of resisting the law and courting
arrest. Gandhi's indomitable spirit and impeccable language were so

---

10 Lelyveld, *Great Soul*, 5.
11 Gopalkrishna Gandhi, "A Barrister Was Thrown Off a Train. He Arose a Revolutionary,"
    The Wire, June 10, 2018, https://thewire.in/history/a-barrister-was-thrown-off-a-train-he
    -arose-a-revolutionary.

infectious that people were willing to pay the price! It was not always the vocabulary of fasting and silent coercion that Gandhi indulged in. Wherever he could use the lexicon of resistance, he did. When a three-pound tax was imposed on the indentured Indians in 1913, Gandhi initiated another satyagraha campaign, and the South African government finally gave in to the power of this "soft-spoken" saint. This language of defiance was possible because "Gandhi was transformed by his deep-running, passionate love of other people, wherein he found God and an increasing desire to lose himself in salving their wounds and sorrows."[12]

Gandhi's resolve to fight injustice intensified even when he was aging. One event that highlighted Gandhi's silence as "concentrated action" was his Salt March to Dandi Beach at the age of sixty-one, when his health was failing and his body was ailing. This conquering hero's courageous actions shook the pillars of the Raj. Even after his arrest, hundreds of men and women, led by Sarojini Naidu, were willing to expose themselves to horrendous police atrocities and violence. That was the power of his silent action. His life was a lesson. No wonder Sarojini Naidu hailed Gandhi as the "Deliverer" and Jawaharlal Nehru congratulated him for the new India he had created by the magic of his words. The language of silence and satyagraha even in the face of untold atrocities was possible for Gandhi because he was deeply convinced that we rule our lives by the law of Truth at any cost. In his first book, *Hind Swaraj*, Gandhi pronounced that violence was no remedy for India's ills, that Indian civilization required a different and higher strategy for self-protection. He said of his book that it "teaches the gospel of love in place of hate. It replaces violence with self-sacrifice. It pits soul-force against brute force."[13] For Gandhi, it meant that "you may not offend anybody; you may not harbour an uncharitable thought, even in connection with one who may consider himself to be your enemy. . . . If we return blow for blow we depart

---

12 M. K. Gandhi, *The Essential Gandhi*, ed. Louis Fischer, 2nd ed. (New York: Vintage Spiritual Classics, 1962), xxi.

13 Gandhi, 104.

from the doctrine of non-violence."[14] Truth was Gandhi's highest principle. He would rather prefer that Truth is God than that God is truth. Truth was not only Gandhi's highest principle; it was for him a practice rooted in love. This has become the grammar and syllable of his language of ahimsa. As he wrote in his letter to Basil Matthews, "Truth and Love have been jointly the guiding principle of my life. If God who is indefinable can be at all defined, then I should say that God is Truth. It is impossible to reach Him, that is, Truth, except through Love."[15]

Performing Truth

Gandhi did not just preach or teach about Truth and love but practiced them. His statement about himself—"My life is my message"—was no exaggeration! His life in itself was a powerful language; his deeds and his communicative silence talked louder and clearer than words that the masses could understand. He saw in Jesus a similar kind of love and life that caused him to state, "To me, he [Jesus] was one of the greatest teachers humanity has ever had.... My interpretation, in other words, is that Jesus' own life is the key of his nearness to God; that he expressed, as no other could, the spirit and will of God."[16] Gandhi's actions spoke louder than words and kindled in people a sense of surrender to his virtues.

Gandhi used his language of love and silence very effectively in 1932 in his struggle against untouchability. Gandhi armed himself with the powerful tool of fasting as performative action when he contended against the evils of untouchability and Indian nationalism. With every new challenge he faced, Gandhi had to evolve a new strategy, a new language to appeal to the authorities and to the common people to suit the situation. This time, Gandhi took to fasting. Gandhi, as a persuasive politician, was well aware that his fasts would exercise a moral

---

14 Maurer, *Great Soul*, 47.
15 Mohandas K. Gandhi to Basil Mathews, June 8, 1927, in *Hindutva: An Indian Christian Response*, ed. J. Mattam and P. Arockiadoss (Bangalore: Dharmaram, 2002), 230.
16 Mohandas K. Gandhi, *The Message of Jesus Christ* (Chennai: Bharatiya Vidya Bhavan, 1986), 67.

pressure on people, prick their conscience, and communicate to them the powerful message that he was anguished at the monstrous social tyranny of untouchability. This language of fasting generated much greater influence than the perpetrators of castes dreamt of. As a result of Gandhi's performative action, for the first time, "there was a spontaneous upsurge of feeling; temples, wells and public places were thrown open to the untouchables. A conference of the leaders of caste Hindus and untouchables was convened."[17]

Gandhi's language of love and liberation was received more powerfully when he undertook menial and manual but meaningful deeds and called upon people mild and mellow in manner to do likewise. Such actions may seem trivial, but from these simple actions, one can learn profound lessons of work ethic and right use of time and resources. In Lloyd and Susanne Rudolph's words, "Gandhi's more mundane contributions to political modernization include introducing in the conduct of politics a work ethic and economizing behavior with respect to time and resources, and making India's political structures more rational, democratic, and professional."[18] In South Africa as well as in India, he took long marches, spading the soil in great heat until his hands became covered with oozing blisters. In South Africa, while in jail, when the head jailer asked him for names of men to clean the latrines, Gandhi was the first to volunteer. It is most fitting that Maurer lauds Gandhi thus: "He asked of others only what he had already done himself. He did not ask of any man anything far distant from that man's inward growth, for he knew from his own experiences that Truth moves more often like rain sinking into soil than like lightning striking a tree. . . . Gandhi saw Truth as it lives here and now, and he refused to put it forth as an unbending set of laws."[19] This language can transcend borders and bring tears from the hardest of hearts and extract work from the laziest of people. It did not mean that Gandhi was a "softie" and could be taken for granted. His followers sensed the firmness and the relentless discipline that he imposed upon himself and others around him. He was friendly and firm at the same time. Gandhi's amazing power over the crowds could be seen in his ability to muster volunteers to serve during the Boer War. In an environment where the British believed that Indians were cowards and incapable of taking risks, and when many threw cold water on his plans of volunteering, through the daring deeds extended by himself and his followers, he proved that there was power in his words.

Language and Conflict: The Gandhi-Ambedkar Encounter

The Gandhi-Ambedkar encounter, as Joseph Lelyveld narrates in *Great Soul*, once again attests to the power of words. It could rightly be considered a "war of words." Lelyveld unfolds the battle between these two stalwarts at the heart of India's national movement. While for Gandhi, "silence" is waiting for the inner voice, for Ambedkar, it is refusing to acknowledge the social structures that stole the voices of the marginalized. Ambedkar would contend that silence in the face of evil is itself evil. Though Gandhi's "eloquent silence" helped him manage many difficult situations, it could not take him further than mere squabble and wrangle with the Hindus on issues of Hindu-Muslim unity and with Ambedkar and the caste Hindus on issues of untouchability. Amid this dark despair, he had the courage to confess he was "not a quick despairer," thus displaying his winsome buoyancy. As a shrewd politician, he would easily decipher the intentions of his critics. Yet Gandhi's confessions at Vaikom when cross-examined by Indanthuruthi Nambiatiri, his reluctance to confront the orthodox, and his supposed retreat from the Devi temple at Kanyakumari all make one wonder how genuine Gandhi was when it came to the issue of untouchability. Is Ambedkar justified, then, in calling this mahatma a devious, untrustworthy, and crafty politician? To some extent, Ambedkar blurred the gorgeous edifice of Gandhi built by many deft hands of writers. But it is to be understood that at the core of Gandhi's life and thinking was not just abolishing untouchability. Independent India was his top priority, his dream and passion, and Hindu-Muslim unity was his mission. Anything else seemed an impediment that impinged upon his goal. He juggled with too many hats on his weary head. So we cannot pin easy labels on this cosmic hero, calling him a fair-weather friend or no friend of the untouchables or an untrustworthy politician.

Yet at Alwaye (Aluva), his actions caused controversy in the little town. For this man of action, deeds helped when words failed! Lelyveld, in his own subtle way, shields Gandhi thus: "And, as so often in his unusually well-recorded life, it's the action rather than the always earnest, sometimes contradictory, sometimes moving words that leaps off the page."[20] At times, Gandhi could become manipulative in his actions. One example occurred when the British government announced its decision to award the untouchables a separate electorate. Gandhi was vehemently opposed to this demand of Ambedkar. From the prison in Poona, Gandhi announced that unless the decision of a separate electorate was revoked, he would fast unto death. Arundhati Roy, in her brilliant attempt to resurrect Ambedkar's intellectual achievements and contributions in her book *The Doctor and the Saint*, accurately comments on Gandhi's threat to fast unto death, "It was barefaced blackmail, nothing less manipulative than the threat of public suicide."[21] At a time when Gandhi was hero-worshipped in India, Ambedkar had the courage to reprimand Gandhi for his views on separate electorate. Gandhi was hurt and his ego was bruised by Ambedkar's sharp and pragmatic words and views.[22] Gandhi's political astuteness is not to be doubted, but at the same time, the complexities involved in his political strategies and personal convictions cannot be ignored. Of the four pillars of Gandhi's Swaraj, two were already crumbling. He could not succeed either in bringing Hindu-Muslim unity or in eradicating untouchability. Gandhi's rebuff of Ambedkar was also painful. Gandhi's avowal, "I did not know [Ambedkar] was a

---

20 Lelyveld, *Great Soul*, 196.
21 Arundhati Roy, *The Doctor and the Saint: The Ambedkar-Gandhi Debate: Caste, Race and Annihilation of Caste* (New Delhi: Penguin Random House, 2019), 84.
22 Roy, 84.

Harijan. I thought he was some Brahman who took a deep interest in Harijans and therefore talked intemperately,"[23] is quite annoying. No wonder it evoked Ambedkar's angry remark, calling Gandhi "a more ignorant and more tactless representative. . . . Gandhi claimed to be a unifying force and a man full of humanity . . . but he had shown how petty he could be."[24] Lelyveld exposes their strengths and weaknesses and also brings a clear distinction between the objectives of Gandhi and Ambedkar. Gandhi believed that moral suasion of the caste Hindus was the best attack against untouchability. Ambedkar disagreed with Gandhi. He believed that the untouchables had to become educated and fight for their own freedom and equality. Ambedkar, as well as many untouchables, was not happy about Gandhi christening them as "harijans," which means children of God. Ambedkar wanted to see the marginalized people as full-fledged children of the soil with equal rights and privileges and not merely as "touchables" under the guise of another name.[25] Ambedkar was all out for the cause of the untouchables, but at the core of Gandhi's life and thinking was not just abolishing untouchability. He had other priorities. He had made Hindu-Muslim unity the mission of his life. Though there are writers who portray Gandhi as a picture-perfect peace warrior and a "Karma Yogi," some—like Vinayak Savarkar, A. P. Aiyar, and Ambedkar—bring to focus his struggles and failures. Their attacks did not spare the Mahatma from pain and are more than enough to tarnish the saint-like stature conferred on Gandhi and to portray his efforts as a series of failures. However, his response to criticism, which is self-effacing and never insulting, embellished the edifice that had been mercilessly smeared with blemish. In his confession, Gandhi said, "If one has completely merged oneself with Him [God] one should be content to leave good and bad, success and failure to Him and be careful for nothing. I feel I have not attained

---

23 Lelyveld, *Great Soul*, 213.
24 Lelyveld, 219.
25 Harold Coward, *Indian Critiques of Gandhi* (Albany: State University of New York Press, 2003), 41.

that state and, therefore, my striving is incomplete."[26] Gandhi was not unaware of his weaknesses and failures. He had the utmost humility that gave him the ability to accept his weakness, to let go of privileges, and to energize his relationship with God and human. He knew the power of the language of surrender!

Gandhi's Relevance for Today's India

How relevant is Gandhi to the India of today? How well can Gandhi's language of love mend the cracks caused by terror, by the sinister fascist factions? As B. R. Nanda puts it, "Gandhi instigated, if he did not initiate, three major revolutions of our time, the revolution against racialism, the revolution against colonialism, and the revolution against violence. He lived long enough to see the success of his efforts in the first two revolutions, but the revolution against violence was hardly under way, when an assassin's bullet removed him from the scene."[27] In a nation like India, where "people like Napoleon who perpetrate unimaginable violence without any sense of shame become heroes in the eyes of the public,"[28] how effective would Gandhi's language of resistance to achieve liberation be? The grim picture of India, as we see today and as captured by I. K. Shukla, makes one wonder if Gandhi's passive activism would ever help the country in convalescing from the bleeding injuries. Shukla had the courage to name the fundamentalists as "communal marauders." He offers a scathing rebuttal of the Hindutva philosophy and its justification of its savagery in his book *Hindutva: An Autopsy of Fascism as a Theoterrorist Cult and Other Essays*. Shukla, in scalding language, states that these communal marauders don't deserve compassion. He lays bare the brutal agenda of the fundamentalist Hindu leaders and, in merciless language, comments, "They have signally succeeded in making India an abomination,

---

26 Gandhi quoted in J. B. Kripalani, *Gandhi: His Life and Thought* (New Delhi: Creative Media Partners, 2015), 35.

27 Nanda, *Gandhi and His Critics*, 153.

28 U. R. Ananthamurthy, *Hindutva or Hind Swaraj* (Noida, India: Harper Perennial, 2018), 32.

a vast torture chamber, a concentration camp, a killing field, a hell-hole of horrors, an unending nightmare."[29] Juxtaposing the verve, nerve, and vivacity exhibited by Shukla in this book with the calmness and composure of matter and manner in Gandhi's *Hind Swaraj*, one cannot but be impressed and persuaded by Gandhi's philosophy of satyagraha! Gandhi wrote *Hind Swaraj* during the turbulence triggered by his passive resistance to the denial of basic human rights to the Indians living in South Africa. He argues that political freedom and a world of peace can be attained through satyagraha. In the foreword to the book, Gandhi explains his encounter with Indian revolutionaries in London. Though he was impressed with their zeal for India's freedom, he was not for their violent means. Gandhi was deeply convinced that violence is not the way to fight for justice. Gandhi's life and language drive home the message that remaining silent spectators to injustice, to the evils of society, and to the discrimination based on caste, culture, and creed is an unforgivable sin. Yet violent means were strictly forbidden.

How can one be not silent and not violent at the same time and still react to injustices around? This paradox was not problematic for Gandhi because of the clarity he had about his policy. For Gandhi, nonviolence was not the absence of war or something that was passive. In Gandhi's language, nonviolence was a radical force; it was positive nonviolence. He called it satyagraha, which involved the "truth-force," "love-force," and "soul-force." This force, he believed, can move mountains. But it involved voluntary suffering.[30] As Jean-Marie Muller points out, "Gandhi's non-violence is both a wisdom founded on a spiritual demand and a strategy founded on political realism."[31] In other words, it demanded sacrifice as well as courage and conviction. Gandhi inculcated in people that violence was the language of brutes. As Shiv Visvanathan affirms in his foreword to *Hindutva or Hind Swaraj*, "Gandhi possessed a truth that needed no militancy, no logic of

29 I. K. Shukla, *Hindutva: An Autopsy of Fascism as a Theoterrorist Cult and Other Essays* (New Delhi: Media House, 2003), 41.
30 Siby K. Joseph and Bharat Mahodaya, eds., *Contemporary Perspectives on Peace and Nonviolence* (Wardha, India: Institute of Gandhian Studies, 2010), 2.
31 Joseph and Mahodaya, iv.

brutality."[32] Having practiced what he preached on peace, Gandhi had every right to promote his belief that peace could be achieved only by peaceful means. Only a saintly soul who struggled and surged above sorrows can say, "When I despair, I remember that all through history the ways of truth and love have always won. There have been tyrants and murderers, and for a time they can seem invincible, but in the end they always fail."[33] He firmly believed that violence, though it at times brought some "good," was fleeting and fugacious. But the evil it perpetrates is perpetual and permanent. Victory gained by vehemence and violence is worthless and momentary.

Through his speeches and writings, Gandhi strove to cultivate the culture of nonviolence, which is essential for the attainment of peace within and peace in the world. He was deeply convinced that violence can only destroy and cannot serve to shape history for the better. He dreamt of a Ram Raj (rule of God) in India where people will be free from suffering and leaders will keep duties before rights. In this Ram Raj, even the divine king is not spared of his obligations. The divine king Rama goes into exile. His wife Sita goes through fire. Rama's brother refuses to become king. He pays the boatman who helps him cross the river Ganga. The king talks about duties and not about rights. Goodness abounds in that realm. It sounds like a far-fetched dream for a present-day Indian. As a country where "one particular religious majority has taken upon itself the task of defining and creating this collective identity [Hindu nationalism] in a very biased manner based on the narrow confines of Hindu religion,"[34] this ideal setup of Ram Raj sounds utopian, and Gandhi's ideas seem too ideal to be practiced.

At a time when humans are not allowed to see the splendor of humanity in all its variety, when "unity in diversity" has only become a cliché, when thought control has become an imperative of fascism, when corruption conglomerates with coercion in every form, when the nation is slowly

---

32 Ananthamurthy, *Hindutva or Hind Swaraj*, xix.
33 Gandhi quoted in "Champions of Human Rights: Mahatma Gandhi (1869–1948)," Youth for Human Rights, accessed October 14, 2021, https://www.youthforhumanrights .org/voices-for-human-rights/champions/mahatma-gandhi.html.
34 Mattam and Arockiadoss, *Hindutva*, 11.

turning into a ghetto, literally and metaphorically, how could one ever dream of a reign as perceived by Gandhi? It is true that violence begets violence, making the wide world a valley of tears, a volley of curses. But where is the space for peace when a large percentage of the population is dehumanized, exposed to a culture of cruelty and mockery? As Sathianathan Clarke rightly observes, India is where "Hindu fundamentalism came to define itself by denouncing the non-Hindu Other" and where it is believed "Muslims and Christians cannot really be part of the Indian nation in its Hinduized polity since they are misfits within this civilization, and their allegiance to the nation is divided."[35] Hearts bleed and plead for a peaceful nation amid the turmoil and turpitude in my country. We should once again find solace in Gandhi's words: "I have found that life persists in the midst of destruction, and therefore there must be a higher law than that of destruction. The higher law was that of love, of nonviolence."[36] Let us believe that one day very soon, Gandhi's dream will come true and people will believe in God not merely with their intellect but with their whole being. We will love all mankind like our mahatma, without any distinction of race or class, nation or religion, and will be able to confess like Gandhi, "By a long process of prayerful discipline I have ceased . . . to hate anybody."[37] There is still hope for us to reimagine a religiously plural and inclusive nationalism if each individual owns the responsibility to make amends and is willing to pay the price. As the newly elected president of Malawi, Dr. Lazarus Chakwera, puts it, the only way to rebuild an "unbuilt" nation is to have a collective sense of responsibility over our national sins and national solutions.[38] U. R. Ananthamurthy puts forward this point most forcefully and

---

35 Sathianathan Clarke, *Competing Fundamentalisms: Violent Extremism in Christianity, Islam, and Hinduism* (Kentucky: Westminster John Knox, 2017), 102.

36 T. N. Khoshoo and John S. Moolakkattu, *Mahatma Gandhi and the Environment* (New Delhi: TERI, 2009), 89.

37 Krishna Kripalani, ed., *All Men Are Brothers: Autobiographical Reflections Mahatma Gandhi* (New York: Continuum, 1958), viii.

38 "Inaugural Address by the State President of the Republic of Malawi, His Excellency Dr. Lazarus McCarthy Chakwera" (speech, Lilongwe, Malawi, July 6, 2020), https://www.malawiembassy.de/.cm4all/uproc.php/0/INAUGURAL%20ADDRESS.pdf?_=1740add2820&cdp=a.

pronounces these propitious and promising words: "Recognizing that the evil that has tasted power is inside us, and striving to overcome it is the Gandhian path."[39]

The solution for poverty alleviation proposed by Gandhi seems to have disappeared with the rapidly expanding transnational supermarkets threatening the livelihoods of small-scale traders and vendors. We have forgotten that safeguarding and strengthening the livelihood and security of the rural and urban poor should be the bottom line of all trade and investment policies. We live in a time when, as Dr. M. S. Swaminathan puts it, environmental degradation, economic and gender inequity, and jobless economic growth are growing concurrently with unprecedented progress in biotechnology and information technology. Are we aware that without ethics, technological progress may become a curse rather than a blessing and without love for diversity and pluralism in human societies, human peace is unachievable? Gandhi's swadeshi principle is more relevant today than it was in his time. Gandhi's vision of development is that technology should be wisely used to meet basic human needs like food, drinking water, shelter, and work. Swaminathan affirms that "India must pass a law granting women equal rights to land as men if the country is to ensure more food is grown for its more than 1 billion people and greater respect for the environment" and that diffusion of new innovation will be rapid only when technological empowerment begins with the poor and with women.[40] This is the only hope for the world ruled by corporates. Gandhi, the great soul, is the most modern of all modern thinkers. He talked, walked, and wrote. He had a finely tuned deployment of language, a dexterous and fearless ability to handle crisis, and a dedication to service. In these ways, Gandhi proved to the world that love could conquer hatred, nonviolence could triumph over violence, and truth could surmount untruth.

---

39 Ananthamurthy, *Hindutva or Hind Swaraj*, 10.

40 M. S. Swaminathan quoted in "Only a New Law Will Guarantee Indian Women Have Rights to Land: M. S. Swaminathan," Club of Mozambique, accessed October 14, 2021, https://clubofmozambique.com/news/new-law-will-guarantee-indian-women-rights-land-m-s-swaminathan/.

His vision was captured so eloquently in Rabindranth Tagore's words: "Into that heaven of freedom, my Father, let my country awake."[41]

Bibliography

Ananthamurthy, U. R. *Hindutva or Hind Swaraj*. Noida, India: Harper Perennial, 2018.

Chakwera, Lazarus. "Inaugural Address by the State President of the Republic of Malawi, His Excellency Dr. Lazarus McCarthy Chakwera." Speech, Lilongwe, Malawi, July 6, 2020. https://www.malawiembassy.de/.cm4all/uproc.php/0/INAUGURAL%20ADDRESS.pdf?_=1740add2820&cdp=a.

Clarke, Sathianathan. *Competing Fundamentalisms: Violent Extremism in Christianity, Islam, and Hinduism*. Louisville, KY: Westminster John Knox, 2017. Kindle.

Club of Mozambique. "Only a New Law Will Guarantee Indian Women Have Rights to Land: M. S. Swaminathan." Accessed October 14, 2021. https://clubofmozambique.com/news/new-law-will-guarantee-indian-women-rights-land-m-s-swaminathan/.

Coward, Harold. *Indian Critiques of Gandhi*. Albany: State University of New York Press, 2003.

Ezekiel, Nissim. "Poet, Lover, Birdwatcher." All Poetry. Accessed October 14, 2021. https://allpoetry.com/Poet,-Lover,-Birdwatcher.

Gandhi, Gopalkrishna. "A Barrister Was Thrown Off a Train. He Arose a Revolutionary." The Wire, June 10, 2018. https://thewire.in/history/a-barrister-was-thrown-off-a-train-he-arose-a-revolutionary.

———. "Mahatma Gandhi Wrote to Convey Not to Impress." *National Herald*, September 28, 2019. https://www.nationalheraldindia.com/india/mahatma-gandhi-wrote-to-convey-not-to-impress.

Gandhi, Mohandas K. *Autobiography: The Story of My Experiments with Truth*. New York: Dover, 1983.

———. *The Essential Gandhi*. Edited by Louis Fischer. 2nd ed. New York: Vintage Spiritual Classics, 1962.

———. *The Message of Jesus Christ*. Chennai: Bharatiya Vidya Bhavan, 1986.

Holy Bible: New Living Translation. Wheaton, IL: Tyndale, 2007.

Joseph, Siby K., and Bharat Mahodaya, eds. *Contemporary Perspectives on Peace and Non-violence*. Wardha, India: Institute of Gandhian Studies, 2010.

Khoshoo, T. N., and John S. Moolakkattu. *Mahatma Gandhi and the Environment*. New Delhi: TERI, 2009.

Kripalani, J. B. *Gandhi: His Life and Thought*. New Delhi: Creative Media Partners, 2015.

Kripalani, Krishna, ed. *All Men Are Brothers: Autobiographical Reflections Mahatma Gandhi*. New York: Continuum, 1958.

---

41 Rabindranath Tagore, "Gitanjali 35," Poetry Foundation, accessed October 14, 2021, https://www.poetryfoundation.org/poems/45668/gitanjali-35.

Lelyveld, Joseph. *Great Soul: Mahatma Gandhi and His Struggle with India*. New Delhi: HarperCollins, 2011.

Mattam, J., and P. Arockiadoss, eds. *Hindutva: An Indian Christian Response*. Bangalore: Dharmaram, 2002.

Maurer, Herrymon. *Great Soul: The Growth of Gandhi*. New York: Country Life, 1948.

Nanda, B. R. *Gandhi and His Critics*. New Delhi: Oxford University Press, 1985.

Roy, Arundhati. *The Doctor and the Saint: The Ambedkar-Gandhi Debate: Caste, Race and Annihilation of Caste*. New Delhi: Penguin Random House, 2019.

Rudolph, Lloyd I., and Susanne Hoeber Rudolph. *Postmodern Gandhi and Other Essays*. London: Oxford University Press, 2006.

Setterfield, Diane. *The Thirteenth Tale*. New York: Washington Square, 2007.

Shukla, I. K. *Hindutva: An Autopsy of Fascism as a Theoterrorist Cult and Other Essays*. New Delhi: Media House, 2003.

Tagore, Rabindranath. "Gitanjali 35 by Rabindranath Tagore." Poetry Foundation. Accessed October 14, 2021. https://www.poetryfoundation.org/poems/45668/gitanjali-35.

Voelz, Johannes. *Transcendental Resistance: The New Americanists and Emerson's Challenge*. Hanover, NH: University Press of New England, 2010.

Youth for Human Rights. "Champions of Human Rights: Mahatma Gandhi (1869–1948)." Accessed October 14, 2021. https://www.youthforhumanrights.org/voices-for-human-rights/champions/mahatma-gandhi.html.

CHAPTER 6

King, Gandhi, and Jesus

Nonviolence in the Age of Covid-19

Josiah Ulysses Young III

Abstract: Placing the legacies of Jesus, Mahatma Gandhi, and Martin Luther King Jr. within the context of the Covid-19 pandemic, this chapter examines the violent abuse of Black lives in the United States and the misanthropic mores from which such abuse stems. King's nonviolent civil rights leadership is reexamined in the darkness of the violence that erupted in the aftermaths of George Floyd's and Breonna Taylor's deaths at the hands of police officers. Of special interest is King's sermonic assertion that "Christ showed us the way, and Gandhi showed it could work." I argue that King's assertion reflects his personalist metaphysics and its relation to Gandhi's embodiment of satyagraha and ahimsa. I point out, in addition, that King's assertion is wed to his radical praxis—his human rights activism that led to his denunciations of white supremacy, the war in Vietnam, and global poverty. The essay concludes with a question about the future of nonviolence and the legacies of King, Gandhi, and Jesus.

Introduction

During the Covid-19-ridden year of 2020, Derek Chauvin, a white policeman in Minneapolis, Minnesota, murdered George Floyd, an unarmed Black man. As Chauvin pressed his knee into Floyd's neck, choking him to death to tortuous degrees, fellow officers helped him restrain Floyd. Bystanders' videos of the event moved thousands of people to take to the streets in protest despite Covid's virulence. Violence erupted on US streets, proving once again that police brutality catalyzes violent social protest. Remember New York's Harlem in 1964, California's Watts in 1965, Michigan's Detroit in 1966, and New Jersey's Newark in 1967? In 1992, Los Angeles erupted once again in the wake of the acquittal of police officers who, with nightsticks, brutally pummeled Rodney King, an unarmed and defenseless Black man. And in 2014, violence erupted in Ferguson, Missouri, in the wake of a police officer's killing of Michael Brown, an unarmed Black youth.

Influenced by Mahatma Gandhi's nonviolent praxis, Dr. Martin Luther King Jr., the head of the Southern Christian Leadership Conference (SCLC), held that violence, whether in the form of riots or war, spreads chaos and death. For when violence erupts like an infection that has been "sleeping" in the body politic, the contagion imperils property and life. For King, as for Gandhi, nonviolent persons refuse to spread destruction through violent rhetoric and actions. King's approach to social protest was not, however, the only one. Blacks who called upon a long history of what one may call the "freedom-by-any-means-necessary" approach to struggle rejected King's Gandhian and Christ-influenced praxis. Typified by persons such as Minister Malcolm X Shabazz and by the Black Panther Party for Self-Defense, which Malcolm X inspired, the call to resist racist oppression by any means necessary is as old as the revolts of enslaved Africans who picked up arms rather than acquiesce in racist oppression in the Americas. Dr. King nonetheless personifies nonviolent protest, and his legacy has been lifted up many times during the recent Covid-19 pandemic because of the ways in which the virus has thrown painful light on the depth and scope of America's excessive privileging of white people.

When one juxtaposes Covid-19 with the police officer's killing of Floyd—and when one remembers Breonna Taylor, an innocent woman whom police officers shot to death after barging into her home shortly before Chauvin killed Floyd—one realizes that the pandemic is an apt metaphor for white privilege. It's not that whites are immune to the virus, of course, but the system highly favors them, which is why their Covid-19 deaths are substantially fewer than Blacks'.[1] That is because white privilege, qua white supremacy, is as widespread as the killer

---

1 APM Research Lab Staff, "The Color of Coronavirus: COVID-19 Deaths by Race and Ethnicity," APM Research Lab, March 5, 2021, https://www.apmresearchlab.org/covid/deaths-by-race.

virus that has taken a tragic toll on Black bodies. According to one source, "Housing segregation is arguably the root cause of" Blacks' high susceptibility to Covid-19. Such "disparities, a manifestation of the systemic racism that has plagued Black Americans' health since the age of slavery . . . can be blamed on what was called 'redlining' during the mid-20th century."[2] Redlining confined Blacks to marginalized areas with a scarcity of quality grocery stores and a dearth of social services like garbage removal and vermin control. What is more, David R. Williams and Lisa A. Cooper write,

> Segregation . . . *adversely* affects health because the concentration of poverty, poor-quality housing, and neighborhood environments leads to elevated exposure to chronic and acute psychosocial (e.g., loss of loved ones, unemployment, violence) and environmental stressors, such as air and water pollution. Exposure to interpersonal discrimination is also linked to chronic disease risk. Greater exposure to and clustering of stressors contributes to the earlier onset of multiple chronic conditions (e.g., hypertension, heart disease, diabetes, asthma), greater severity of disease, and poorer survival for African American individuals than white persons. For example, exposure to air pollution has been linked to hypertension and asthma, as well as more severe cases of and higher death rates due to COVID-19.[3]

By confining many Black people to ghettos, miseducating and overincarcerating us, reclaiming our dying neighborhoods through systemic gentrification, white privilege deprives millions of Blacks of a good quality of life. It is no wonder, then, that a disproportionate number of African Americans have perished from Covid-19. The morbidities emergent from systemic inequities in health care—in diabetes, breast and prostate cancers, hypertension, HIV/AIDS, and infant mortality, for example—are, it bears repeating, disproportionately common among marginalized and brutally policed African Americans. Let me

2 Dylan Scott and Christina Animashaun, "One in 1,000 Black Americans Has Died from Covid-19," Vox, October 2, 2020, https://www.vox.com/coronavirus-covid19/ 2020/10/2/21496884/us-covid-19-deaths-by-race-black-white-americans.

3 David R. Williams and Lisa A. Cooper, "COVID-19 and Health Equity—a New Kind of 'Herd Immunity,'" Jama 323, no. 24 (May 2020): 2478–80, https://jamanetwork.com/ journals/jama/fullarticle/2766096.

add that millions of African Americans are in service jobs and live in high-density areas, both of which have increased rates of Covid-19 infection. Yes, people who perish unfairly from preventable disease while being unfairly policed are victims of violence. What is more, the overall climate in the United States during the pandemic and the inflammatory rhetoric of the forty-fifth president made conditions ripe for violent conflict in US cities. Witness the skirmishes between the Black Lives Matter protestors and Donald Trump's clandestine law-and-order forces in Portland, Oregon, an aftershock of Floyd's murder.[4] Witness, too, the rise of Black and white militias who exist at cross purposes. Blood would run in the streets if the Not Fucking Around Coalition (NFAC)[5] and the Proud Boys[6] squared off. It seems to me that Dr. King's legacy needs to be lifted up more now than ever. Allow me to lift up some things about it by discussing Gandhi's influence on King in more detail.

Gandhi, Satyagraha, Ahimsa, and King

Mohandas Gandhi was an indispensable sage in Dr. King's life. Two Gandhian principles, satyagraha and ahimsa, were of special interest to King. Gandhi discovered satyagraha, or truth-force, in the context of early twentieth-century South Africa. That protoapartheid state brutally curtailed the human rights of the Indian immigrants and the indigenous Africans, whom Gandhi disdained at one time.[7] Refusing to comply with white supremacist law for the sake of the *Indians* rather than the Africans, Gandhi, then a barrister in South Africa, provided this

4 Casey Michel, "How Portland Became a Nightmare for Democrats," *Politico*, September 23, 2020, https://www.politico.com/news/magazine/2020/09/23/portland-problem -democrats-cant-solve-420152.

5 Ali Bouldin, "The Birth of the NFAC; America's Black Militia," *Chicago Defender*, July 31, 2020, https://chicagodefender.com/the-birth-of-the-nfac-americas-black-militia/.

6 Katie Shepherd, "Portland Police Stand by as Proud Boys and Far-Right Militia Flash Guns and Brawl with Antifa Counterprotesters," *Atlantic*, August 22, 2020, https:// www.washingtonpost.com/nation/2020/08/22/portland-police-far-right-protest/.

7 Aswin Desia and Goolam Vahed, *The South African Gandhi: Stretcher-Bearer of Empire* (Stanford, CA: Stanford University Press, 2016).

definition of satyagraha: "Truth (Satya) implies Love, and Firmness (Agraha) engenders and therefore serves as a synonym for force . . . that is to say, the Force which is born of Truth and Love or Non-violence."[8] The satyagrahi—the one who embodies satyagraha—will not lash out hatefully to attain the goal of justice. Consequently, the nonviolent resister is at the mercy of the violent upholders of the unjust laws one cannot obey.[9] In taking the oppressors' hatred on the chin, the satyagrahi holds that "real suffering bravely born melts even a heart of stone."[10]

Ahimsa, the other principle, is the Hindu "principle of noninjury to living beings."[11] Gandhi informs us that "eating, drinking," and "moving about necessarily involves some *himsa*, destruction of life" (note the absent *a*).[12] According to Gandhi, an *ahimsa* "votary . . . shuns to the best of his ability the destruction of the tiniest creature" and therefore "incessantly tries to be free from the deadly coil of *himsa*."[13] Ahimsa thus entails benign ways of living in harmony with all life-forms. Given his belief in reincarnation (*samsara*) and one's eventual liberation from it (*moksha*), Gandhi thought one's perfection of ahimsa could take lifetimes. "But why worry" about the time involved, for satyagraha "is the only permanent thing in life . . . the only thing that counts."[14] Those who grow perfect in this kind of love willingly suffer lifetimes of struggles with himsa until ahimsa characterizes their conscious and unconscious being. To quote Gandhi, "You do not become nonviolent by merely saying, 'I shall not use force.' It must be felt in the heart. . . . When there is that feeling it will express itself through some action.

---

8 M. K. Gandhi, *The Essential Gandhi: An Anthology of His Writings on His Life, Work, and Ideas*, ed. Louis Fischer, 2nd ed. (New York: Vintage Spiritual Classics, 2002), 77.

9 Gandhi, 78.

10 Gandhi, 79.

11 Dictionary.com, "ahimsa (n.)," accessed May 27, 2020, https://www.dictionary.com/browse/ahimsa.

12 Mohandas K. Gandhi, *An Autobiography: The Story of My Experiments with Truth* (Boston: Beacon, 1993), 349.

13 Gandhi, 349.

14 Gandhi quoted in Quinton Dixie and Peter Eisenstadt, *Visions of a Better World: Howard Thurman's Pilgrimage to India and the Origins of African American Nonviolence* (Boston: Beacon, 2011), 109.

It may be a sign, a glance, even silence."[15] Sue Bailey Thurman, wife of Howard Thurman, asked Gandhi during their visit to India in 1935–36 how one should respond to brutes who lynch one's brother.[16] Gandhi told her, "There is such a thing as self-immolation. . . . Supposing I was a Negro, and my sister was ravished by a White or lynched by a whole community, what would be my duty?—I ask myself. And the answer comes to me: I must not wish ill to these, but neither must I co-operate with them."[17] According to Quinton Dixie and Peter Eisenstadt's book *Visions of a Better World: Howard Thurman's Pilgrimage to India and the Origins of African American Nonviolence*, Gandhi hosted an American contingent in 1937 that included Dr. Benjamin E. Mays.[18] Dr. Mays, one of King's mentors, was the president of Morehouse College during the time King studied there. During Mays's encounter with Gandhi, the matter of self-immolation came up insofar as Gandhi pronounced that the Ethiopians who threw their spears at Italian tanks in defense of their land missed an opportunity to make an unforgettably powerful statement. For Gandhi, the Africans should have "retired from the field and allowed themselves to be slaughtered."[19]

In the "guest book of the Mani Bhavan Gandhi Sangrahalaya in Bombay, India," Dr. King wrote that his visit to India in 1959 "was an experience [he would] never forget."[20] The entire experience deepened his conviction that "it is better to be the recipient of violence" (as in self-immolation?) than to inflict it. Violent behavior just adds to the "bitterness in the universe."[21] One who refuses to hit back, however,

---

15 Gandhi, *Essential Gandhi*, 281.

16 Dixie and Eisenstadt, *Visions of a Better World*, 109. According to the authors, Mrs. Thurman asked Gandhi, "How am I to act . . . supposing my own brother was lynched before my very eyes?"

17 Gandhi quoted in Dixie and Eisenstadt, 109.

18 Dixie and Eisenstadt, 109.

19 Dixie and Eisenstadt, 109.

20 Clayborne Carson, ed., *The Papers of Martin Luther King, Jr.*, vol. 5, *Threshold of a New Decade. January 1959–December 1960*, ed. Tenisha Hart Armstrong, Adrienne Clay, Susan Carson, and Kieran Taylor (Berkeley: University of California Press, 2005), 134.

21 *The Autobiography of Martin Luther King, Jr.*, ed. Clayborne Carson (New York: Warner, 1998), 130.

may "develop a sense of shame in the opponent, and thereby bring about a transformation and change of heart."[22] Dr. King left India "more convinced than ever before that the method of nonviolent resistance is the most potent weapon available to oppressed people in their struggle for justice and human dignity."[23] What is more, Dr. King came away convinced that Gandhi "embodied in his life certain universal principles that are inherent in the moral structure of the universe, and . . . as inescapable as the law of gravitation."[24] For King, in addition, Gandhi more than anyone else embodied the nonviolent wisdom of Jesus of Nazareth. King reportedly said, "Christ showed us the way, and Gandhi showed it could work."[25] Let's examine King's assertion under the following headings: (1) King, Jesus, and the Drum Major Instinct; (2) King, Gandhi, and Ahimsa; (3) "Can I Threaten Them with Death or Must I Not Share with Them My *Life*?"; and (4) King, Gandhi, and the Spirit of Christ: A Palm Sunday Sermon.

King, Jesus, and the Drum Major Instinct

In his "Drum Major Instinct" sermon delivered in 1968, King asserts that humankind has "a kind of drum major instinct—a desire to be out front, a desire to lead the parade, a desire to be first. . . . Sigmund Freud used to contend that sex was the dominant impulse, and [Alfred] Adler came with a new argument saying that this quest for recognition, this desire for attention, this desire for distinction is the basic impulse, the basic drive of human life, this drum major instinct."[26] Throughout the sermon, Dr. King explores how the drum

---

22 *Autobiography of King*, 130.
23 King, "Farewell Statement for All India Radio, 9 March 1959," in Carson, *Papers of King*, 5:136.
24 King, 136.
25 Kanishk Tharoor, "The Debt MLK Owed to India's Anti-colonial Fight," *Atlantic*, April 4, 2018, https://www.theatlantic.com/international/archive/2018/04/mlk-postcolonial-struggles/557150/.
26 Martin Luther King Jr., "The Drum Major Instinct," in *A Testament of Hope: The Essential Writings of Martin Luther King, Jr.*, ed. James Melvin Washington (New York: Harper & Row, 1986), 260.

major instinct evinces that "man" is either a wolf or a guardian angel
to man. Enmity among nations exemplifies the drum major instinct's
wolfish modality. Dr. King asserts that the Cold War—brutally raging
in Vietnam in 1968—sprang from "a bitter, colossal contest for supremacy," a *"suicidal thrust"* none can halt if a world power launches a nuclear
missile at its nemesis. The "dominos" would surely fall then, for, King
preaches, the Soviet Union's "twenty-megaton bombs" would take out
"New York in three seconds, with everybody wiped away, and every
building. And we [Americans] can do the same thing to Russia and
China."[27] King believes nonetheless that we can rise above the lex tali-
onis and seek to be first in a Christlike way. This, one might say, is the
drum major instinct's ecclesiological modality. King's faith was that
the biblical God created humankind in "His" image, which is Christological in Fredrich Schleiermacher's sense of Jesus's "God-consciousness."
Here Jesus—an extraordinary theologian and the quintessence of
virtue—is not, truth be told, the Trinity's incarnate logos for King. He
is, rather, the *teacher par excellence.* Another name for this Christlike
God-consciousness for Dr. King is *"personality,"* in the metaphysical
sense of the self-consciousness and self-direction proffered by Boston personalists Bordon Parker Bowne, Albert Cornelius Knudson,
and Edgar S. Brightman.

Boston personalists hold that the universe has too much order and
symmetry to be a random development from chaos. An intelligent
mind must be at work. Judaism, Christianity, and Islam corroborate this
conclusion, as each tradition conceives of the Creator as self-directed,
supremely rational, and uniquely personal. In the Jewish-Christian traditions, moreover, the human being is deemed to be the image of God
precisely because God has given the human being a "spirit"—rational,
ethical, emotive, and uniquely personal—which mirrors God (Genesis 2:7). But where the human being is mortal and contingent, God is
immortal and essential—without a beginning or an end. For Bordon
Parker Bowne (1847–1910), the "father" of Boston personalism, God
is a "self-sufficient, self-possessing, all-embracing intelligence" who is

27 King, 264 (emphasis added).

"superior to our finite temporal limitations" without being "a statically immovable and intellectually monotonous being."[28] God is "the perfect fullness of life, without temporal ebb or flow," one who relates himself "to the world of finite spirits."[29]

For Dr. King, every human being who has a moral consciousness mirrors the divine person and is, as such, sacred, for they have an innate ability to choose truth over falsehood and thus nonviolence over violence. To go with God, moreover, is to follow the example and teachings of Jesus of Nazareth, "the Son of God," and thus acknowledge a *self-sufficient, self-possessing, all-embracing intelligence* at work in him and all who seek to build the beloved community with others, regardless of their so-called race. According to Bowne's student Albert Knudson, "the believer in Christ" upholds the personalities of both "God and man" as "a matter of unique and vital concern."[30] For Christ, "God was in his essential nature a personal Being, a Being with whom he could hold fellowship, and the individual man was a being of infinite worth, an end in himself."[31] Furthermore, human beings with focused hearts and minds can in following Jesus strengthen their God-consciousness and subdue their violent impulses.

Edgar S. Brightman, with whom King went to Boston to study, holds, much to King's displeasure, that even God, the quintessential person, has a subordinate nature he must subdue. To quote from Brightman's book *The Problem of God*, "God is a conscious Person of perfect good will . . . the source of all value and . . . worthy of worship and devotion. He is the creator of all other persons and gives them the power of free choice. Therefore his purpose controls the outcome of the universe. His purpose and his nature must be inferred from the way in which experience reveals them, namely, as being gradually attained through effort, difficulty, and suffering. Hence there is in God's very nature

---

28 Borden Parker Bowne, *Personalism* (London: Forgotten, 2012), 149–50.
29 Bowne, 149.
30 Alfred Knudson, *The Philosophy of Personalism: A Study in the Metaphysics of Religion* (New York: Abingdon, 1927), 79.
31 Knudson, 79.

something which makes the effort and pain of life necessary."[32] For Brightman, God is creatively and salvifically at work in the world. And yet, "a passive element . . . enters into every one of [God's] conscious states, as sensation, instinct, and impulse enter into ours, and constitutes a problem for him. This element we call The Given."[33] Natural and moral evil occur, therefore, because God, in the final analysis, is responsible for all that has transpired. Otherwise, there would be nothing rather than something. According to Brightman, "The evils of life and the delays in the attainment of value, in so far as they come from God and not from human freedom, are thus due to his nature, yet not wholly to his deliberate choice. His will and reason acting on The Given produce the world and achieve value in it."[34] Brightman sums up his doctrine of God this way: "God is a . . . supremely conscious, supremely valuable, and supremely creative [Person] . . . limited both by the free choices of other persons and by restrictions within his own nature."[35] Although King rejects Brightman's idea that God must contend with an irrational element within the divine being, he agrees that Jesus of Nazareth exemplifies this consciousness of God as a "supremely valuable, and supremely creative" person.[36] For the sake of his God, Jesus embodied ethical wisdom and prophetic insight and was limited by those who disagreed with his message to such an extent that they crucified him. King thus thinks it's worth remembering the great price Jesus paid for his holiness. For King, the possibility of nuclear devastation suggests, moreover, that the Christianized principalities and powers—principally the United States—have forgotten Jesus altogether.

Gandhi had come to feel similarly about the future in the wake of the destruction of Hiroshima, Japan. The radioactive fire—"the

32 Edgar S. Brightman, *The Problem of God* (New York: Abingdon, 1930), 113.
33 Brightman, 113.
34 Brightman, 113.
35 Brightman, 113.
36 Martin Luther King Jr., "The Doctrine of God," in Carson, *Papers of King*, vol. 2, *Rediscovering Precious Values, July 1951–November 1955*, ed. Ralph E. Luker, Penny A. Russell, and Pete Holloran (Berkeley: University of California Press, 1994), 82–85.

wholesale destruction of men, women and children"—epitomized the monstrous usage of science. He prophesized "suicide for mankind" if the world failed to see the necessity of nonviolence after Hiroshima.[37] Gandhi wants one to know, however, that truth lovers may perish in the struggle for human rights, but Truth will march on. Gandhi's Jesus, in addition, exemplifies Aldous Huxley's wise axiom, "The law of the survival of the fittest is the law for the evolution of the brute, but the law of self-sacrifice is the law of evolution for the man."[38] Jesus's insistence that one should take the clothes off his back to accommodate a thief and turn the other cheek to the assaulter epitomizes the satyagrahi's soul-force for Gandhi. He realizes that soul-force—"the human law of self-sacrifice"—is in short supply in "modern civilization."[39] The truth is the light, nonetheless. Gandhi avows that "brute force will avail against brute force only when it is proved that darkness can dispel darkness. . . . If light can come out of darkness, then alone can love emerge from hatred."[40] For Gandhi, Jesus, whom he called the "Asian prophet," "bade us love our enemies—a hard task! But there is no escape from it" if the light is to overcome the darkness.[41]

The lynching of fourteen-year-old Emmett Till exemplifies for some of us the hard task of loving our enemies. His 1955 murder marks what Blacks were (and *are*) up against. An all-white jury acquitted the white men who stripped Till naked, beat him, gouged out his eye, and shot him in the head. They threw his weighted-down corpse in the Tallahatchie River, and all because a white woman—Carolyn Bryant, wife of one of the killer—said Emmett flirted with and even dared to touch her. In opening Emmett's coffin, Mrs. Mamie Till-Mobley, Emmett's mother, revealed the disfigured system that exonerates brutes who rip children apart. If she had insisted on a closed coffin, the butchery would not

37 Mohandas K. Gandhi, "Nuclear War," in *The Mind of Mahatma Gandhi*, comp. and ed. R. K. Prabu and U. R. Rao (Ahmedabad: Navajivan Mudranalaya, 1960), chap. 94, accessed May 25, 2020, https://www.mkgandhi.org/momgandhi/chap94.htm.
38 Gandhi, *Essential Gandhi*, 79.
39 Gandhi, 80.
40 Gandhi, 80.
41 Gandhi, 80.

have been exposed. Rosa Parks said she was thinking of Emmett Till when she refused to rise from her bus seat to accommodate a white person, as was required of her by law. History credits her with being the catalyst for the Montgomery Bus Boycott and the meteoric rise of Dr. King, who surely became a model of nonviolence. Dr. W. E. B. Du Bois once thought that Dr. King "could be the American Gandhi."[42]

King, Gandhi, and Ahimsa

Just a few weeks after the 1963 March on Washington, Robert Chambliss, an Alabama Klansman known as "Dynamite Bob," and his Klan henchmen planted explosives in the Sixteenth Street Baptist Church and murdered four Black girls on a Sunday morning in Birmingham, Alabama. The blast beheaded one of them and embedded mortar in the skull of another. The sister of one of the victims survived but lost an eye. In his eulogy for the murdered children, Dr. King made the point that the damage done to the community was not merely the act of a crazed Klansman. *The whole Jim Crow system had blood on its hands.* Maybe the four girls' "innocent blood" might help reform the system. King's notion of redemptive suffering is staurological, and yet it brings Gandhi's satyagraha to mind. King held that African Americans *must* keep faith with their "white brothers" who were complicit in the terrorism that destroyed Black children. "Somehow"—but *why* exactly?— Black folk, according to King, "must believe that the most misguided among [the whites] can learn to respect the dignity and the growth of all human *personality.*"[43] When considering King's eulogy for the children, ahimsa comes to mind too. Ahimsa signifies one's grief over the four girls, the intensification of truth-force, and thus the refusal to take up arms as a species of *violent* self-immolation. One takes the

---

42 Ibram X. Kendi, *Stamped from the Beginning: The Definitive History of Racist Ideas in America* (New York: Bold Type, 2017), 366.

43 King, "Eulogy for the Martyred Children," in *Testament of Hope*, 222 (emphasis added).

struggle to another level, or so Dr. King thought, in asserting that God wrings "good out of evil" and that "unmerited suffering is redemptive."[44]

King attempted to expand his nonviolent praxis to the urban north—Chicago—three years after his Birmingham campaign. About *ten thousand* incensed whites came out to oppose King's efforts to integrate white Chicago neighborhoods. The intensity of this anti-Black racism was new to him. King lived for months in one of Chicago's Black ghettos and experienced the hurt that white Chicago inflicted on Blacks by intentionally walling them off in every conceivable way to keep them from interacting with whites competitively and fairly. The toll such segregation took on Chicago's Black children distressed King. He writes of how inadequately dressed they were for Chicago's frigid winters. He laments their sickliness due to insufficient medical care. "The 'runny noses' of ghetto children," King writes, graphically symbolize "medical neglect in a society which has mastered most of the diseases from which they will soon die." "There is," Dr. King writes, "something wrong in a society that allows this to happen."[45] That truth hit Dr. King hard in Chicago, but it was not only whites' disdain for African Americans that deepened King's awareness of what he was facing in 1966. He was also facing a change in how African Americans were responding to anti-Black violence.

A number of Student Nonviolent Coordinating Committee (SNCC) members embraced Malcolm X's Pan-Africanist values and his clarion call to self-defense "by any means necessary!" Their militancy placed them at odds with King's organization, the Southern Christian Leadership Conference (SCLC). SNCC luminary Stokely Carmichael (Kwame Ture) was the most well-known SNCC militant to challenge King's nonviolence praxis with the cry of Black Power. King thought that Black Power, despite its merits, was "a nihilistic philosophy born out of the conviction that the Negro can't win."[46] For Dr. King, Black

---

44 King, 221–22.
45 Martin Luther King Jr., *Where Do We Go from Here: Chaos or Community?* (Boston: Beacon, 1986), 121–22.
46 King, 45.

Power rhetoric had value as a call to a certain Bookerite self-sufficiency within the African American community. But Black Power advocates' self-directed separation from whites and intention to pick up arms against white terrorists was anarchic to King. Black-run banks, schools, and churches were fine, but urban warfare like that which broke out in Newark, New Jersey, in 1967 would undermine the struggle for human rights.[47] In its rejection of ahimsa, moreover, the Black Power imperative eschewed the precedent Gandhi set. "Mahatma Gandhi's movement in India," King writes, "mounted a revolution on hope and love, hope and nonviolence."[48] He thought Blacks' struggle for a good quality of life had to be revolutionary in precisely that way. But many African Americans were abandoning Gandhi for Frantz Fanon, the Black psychiatrist whose book *The Wretched of the Earth* championed revolutionary violence.[49] The lionization of Minister Malcolm's legacy in the world of color, the rise of Black Power rhetoric, and Fanon's growing popularity unveiled that Dr. King represented only a portion of Black America. The recent documentary on King's devotion to nonviolence, *King in the Wilderness*, brings out poignantly how Dr. King nonetheless sought out creative dialogue with those who were, in their way, about the same struggle. He was keen to talk to them because he believed that all rational and humane human beings would see that nonviolence is the only way to bring about a viable future.

"Can I Threaten Them with Death or Must I Not Share with Them My *Life*?"

Despite the accolades he had won—*Time Magazine*'s Man of the Year and a Noble Peace Prize (1964)—the mainstream press vilified Dr. King for opposing the war in Vietnam. President Lyndon Johnson reportedly

---

47 Rick Rojas and Khorri Atkinson, "Five Days of Unrest That Shaped, and Haunted, Newark," *New York Times*, July 11, 2017, https://www.nytimes.com/2017/07/11/nyregion/newark-riots-50-years.html.

48 King, *Where Do We Go?*, 45.

49 King, 67.

took to calling Dr. King that "nigger preacher"[50] when King denounced the war, and even some SCLC members questioned the wisdom in King's stepping from domestic matters into foreign affairs. Perhaps the stunning King monument in Washington, DC, has vindicated his stand against the Vietnam War and his devotion to the drum major instinct that undergirded his antiwar consciousness, but at the time of his assassination on April 4, 1968, he was the odd man out primarily because of what he said in his 1967 address, "Beyond Vietnam: A Time to Break Silence."

Delivered exactly one year before his assassination, "Beyond Vietnam" acknowledged Vietnamese nationalist Ho Chi Minh, who led a decades-old struggle against the foreign invaders, principally the French, the Japanese, and the Americans. As Dr. King saw it, the Americans "rejected a revolutionary government seeking self-determination." He made the point that "the peasants" desired "this new government." It would have "meant real land reform, one of the most important needs in their lives."[51] Rather than demonize Hanoi and its Marxist and Maoist allies as "Gog and Magog," Dr. King thought the United States should cool its weapons and seek negotiations with the North Vietnamese Army and the Viet Cong. He thus set no great stock in the decree that South Vietnam, which the United States propped up, was the last great bastion against Asian communism. Dr. King saw the folly of the Americans' Cold War strategy and credited his awareness of it to Jesus Christ—"the one who loved his enemies so fully that he died for them."[52] King asks, "Can I as . . . a faithful minister of" Jesus Christ wish *death* upon "the Vietcong or . . . Mao? . . . Can I threaten them with death or must I not share with them my *life?*"[53] One's life here is unrestricted by "race or nation or creed," for life, King avows, expands in an inviolable commitment to worldwide siblinghood for the

50 Scott Saul, "Sweet Martin's Baddass Song," *The Nation*, May 1, 2008, https://www.thenation.com/article/archive/sweet-martins-baddass-song/.
51 King, "A Time to Break Silence," in *Testament of Hope*, 235.
52 King, 234.
53 King, 234.

sake of Jesus's deity, whom he called Father.[54] The oppressed make up the plumb line here as they measure the straightness and soundness of our global morality for Christ's sake. Bringing to mind Matthew 25:31–46, King told those assembled at New York City's Riverside Church to hear "Beyond Vietnam" that humane souls search out "allegiances and loyalties which are broader and deeper than nationalism" and thus go "beyond our nation's self-defined goals and positions."[55] This characteristic of the drum major instinct typifies those who "speak for the weak, for the voiceless, for victims of our nation and for those it calls enemy, for no document from human hands," King offers, "can make these humans any less our" siblings.[56]

In the name of democracy, free enterprise, and "almighty God," the United States unleashed its bone-crushing technology on the land while forcing the peasants into "strategic hamlets," which Dr. King calls "concentration camps." He told the Riverside ecclesia that the peasants, *les damnés de la terre*, "languish under our bombs and consider us—not their fellow Vietnamese—the real enemy. They move sadly and apathetically as we herd them off the land of their fathers into concentration camps where minimal social needs are rarely met. They know they must move or be destroyed by our bombs. So they go—primarily women and children and the aged." The Americans' Agent Orange and other toxic weaponry poisoned the people's water and destroyed millions of acres of their life-sustaining grain. Dr. King surmises that American weaponry may have killed over a million—"mostly children." King asks, "What do they think as we test our latest weapons on them, just as the Germans tested out new medicine and new tortures in the concentration camps of Europe?"[57]

The war's immorality is seen as well in the toll it took on dispensable Americans, the poor, the "grunts." Dr. King points out that the United States was "taking the black young men who had been crippled

---

54 King, 234.
55 King, 234.
56 King, 234.
57 King, 236.

by our society and sending them eight thousand miles away to guarantee liberties in Southeast Asia which they had not found in southwest Georgia and East Harlem." One commonly saw Black "and white boys on TV screens . . . kill and die together for a nation . . . unable to seat them together in the same schools." They burn "the huts of a poor village" as comrades in arms but "would never live on the same block in Detroit."[58] Foreshadowing what he would say in "The Drum Major Instinct" in 1968, Dr. King held that the United States could "lead the way in [a] revolution of values." Seeming to allude to Sigmund Freud's *Beyond the Pleasure Principle*, King declared at Riverside Church, "There is nothing, except a tragic *death wish* to prevent [the United States] from reordering our priorities, so that the pursuit of peace will take precedence over the pursuit of war."[59]

King, Gandhi, and the Spirit of Christ: A Palm Sunday Sermon

In 1959, King delivered a Palm Sunday sermon to his congregation, the Dexter Avenue Baptist Church in Montgomery, Alabama. He linked Palm Sunday to Gandhi's legacy. The juxtaposition of the two no doubt reflects Dr. King's liberal education. He read Edgar S. Brightman's A *Philosophy of Religion* in seminary and seems to have taken his definition of the discipline to heart: "Philosophy of religion [discovers] by rational interpretation of religion and its relations to other types of experience, the truth of religious beliefs and the value of religious attitudes and practices."[60] King's receptiveness to the truth claims of other religions partially accounts for his assertion that Gandhi "caught the spirit of Jesus Christ and lived it more completely in his life . . . than anybody else in the modern world."[61]

Two Johannine pericopes frame Dr. King's Christianized portrait of Gandhi: (1) John 10:16, in which Jesus says, "I have other sheep

---

58 King, 233.
59 King, 241 (emphasis added).
60 Edgar S. Brightman, A *Philosophy of Religion* (New York: Prentice-Hall, 1940), 22.
61 King, "Palm Sunday Sermon on Mohandas K. Gandhi, Delivered at Dexter Avenue Baptist Church," in Carson, *Papers of King*, 5:146.

that do not belong to this fold"; and (2) John 14:12, where Jesus says, "One who believes in me . . . will do greater works than these." In the first pericope, Jesus identifies himself as the good shepherd and suggests that those who hear his voice are righteous Jews like him. When the world recognizes his import, however, the gentiles—principally Gandhi here—will take up the nonviolent cross. Gandhi fulfills the second pericope's prophecy too. King offers that Jesus lived his first-century life entirely in Palestine. His spatiotemporal limitations thus made it impossible for him to do what Gandhi did, to "achieve for his people independence from . . . the British Empire without lifting one gun or . . . uttering one curse word."[62] Dr. King would have one believe that Gandhi did what he did because he embraced "the spirit of Jesus Christ . . . and the love of God . . . without picking up a gun or without any ammunition." Gandhi freed his people "from the largest empire in the history of this world."[63]

I, for one, doubt Gandhi would have thought of his work in such Christian terms. He respected Christ's Sermon on the Mount but was far more moved by the Bhagavad Gita. It seems to me, then, that he would have anchored his understanding of ahimsa in Arjuna rather than Jesus. It seems to me, in addition, that Gandhi thought Christianity was far too wed to European consciousness to be of any great use to people of color. Gandhi wondered why African Americans were so loyal to the church. According to one source, Gandhi held that "God-given faith . . . could . . . fight the oppression of white American segregation and he challenged [Howard] Thurman" during their 1935–36 conversations "to rethink the idea of Christianity as a religion used by whites to keep blacks" oppressed.[64] The "images of a white Christ and ideas of a land of milk and honey in the great beyond"[65] did not elevate Black self-esteem or move Blacks to change their situation. Gandhi thought "Hindu principles offered Indians a basis for nonviolent opposition to

---

62 King, 148.

63 King, 148.

64 "Howard Thurman," This Far by Faith, PBS, accessed June 8, 2020, https://www.pbs .org/thisfarbyfaith/people/howard_thurman.html.

65 "Howard Thurman."

British power. . . . Did Christianity have a similar power to overcome white racism?"[66] After all, the people who enslaved Black Americans' African ancestors forced Christianity on their American-born progeny by and large. The North American white churches did precious little to overcome such a racist system. Nonetheless, the point Dr. King made is highly significant. We live in an age in which nuclear missiles can incinerate life. Dr. King tells his Palm Sunday congregation that "the choice" is not, in truth, "between violence and nonviolence." The choice is between "nonviolence [and] nonexistence." King concludes his sermon by linking Gandhi to "God's appeal to this age, an age drifting to its doom." This appeal is a warning: "He who lives by the sword will perish by the sword" (Matt 26:52; paraphrased).[67]

Conclusion

King contends that we have within us a self-conscious and self-directed drum major instinct that ennobles humankind and gives glory to God. He appropriated Gandhi's satyagraha and ahimsa principles in an effort to show the world the practicality of this self-consciousness and self-direction. Although Gandhi did not think in terms of Dr. King's Christian personalist categories, he greatly respected Jesus of Nazareth, as did Dr. King. I have found no evidence that King and Gandhi took a Trinitarian view of Jesus to heart. They did not take the dogmas on Christ's incarnation, two natures, bodily resurrection, and ascension literally. They did not expect the Parousia and the descent of the heavenly Jerusalem. They did not expect Christ to appear on the clouds to save us. Our salvation depends on the drum major instinct we decide upon—the one that promotes life or the one the that promotes death.

Is Dr. King right that "we still have a choice today: nonviolent coexistence or violent coannihilation"?[68] Is Gandhi correct that "human

---

66 "Howard Thurman."
67 King, "Palm Sunday Sermon," in Carson, *Papers of King*, 5:156.
68 King, *Where Do We Go?*, 202.

nature will find itself only when it fully realizes that to be human it has to cease to be beastly or brutal"?[69] Is there truly a chance that human-kind will adopt Jesus's axiom, "love [*agapate*] your enemies and pray for those who persecute you" (Matt 5:44)? One tends to doubt it today. It seems utterly illusory to hold that the United States, China, Russia, North Korea, India, and Pakistan will soon denuclearize themselves and swear off violence from now on. In the United States, policemen's killing of George Floyd and Breonna Taylor and the high toll Covid-19 has taken on the Black community, and other communities of color, demonstrate white supremacists' systemic violence. More and more, persons around the world are realizing how police brutality and sadis-tic white privilege take Blacks' breath away. The thousands of peo-ple who took to the streets in protest of Floyd's murder despite the pandemic were nonviolent for the most part. But the *injustice* itself— the four centuries of virulent racism—provokes violence, a sad fact observed recently in cities such as Atlanta, Minneapolis, and Wash-ington, DC. The irony here is bitter. Violence took the lives of King, Gandhi, and Jesus and seems to be the dominant force in the world today. Their legacies seem to prove that there is something quixotic about the notions of "turn the other cheek," ahimsa, and satyagraha. And yet one would be too cynical to hold that human beings are bound to be wolves to one another. One would also be wrong to think that human beings have nothing to worry about. None can afford to be san-guine about the survival of the human race. I think Dr. King said it best in "Beyond Vietnam": "We must move past indecision to action. We must find new ways to speak for peace . . . and justice through-out the developing world, a world that borders on our doors. If we do not act, we shall surely be dragged down the long, dark, and shame-ful corridors of time reserved for those who possess power without compassion, might without morality, and strength without sight."[70] Are those in power, and those who will them to power, equipped to realize

---

69 Gandhi, *Essential Gandhi*, 289.
70 King, "Time to Break Silence," in *Testament of Hope*, 243.

the wisdom of King's either-or, Gandhi's humane spirituality, or Jesus's self-immolating cross? Time will tell.

Bibliography

APM Research Lab Staff. "The Color of Coronavirus: COVID-19 Deaths by Race and Ethnicity." APM Research Lab, March 5, 2021. https://www.apmresearchlab.org/covid/deaths-by-race.

Bouldin, Ali. "The Birth of the NFAC; America's Black Militia." *Chicago Defender*, July 31, 2020. https://chicagodefender.com/the-birth-of-the-nfac-americas-black-militia/.

Bowne, Borden Parker. *Personalism*. London: Forgotten, 2012.

Brightman, Edgar S. *A Philosophy of Religion*. New York: Prentice-Hall, 1940.

———. *The Problem of God*. New York: Abingdon, 1930.

Carson, Clayborne, ed. *The Papers of Martin Luther King, Jr.* Vol. 2, *Rediscovering Precious Values, July 1951–November 1955*, edited by Ralph E. Luker, Penny A. Russell, and Pete Holloran. Berkeley: University of California Press, 1994.

———. *The Papers of Martin Luther King, Jr.* Vol. 5, *Threshold of a New Decade. January 1959–December 1960*, edited by Tenisha Hart Armstrong, Adrienne Clay, Susan Carson, and Kieran Taylor. Berkeley: University of California Press, 2005.

Desia, Aswin, and Goolam Vahed. *The South African Gandhi: Stretcher-Bearer of Empire*. Stanford: Stanford University Press, 2016.

Dictionary.com. "ahimsa (n.)." Accessed May 27, 2020. https://www.dictionary.com/browse/ahimsa.

Dixie, Quinton, and Peter Eisenstadt. *Visions of a Better World: Howard Thurman's Pilgrimage to India and the Origins of African American Nonviolence*. Boston: Beacon, 2011.

Gandhi, Mohandas K. *An Autobiography: The Story of My Experiments with Truth*. Boston: Beacon, 1993.

———. *The Essential Gandhi: An Anthology of His Writings on His Life, Work, and Ideas.* Edited by Louis Fischer. 2nd ed. New York: Vintage Spiritual Classics, 2002.

———. "Nuclear War." In *The Mind of Mahatma Gandhi*, compiled and edited by R. K. Prabu and U. R. Rao, 554–558. Ahmedabad: Navajivan Mudranalaya, 1960. https://www.mkgandhi.org/momgandhi/chap94.htm.

Kendi, Ibram X. *Stamped from the Beginning: The Definitive History of Racist Ideas in America*. New York: Bold Type, 2017.

King, Martin Luther, Jr. *The Autobiography of Martin Luther King, Jr.* Edited by Clayborne Carson. New York: Warner, 1998.

———. *A Testament of Hope: The Essential Writings of Martin Luther King, Jr.* Edited by James Melvin Washington. New York: Harper & Row, 1986.

———. *Where Do We Go from Here: Chaos or Community?* Boston: Beacon, 1986.

Knudson, Alfred. *The Philosophy of Personalism: A Study in the Metaphysics of Religion.* New York: Abingdon, 1927.

Little, Becky. "How Martin Luther King Jr. Took Inspiration from Gandhi on Nonviolence." Biography, January 19, 2021. https://www.biography.com/news/martin-luther-king-jr-gandhi-nonviolence-inspiration.

Michel, Casey. "How Portland Became a Nightmare for Democrats." *Politico,* September 23, 2020. https://www.politico.com/news/magazine/2020/09/23/portland-problem-democrats-cant-solve-420152.

Rojas, Rick, and Khorri Atkinson. "Five Days of Unrest That Shaped, and Haunted, Newark." *New York Times,* July 11, 2017. https://www.nytimes.com/2017/07/11/nyregion/newark-riots-50-years.html.

Saul, Scott. "Sweet Martin's Baddass Song." *The Nation,* May 1, 2008. https://www.thenation.com/article/archive/sweet-martins-badass-song/.

Scott, Dylan, and Christina Animashaun. "One in 1,000 Black Americans Has Died from Covid-19." Vox, October 2, 2020. https://www.vox.com/coronavirus-covid19/2020/10/2/21496884/us-covid-19-deaths-by-race-black-white-americans.

Shepherd, Katie. "Portland Police Stand by as Proud Boys and Far-Right Militia Flash Guns and Brawl with Antifa Counterprotesters." *Atlantic,* August 22, 2020. https://www.washingtonpost.com/nation/2020/08/22/portland-police-far-right-protest/.

Tharoor, Kanishk. "The Debt MLK Owed to India's Anti-colonial Fight." *Atlantic,* April 4, 2018. https://www.theatlantic.com/international/archive/2018/04/mlk-postcolonial-struggles/557150/.

This Far by Faith. "Howard Thurman." PBS. Accessed June 8, 2020. https://www.pbs.org/thisfarbyfaith/people/howard_thurman.html.

Williams, David R., and Lisa A. Cooper. "COVID-19 and Health Equity—a New Kind of 'Herd Immunity.'" *Jama* 323, no. 24 (May 2020): 2478–2480. https://jamanetwork.com/journals/jama/fullarticle/2766096.

CHAPTER 7

Gandhi, Bonhoeffer, and the Sermon on the Mount

Peter Hooton

Abstract: The German theologian Dietrich Bonhoeffer (1906–45) mentions his hopes of visiting Gandhi in a July 1934 letter from London to his friend and former teacher Reinhold Niebuhr. It is time, he tells Niebuhr, to bring the focus of German church opposition to Hitler back to the Sermon on the Mount. Bonhoeffer wanted to explore new ways of countering religion's subordination to the totalitarian aims of the state and believed Gandhi might be able to help him in this endeavor. By November, he had secured an invitation from Gandhi to visit him. But it wasn't to be. Bonhoeffer was called back to Germany. After laying out this background, the essay goes on to consider the still intriguing what-if question. If they had met early in 1935 in the small market town of Wardha in central India—where Gandhi had finished his countrywide crusade against untouchability in August 1934—what may the young Bonhoeffer have taken away from the encounter? Might he have warmed to the Mahatma's injunction to "melt Hitler's heart" with acts of nonviolent resistance, or is he, perhaps, even then more likely to have concluded that the surging tide of Nazism and a Raj on the ebb presented very different challenges, demanding very different solutions?

Introduction

The German theologian Dietrich Bonhoeffer (1906–45) was strongly drawn to India as a possible source of spiritual renewal for Western Christianity and to Gandhi's teaching and practice of nonviolent resistance and community life. Bonhoeffer credited Gandhi with extending the Vedic sense of the soul's oneness with the universe from the individual to a whole people. It was, he said, "the powerful act of Gandhi to extend this teaching of life . . . toward a people in a national question and now, too, to place the community under the commandment: You should not destroy any life; suffering is better than living with vio-lence."[1] If they had met, as both once loosely anticipated, early in 1935, what may the young Bonhoeffer have taken away from the encounter? Might he have warmed to the Mahatma's injunction to "melt Hitler's heart" with acts of nonviolent resistance, or is he, perhaps, even then more likely to have concluded that the surging tide of Nazism and a Raj on the ebb presented very different challenges, demanding very different solutions?

Bonhoeffer's Dream of India

Bonhoeffer had been contemplating a visit to India, on and off, since his grandmother first suggested the idea to him in 1928, when he was just twenty-two and an assistant pastor to a German-speaking congregation in Barcelona.[2] But it was in London, in 1934, that the most explicit plans for a visit to India were made. Whereas initially, he was drawn to India simply by "the desire for a wider experience of the world,"[3] now he hoped to find there new sources of inspiration for a Western Christianity in decline.[4] Bonhoeffer had left Berlin for London in October 1933 partly as a result of the failure of Germany's church opposition to produce, in the Bethel Confession of August 1933, a confession of faith that chal-lenged the religious ethno-nationalism of the German Christians—an ethno-nationalism embodied in the conviction that the German Protestant Church must become a Reich Church for Christians of the Aryan race. He was nonetheless encouraged by the subsequent

---

1 Dietrich Bonhoeffer, "The Right to Self-Assertion," in *Dietrich Bonhoeffer Works* (*DBWE*), ed. Victoria J. Barnett, vol. 11, *Ecumenical, Academic, and Pastoral Work: 1931–1932*, ed. Victoria J. Barnett, Mark S. Brocker, and Michael B. Lukens, trans. Anne Schmidt-Lange et al. (Minneapolis: Fortress, 2012), 251.

2 Eberhard Bethge, *Dietrich Bonhoeffer: A Biography*, ed. Victoria J. Barnett, rev. ed. (Min-neapolis: Fortress, 2000), 105. See also Reinhart Staats, afterword to the German edition of *DBWE*, ed. Victoria J. Barnett, vol. 10, *Barcelona, Berlin, New York: 1928–1931*, ed. Clifford J. Green, trans. Douglas W. Stott (Minneapolis: Fortress, 2008), 620.

3 Bethge, *Bonhoeffer*, 409.

4 Dietrich Bonhoeffer, "Letter to Karl-Friedrich Bonhoeffer," in *DBWE*, ed. Victoria J. Bar-nett, vol. 13, *London: 1933–1935*, ed. Keith Clements, trans. Isabel Best (Minneapolis: For-tress, 2007), 81.

emergence, from "the ruins of the destroyed church" and in conjunction with the "intact churches"[5] and the Pastors' Emergency League,[6] of a new, consolidated Confessing Church opposition with its own confession[7] and administration. In England, Bonhoeffer was able to mobilize considerable support for the Confessing Church among the German congregations there, but he was unable, at an ecumenical level, to persuade the European churches to recognize the Confessing Church as "the true, constitutionally grounded Evangelical [Protestant] Church in Germany."[8]

Bonhoeffer knew, though, that the real threat to Christianity in Germany came not from the poorly organized German Christians but from the Nazi state that manipulated and coerced them. In September 1934, he wrote to a Swiss friend, Erwin Sutz, "It is . . . time for a final break with our theologically grounded reserve about whatever is being done by the state—which really only comes down to fear. 'Speak out for those who cannot speak' [Prov 31:8]—who in the church today still remembers that this is the very least the Bible asks of us in such times as these?"[9] Bonhoeffer had little confidence overall in the church's capacity for serious and sustained opposition to state-sanctioned injustice. "Must it be that Christianity, which began in such a tremendously revolutionary way long ago, is now conservative for all time?" he asked in a sermon given in Berlin in June 1932, some six months prior to Hitler's appointment as chancellor of Germany. "That . . . time after time the church does not see what has actually happened until twenty years after the fact?"[10]

---

5 The words *destroyed* and *intact* were used to distinguish between those German Protestant churches that were dominated by German Christian supporters of the Nazi Party and those predominantly South German provincial churches that were not. Ferdinand Schlingensiepen, *Dietrich Bonhoeffer 1906–1945: Martyr, Thinker, Man of Resistance*, trans. Isabel Best (London: T&T Clark, 2012), 133.

6 The Pastors' Emergency League was established in September 1933 in order to resist the Nazification of Scripture and the Protestant Confession.

7 The Barmen Theological Declaration of May 1934.

8 Schlingensiepen, *Bonhoeffer*, 168.

9 Bonhoeffer, "Letter to Erwin Sutz," in *DBWE*, 13:217.

10 Bonhoeffer, "Sermon on Colossians 3:1–4, Berlin, June 19, 1932," in *DBWE*, 11:459.

In a sermon that is thought to have been preached in London sometime in 1934, Bonhoeffer addressed the issue of human vulnerability and the church's response to it. "Have you ever thought," he asked the congregation, "what outlook on life a cripple, a hopelessly ill man, a socially exploited man, a coloured man in a white country, an untouchable—may have? And if so, did you not feel that here life means something totally different from what it means to you and that on the other hand you are inseparably bound together with the unfortunate people, just because you are a man like them . . . and just because in all your strength you will feel their weakness?"[11] Bonhoeffer was convinced that Christianity's credibility depended finally, and unequivocally, on "its revolutionary protest against violence, arbitrariness and pride of power" and on "its apologia for the weak." And he was painfully aware that its record, in practice, left much to be desired. Christianity, he believed, had "adjusted itself much too easily to the worship of power. It should give much more offence, more shock to the world, than it is doing."[12]

Consistent with these views, Bonhoeffer feared the Confessing Church would find ways of accommodating itself to the demands of a progressively more belligerent religious nationalism and became increasingly disillusioned with its all too frequent failure to stand up for Christ in the face of Nazi tyranny and brutality. As he said ten years later in a message from prison to those gathered at the baptism of his godson, Dietrich Bethge, "Our church has been fighting during these years only for its self-preservation, as if that were an end in itself. It has become incapable of bringing the word of reconciliation and redemption to humankind and to the world."[13] In Gandhi's India, Bonhoeffer hoped to explore new ways of resisting tyranny and religion's subordination to the totalitarian aims of the state. As his close

11 Bonhoeffer, "Sermon for Evening Worship Service on 2 Corinthians 12:9, London, 1934 (?)," in *DBWE*, 13:401–2.

12 Bonhoeffer, "Sermon on 2 Corinthians 12:9," in *DBWE*, 13:402.

13 Dietrich Bonhoeffer, "Thoughts on the Day of Baptism of Dietrich Wilhelm Rüdiger Bethge," in *DBWE*, ed. Victoria J. Barnett, vol. 8, *Letters and Papers from Prison*, ed. John W. de Gruchy, trans. Isabel Best et al. (Minneapolis: Fortress, 2010), 389.

friend and biographer, Eberhard Bethge, points out, at this stage "it was still unthinkable to Bonhoeffer to join a conspiracy against Hitler; he sought a prototype for passive resistance that could induce changes without violence. . . . He sought a means of fighting Hitler that went beyond the aims and methods of the church struggle [Kirchenkampf] while remaining legitimate from a Christian standpoint."[14]

Bonhoeffer mentioned his hopes of visiting Gandhi in a July 1934 letter to Reinhold Niebuhr, under whom he had studied in New York several years prior. Theological orthodoxy, he told Niebuhr, would not save Germany. It was "high time" to bring the focus of church opposition to the National Socialist state back to the Sermon on the Mount, "to some degree on the basis of a restoration of Reformation theology [*solus christus, sola scriptura, sola fide*], but in a way different from the Reformation understanding. . . . The new church that must come into being in Germany will look very different from the opposition church today. For my part, I am planning to go to India quite soon to see what Gandhi knows about such things and what there is to learn there."[15]

In October 1934, Bonhoeffer set out his reasons for visiting India in a personal letter to Gandhi. He feared, he said, that Europe was again on the verge of war—a war that would be "the spiritual death of Europe." What was now most urgently needed in Europe was "a truly spiritual living Christian peace movement" and a "reborn" Christianity based on the Sermon on the Mount. Europeans were not without great theologians, but they had no one to show them "the way towards a new Christian life in uncompromising accordance with the Sermon on the Mount." This they might learn from Gandhi and his dedication to peace and nonviolence. Bonhoeffer fully understood that Gandhi was not a "baptised Christian, but the people whose faith Jesus praised mostly did not belong to the official Church at that time either." And he was most anxious not to miss "the one great occasion in [his] life to learn the meaning of . . . real community life, of truth and love in reality."[16]

Bonhoeffer asked Gandhi whether he might be able to stay with him in his ashram. He did not, he said, "believe in short interviews." People only got to know one another by living with one another. He enclosed a letter from Gandhi's good friend Charles Freer Andrews and mentioned that he had asked an English friend of his own, George Bell, bishop of Chichester, for a letter of recommendation.[17] Bell described Bonhoeffer to Gandhi as "a most earnest man" who was "probably to have charge of the training of Ordination candidates for the Ministry in the future Confessional Church of Germany." He told Gandhi that Bonhoeffer expected "to be in India for the first two or three months of 1935" and wanted "to study community life as well as methods of training."[18]

Bonhoeffer outlined his dilemma to Sutz—the dilemma of "trying to decide whether to go back to Germany as director of a preachers' seminary that [was] soon to be opened there, stay [in London], or go to India." He had never really believed in the university, he said. "The next generation of pastors . . . ought to be trained entirely in church-monastic schools, where the pure doctrine, the Sermon on the Mount, and worship are taken seriously—which for all three of these things is simply not the case at the university and under the present circumstances is impossible."[19]

Gandhi replied to Bonhoeffer at the beginning of November 1934, encouraging him to visit as soon as possible "so as to get the benefit of such cold weather as we get here" and giving him some idea of the modest costs involved. With reference to Bonhoeffer's expressed

---

16 Clifford Green, "Dietrich Bonhoeffer's Letter to Mahatma Gandhi," *Journal of Ecclesiastical History* 72, no. 1 (2021): 120, doi: 10.1017/S0022046920000093. The full text of the letter has only just been published after Green obtained a copy of the original from the historian Ramachandra Guha. Guha quotes parts of the letter, which is held by the Nehru Memorial Museum and Library in New Delhi, in the second volume of his biography of Gandhi, *Gandhi: The Years That Changed the World, 1914–1948* (New York: Knopf, 2018).

17 Green, "Bonhoeffer's Letter to Gandhi," 120.

18 George Bell to Mahatma Gandhi, October 22, 1934, in *DBWE*, 13:225.

19 Bonhoeffer, "Letter to Sutz," in *DBWE*, 13:217.

desire to share his daily life, Gandhi said, "I may say that you will be staying with me if I am out of prison and settled in one place when you come. But otherwise, if I am travelling or if I am in prison, you will have to be satisfied with remaining in or near one of the institutions that are being conducted under my supervision. If you can stay in any of the institutions I have in mind and if you can live on the simple vegetarian food that these institutions can supply you, you will have nothing to pay for your boarding and lodging."[20]

Bonhoeffer hoped to benefit from Gandhi's experience of nonviolent resistance and faithful life in community. Indeed, Larry Rasmussen speculates that, in the Hindu Gandhi, Bonhoeffer may even have caught a glimpse of Christ himself, "a vision that perhaps here in Gandhi and his India was the gospel in other words and deeds."[21] But it wasn't to be. Bonhoeffer was delayed in London and eventually forced to choose between India and the Berlin-Brandenburg Preachers' Seminary of the Confessing Church of the Old Prussian Union, which opened under his direction at Zingsthof in April 1935.

Gandhi's Law of Love

If Bonhoeffer had visited Gandhi early in 1935, he may have expected to find him in the small market town of Wardha in central India,[22] where Gandhi had finished a countrywide crusade against untouchability the previous August. The crusade followed periods of imprisonment—during which he had fasted on three occasions against untouchability—and signaled a break in the calls for civil disobedience that had prompted Gandhi's detention by the British. In nine months, "he traveled more than 12,500 miles by rail, car, and foot,"

---

20 Mahatma Gandhi to Bonhoeffer, November 1, 1934, in *DBWE*, 13:229–30.
21 Larry L. Rasmussen, "Bonhoeffer, Gandhi, and Resistance," in *Reflections on Bonhoeffer: Essays in Honor of F. Burton Nelson*, ed. Geffrey B. Kelly and C. John Weborg (Chicago: Covenant, 1999), 52.
22 As it happened, Wardha was little more than a mailing address for Gandhi in the months Bonhoeffer had hoped to be in India. The Mahatma was constantly on the road in the "winter" of 1934–35.

raising money for his new harijan[23] fund and "giving three, four, five speeches a day—six days a week, omitting only Mondays, his 'silent day'—mostly to mammoth crowds, drawn by the man rather than his cause."[24] The energy he displayed was, as usual, prodigious, but there is little evidence that his antiuntouchability crusade changed many Hindu minds. Persuasion and fasting were, however, the only tools at his disposal. Untouchability, he said, would not be removed "by any legal enactment." It would happen "only when the Hindu conscience [was] roused to action and of its own accord remove[d] the shame."[25] Gandhi's critics accuse him, with some justice, of being unable to "conceive of a role for Untouchables other than as victims in need of ministration."[26] Although, he once declared that he "would far rather that Hinduism died than that untouchability lived,"[27] it was only as a caste Hindu that he could press for its abolition. There was for Gandhi— despite his youthful flirtations with esoteric Christianity in England and Christian evangelists in South Africa—no other way of being.

Gandhi's decision, following his release from prison in 1933, to give his undivided attention to the issue of untouchability did not impress his colleagues in the Indian National Congress. Their goal was Swaraj (self-rule), and it was Gandhi's job to get them there. Gandhi, for his part, felt that he was losing his grip on the movement he had led for the past fourteen years. He had never seen Swaraj as an end

---

23 After 1932, Gandhi referred to untouchables as harijans (people of God). The term has always been contentious. It symbolized, to some extent, the gap in understanding between Gandhi and his untouchable antagonist, B. R. Ambedkar. Gandhi's aim was to have untouchables embraced by a religion that wrongly excluded them, whereas Ambedkar was forced to conclude that it was time for untouchables to abandon Hinduism altogether.

24 Joseph Lelyveld, Great Soul: Mahatma Gandhi and His Struggle with India (New York: Vintage, 2011), 242.

25 Mahatma Gandhi, Young India, June 30, 1927, in The Essential Gandhi: An Anthology of His Writings on His Life, Work, and Ideas, ed. Louis Fischer, 2nd ed. (New York: Vintage Spiritual Classics, 2002), 218.

26 Arundhati Roy, "The Doctor and the Saint," in B. R. Ambedkar, Annihilation of Caste, ed. S. Anand (London: Verso, 2014), 129.

27 Gandhi, "Speech at Last Meeting of Minorities [Untouchables] Committee, November 13, 1931," in Essential Gandhi, 219.

in itself. Real Swaraj could only be achieved peacefully. There was no place for "the murder of others" in India's struggle for freedom, which Gandhi envisaged as "a voluntary act of continuous self-sacrifice."[28] Real Swaraj also meant, for Gandhi, the peaceful coexistence of Hindus and Muslims in a united India, the rejuvenation of Indian village life, and the end of untouchability. Congress members, on the whole, did not share this view. They wanted power in an independent India and were impatient with Gandhi's conditional support for their objective. Gandhi, for his part, was tired of only having lip service paid to his (and the Congress's) guiding principles.[29] He was ready to move on. He was leaving, he told a meeting of the Congress Subjects Committee, "in order to develop the power that non-violence has—non-violence in thought, word and deed, unadulterated non-violence."[30] And he was leaving, too, because he had lost the power to persuade the Congress to his view: "I have become helpless. It is no use keeping a man like me at the helm of affairs, who has lost his strength.'"[31]

Gandhi formally resigned from the Indian National Congress at its annual meeting in Bombay in October 1934. He then returned to Wardha. As Joseph Lelyveld puts it, "What the Congress hadn't accomplished under his leadership, he now undertook to do on his own."[32] To this end, he established in Wardha the All India Village Industries

---

28 Gandhi, *Young India*, August 27, 1925, in *Essential Gandhi*, 171.
29 Gandhi strove heroically, though ultimately unsuccessfully, over the years for the shared realization of these principles. In October 1934, he told the All India Congress Committee, "I cannot change my mind on the cardinal doctrines of the charkha [village spinning wheel], Hindu-Muslim unity and removal of untouchability, without which you cannot even understand the principles of nonviolence or free the Congress from greed and selfishness. These fundamental things, which are part of our creed, should come naturally to us. I may be told that I am asking human nature to give me too much. That may be so. It does not show that I am wrong in not being able to remain in this institution." M. K. Gandhi, "Speech at Subjects Committee Meeting, A.I.C.C., October 23, 1934," in *The Collected Works of Mahatma Gandhi (CWMG)*, vol. 65 (New Delhi: Publication Division, Government of India, 1999), 215, accessed June 24, 2020, https://www.gandhiashramsevagram.org/gandhi-literature/mahatma-gandhi-collected-works-volume-65.pdf.
30 Gandhi, "Subjects Committee Meeting, October 23, 1934," in *CWMG*, 65:214.
31 Gandhi, 217.
32 Lelyveld, *Great Soul*, 254.

Association (AIVIA), whose job it was to promote the growth and diversification of economic activity at the village level and to improve rural health and hygiene. The association's success depended on volunteers who were assigned to various remote locations, where they generally served initially as village sanitation officers. The volunteers made little headway. While there was no objection to their performing the work of "scavengers" responsible for the collection and sanitary disposal of human feces, their hosts were not inspired to follow their example. In April 1936, Gandhi moved to the village of Segaon in an effort to understand why this was so, but in the early months of 1935 (when Bonhoeffer was planning to visit him), the program was in its infancy, and its deficiencies would not have been obvious to him.

Gandhi never formally rejoined the political movement from which he resigned in 1934, but he remained closely connected to it and continued to exercise very considerable authority, both directly and through his loyal associates in the Congress. A senior British official in the Punjab remarked, some months prior to Gandhi's resignation, that while people were now "more critical of his aims and objects . . . it would be a mistake to regard him as a spent force. Given the occasion, he would still wield very great power and he [was] still more able than any other Indian to organize a big movement against Government."[33] Lelyveld describes Gandhi's resignation as signaling that "he could neither impose his priorities on the movement nor let go of them." It was "a gesture, an expression of his disappointment," but it was also "something of a sham. The party still revolved around him, if not all the time, at least whenever it needed to unravel a tangled issue."[34] Gandhi made it clear, at the time of his departure, that he would continue "to take interest in the welfare of the organization for whose good [he had] left it."[35] He expected the Congress to remain true to his principles, including the principle of nonviolent civil disobedience, and warned that he would not hesitate to criticize

33 Lelyveld, 248.
34 Lelyveld, 256.
35 Gandhi, "Statement to the Press, October 30, 1934," in *CWMG*, 65:265.

its methods, and the actions of its members, whenever he saw the need for it.

Civil disobedience was a powerful weapon in Gandhi's hands, but it was hard to control, and it worried him. He did not use it often. After an angry crowd in Chauri Chaura murdered twenty-two policemen in February 1922, Gandhi responded by suspending—for a third time, and with only the reluctant support of Congress leaders—the nation-wide civil disobedience campaign he had initiated in 1919. Gandhi acknowledged his colleagues' disappointment but was adamant that he could not be "party to a movement half-violent and half non-violent, even though it may result in the attainment of so-called swaraj, for it [would] not be real swaraj as [he had] conceived it."[36] Although he could not have known this at the time, the next mass act of civil disobedience—the famous Salt March of March and April 1930—was now eight years away.

Gandhi first conceived of civil disobedience as "passive resistance" when, in South Africa in 1906, he crafted a response to legislation requiring Indians in the Transvaal to register "for rights of residence they thought they already possessed as 'British Indians.'"[37] But passive resistance was not really what Gandhi had in mind, suggesting as it did to him an unhealthy combination of weakness and willful aggression. He subsequently announced—in his Natal newspaper *Indian Opinion*—"a small prize . . . to be awarded to the reader who invented the best designation for our struggle." A second cousin suggested *sadagraha*, meaning "firmness in a good cause." Gandhi liked the word but decided it was not quite what he was looking for. He therefore "corrected it" to *satyagraha*. "Truth (Satya)," wrote Gandhi, "implies Love, and Firmness (Agraha) . . . serves as a synonym for force . . . that is to say, the Force which is born of Truth and Love or Non-violence."[38] Gandhi argued that proof of the existence of this

---

36 Gandhi, "Letter to Members of Working Committee, Bardoli, February 8, 1922," in *CWMG*, 26:110, accessed June 18, 2020, https://www.gandhiashramsevagram.org/gandhi-literature/mahatma-gandhi-collected-works-volume-26.pdf.

37 Lelyveld, *Great Soul*, 16.

38 Gandhi, *Satyagraha in South Africa*, in *Essential Gandhi*, 77.

force of Truth or Love lay "in the fact that, in spite of the wars of the world, [the world] still lives on." While history records "every interruption of the even working of the force of love or of the soul," every "interruption of the course of nature," the force of love itself, "being natural, is not noted in history."[39]

In satyagraha, "there is not the remotest idea of injuring the opponent." The adversary is overcome by one's own suffering.[40] "Real suffering bravely born melts even a heart of stone,"[41] and it is love that drives the sacrifice. Jesus, Gandhi reminds us, "bade us love our enemies" and just as, for Jesus, love necessarily "embraced the whole of humanity," so in today's violent world, the only way out of humanity's present "misery and affliction" lay in a return to "the law of Love"[42]—in a global "brotherhood of man."[43] Truth, which "implies Love," was Gandhi's God, and nonviolence was "the means of realizing Him."[44] By contrast, to use brute force against brute force was like trying to dispel darkness with darkness.[45]

There is, however, an important exception to this otherwise unambiguous affirmation. The exception arises when we are left with just one choice, a choice between cowardice and violence. In this case, and only in this case, Gandhi advises violence. "I would," he says, "rather have India resort to arms in order to defend her honor than that she should in a cowardly manner become or remain a helpless witness to her own dishonor." There can be no such thing as freedom for a helpless people. While nonviolence will always be "infinitely superior" to violence, and forgiveness "more manly" than retribution, the strength to forgive comes in some measure from a power—"the power

39 M. K. Gandhi, *"Hind Swaraj" and Other Writings*, ed. Anthony J. Parel (Cambridge: Cambridge University Press, 2009), 87–88.
40 Gandhi, *Satyagraha in South Africa*, 78.
41 Gandhi, 79.
42 Gandhi, *Indian Opinion*, July 26, 1913, in *Essential Gandhi*, 80.
43 Gandhi, *Young India*, April 14, 1929, 167.
44 Gandhi, *Young India*, January 8, 1925, 174.
45 Gandhi, *Indian Opinion*, July 12, 1913, 80.

to punish"—foregone. "A mouse," he observes wryly, "hardly forgives a cat when it allows itself to be torn to pieces by her."[46]

Shared Vision, Different Paths

In his letter to Gandhi of October 17, 1934, Bonhoeffer praises Gandhi's commitment to peace and nonviolence, to "truth and its force," and speaks of his own desire to live a "new Christian life" in conformity with the Sermon on the Mount. Bonhoeffer looks to Gandhi to teach him the meaning of "real community life, of truth and love in reality."[47] But by the time Bonhoeffer left London for Zingsthof in April 1935, he already had a reasonably good idea of what a faithful life in community might look like. George Bell had arranged for him to visit several Anglican monastic communities prior to his departure from England, and these made a very positive impression on him. While Bonhoeffer's companion on the tour, Julius Rieger, complained of spiritual straitjackets, Bonhoeffer found this sampling of the monastic life, with its regular rhythms of worship, prayer, contemplation, table fellowship, study, and leisure activities, "positively energizing."[48] At the same time, however, the threat posed by Nazism to human security and decency in Germany, and to peace in Europe, was growing by the day. Bonhoeffer, whose Christian pacifism had "suddenly [come] into focus as something utterly self-evident" only two years earlier,[49] could hardly have been more ready than he was at the end of 1934 for a close-up encounter with Gandhi's concept and practical experience of satyagraha.

Bonhoeffer was already firmly on the public record as an eloquent opponent of violence in its "total war" form. In a lecture he gave at a youth peace conference in Czechoslovakia in July 1932, Bonhoeffer

---

46 Gandhi, *Young India*, August 11, 1920, 137.
47 Green, "Bonhoeffer's Letter to Gandhi," 8.
48 Charles Marsh, *Strange Glory* (New York: Vintage, 2015), 220.
49 Dietrich Bonhoeffer, "Letter to Elisabeth Zinn," in DBWE, ed. Victoria J. Barnett, vol. 14, *Theological Education at Finkenwalde: 1935–1937*, ed. H. Gaylon Barker and Mark S. Brocker trans. Douglas W. Stott (Minneapolis: Fortress, 2013), 134, 134n2.

distinguished between the right to struggle for truth and justice and the right to wage war. "The right to wage war," he said on this occasion, "can be derived from the right to struggle no more than the right to inflict torture can be derived from the necessity of legal process in human society."[50] Bonhoeffer described "today's war" as "absolutely destructive" and a violation of God's "order of preservation." The past could not be changed, "but we must face the next war with all the power of resistance, rejection, condemnation. . . . We should not balk here at using the word 'pacifism.' . . . Certainly this will not lead to an eradication of strife as such from the world. But we are concerned here with a very specific means of struggle forbidden today by God."[51] That same year, he told the ecumenical working group of the German Christian Student Association[52] that Christians are called by "the promise of the Beatitudes . . . [to] become witnesses for peace."[53] War may come, but for Christians, any form of military service, apart from the ambulance corps, is impermissible: "The commandment 'You shall not kill,' the word that says, 'Love your enemies,' is given to us simply to be obeyed."[54]

Bonhoeffer's most famous denunciation of war came just weeks before he wrote the letter to Gandhi—and with Gandhi clearly in mind—at an ecumenical gathering of Christian churches in Fanø, Denmark, in the summer of 1934:

> Why do we fear the fury of the world powers? Why don't we take the power from them and give it back to Christ? We can still do it today. The Ecumenical Council is in session; it can send out to all believers this radical call for peace. The nations are waiting for it in the East and in the West. Must we be put to shame by non-Christian peoples in the East? Shall we desert the individuals who are risking their lives for this message? The hour is late.

50 Bonhoeffer, "Lecture in Ciernohorské Kúpele: On the Theological Foundation of the Work of the World Alliance," in *DBWE*, 11:366.
51 Bonhoeffer, 367.
52 This was the German branch of the World Student Christian Federation. It was not part of the German Christian movement.
53 Dietrich Bonhoeffer, "Christ and Peace," in *DBWE*, ed. Victoria J. Barnett, vol. 12, *Berlin: 1932–1933*, ed. Larry L. Rasmussen, trans. Isabel Best and David Higgins (Minneapolis: Fortress, 2009), 259.
54 Bonhoeffer, 260.

The world is choked with weapons, and dreadful is the distrust which looks out of all men's eyes. The trumpets of war may blow tomorrow. For what are we waiting? Do we want to become involved in this guilt as never before?[55]

Peace, he tells the conference, cannot be guaranteed by treaties, or by money, or by "universal peaceful rearmament," because all of these confuse peace with safety, whereas, in fact, peace "can never be made safe." It can only be risked. Peace cannot bring security because the guarantees that security requires are built on mistrust, and mistrust is one of the principal architects of war. Rather, peace "means to give oneself altogether to the law of God, wanting no security, but in faith and obedience laying the destiny of the nations in the hand of Almighty God, not trying to direct it for selfish purposes. Battles are won, not with weapons, but with God."[56]

Bonhoeffer did not get the chance to discuss the Sermon on the Mount with Gandhi, but his attention remained fixed on it, and it gave rise, at the preachers' seminary where he spent most of the next two and a half years, to what is still his best-known book, *Discipleship*, which takes Matthew chapters 5–7 as its inspiration. Here, in an exegesis of Matthew 5:38–42,[57] Jesus affirms the Old Testament "power of retribution to convict and overcome evil" but expects his followers nonetheless "to renounce their own rights for his sake." Thus, says Bonhoeffer, "Jesus releases his community from the political and legal order, from the national form of the people of Israel, and makes it into what it truly is, namely, the community of the faithful that is not bound by political and national ties." For this community, "retribution means patiently bearing the blow, so that evil is not added to evil." Rather, evil is allowed to "run its course" and, because it encounters no resistance, is left isolated and powerless. There is no other way that "evil can be overcome."[58]

55 Bonhoeffer, "The Church and the Peoples of the World," in *DBWE*, 13:309.

56 Bonhoeffer, 308–9.

57 "'You have heard that it was said, "An eye for an eye and a tooth for a tooth." But I say to you, Do not resist an evildoer'" (Matt 5:38–39).

58 Dietrich Bonhoeffer, *DBWE*, ed. Wayne Whitson Floyd Jr., vol. 4, Discipleship, ed. Geffrey B. Kelly and John D. Godsey, trans. Barbara Green and Reinhard Krauss (Minneapolis: Fortress, 2003), 132–33.

While Bonhoeffer is careful not to interpret this teaching "as general secular wisdom for life in the world"—which would really be "an irresponsible imagining of laws . . . the world would never obey"—he reminds us that, in Jesus Christ, we are not in the presence of a "programmatic thinker." Jesus does not provide flexible ethical guidance for life in a complex and equivocal world. "Rather," Bonhoeffer says, "the one speaking here about overcoming evil with suffering is he who himself was overcome by evil on the cross and who emerged from that defeat as the conqueror and victor. . . . With his command, Jesus calls disciples again into communion with his passion."[59] Only by their readiness to respond selflessly to Jesus's call can his disciples hope to make his passion "visible and credible to the world."[60] Bonhoeffer fully understood that the struggle for the soul of Christianity and against religious nationalism in Nazi Germany would eventually demand real suffering. He told Sutz in April 1934, "I believe that all of Christendom should be praying with us for the coming of resistance 'to the point of shedding blood' [Heb 12:4 NASB] and for the finding of people who can suffer it through. Simply suffering is what it will be about."[61]

There is already evidence here of a tension in Bonhoeffer's theology between Christ's very clear expectations of those who follow him and Bonhoeffer's understanding of the options available to opponents of a savage and remorseless Nazi regime. There are also hints of the profoundly personal sense of responsibility that was always present in his thinking. In February 1929, he told an audience in Barcelona, "Ethical decisions lead us into the most profound solitude, the solitude in which a person stands before the living God. Here no one can help us . . . here God imposes a burden on us that we must bear alone."[62] Jesus's followers, Bonhoeffer says in *Discipleship*, "are always completely

---

59 Bonhoeffer, 136–37.
60 Bonhoeffer, 136.
61 Bonhoeffer, "Letter to Erwin Sutz," 135.
62 Dietrich Bonhoeffer, "Basic Questions of a Christian Ethic," in *DBWE*, 10:367.

alone, single individuals who can act and make decisions finally only by themselves."[63]

Later, in the *Ethics*, Bonhoeffer again conjures this powerful image of standing alone before God when he makes it clear that "those who are responsible act in their own freedom, without the support of people, conditions, or principles." They must "observe, judge, weigh, decide, and act on their own . . . in the midst of the countless perspectives from which every phenomenon is seen," before "surrendering to God the deed that has become necessary and is nevertheless . . . free, surrendering it to God, who looks upon the heart, weighs the deeds, and guides history."[64] By the time he wrote these words, Bonhoeffer was a member of the German Resistance and almost certainly open to participation in tyrannicide, but in early 1935, when Bonhoeffer had hoped to be in India, he was a pacifist who aspired to live in accordance with the teachings of the Sermon on the Mount and was in the very early stages of compiling the material that would later become *Discipleship*. If they had met, what might Bonhoeffer have learned from Gandhi? Would Gandhi have encouraged Bonhoeffer to pursue a more obviously political path? Could Bonhoeffer's resistance to Hitler have assumed some other, more overtly Gandhian shape?

Gandhi was single-minded and idealistic, but he was by no means blind to life's complexities or to its inconsistencies, including his own. Life, he said, "is governed by a multitude of forces," and our actions are never determined "by one general principle." Gandhi could envisage situations where he would consider it his "duty to vote for the military training of those who wish to take it." He knew that not everyone shared his unbending commitment to nonviolence: "It is not possible to make a person or a society non-violent by compulsion."[65] Bonhoeffer, though, already shared Gandhi's nonviolent convictions and in 1937 could still publish a book that spoke of disciples being called to live

63 Bonhoeffer, *DBWE*, 4:135.

64 Dietrich Bonhoeffer, "History and Good (2)," in *DBWE*, ed. Wayne Whitson Floyd Jr., vol. 6, *Ethics*, ed. Clifford J. Green, trans. Reinhard Krauss, Charles C. West, and Douglas W. Stott (Minneapolis: Fortress, 2005), 283–84.

65 Gandhi, *Young India*, September 13, 1928, 181.

"extraordinary" lives of "perfect purity, perfect truthfulness, perfect nonviolence . . . [and] undivided love for one's enemies."[66] There can be little doubt that if they had met early in 1935, Gandhi would have found in him a sympathetic, thoughtful, and spirited interlocutor.

Bonhoeffer would almost certainly have understood Gandhi, but did Gandhi understand the true nature of Fascism and Nazism in Europe in the 1930s? The evidence suggests that he did not. Gandhi emerged from a meeting with Mussolini in December 1931 impressed by the dictator's apparent concern for the welfare of "the peasant class" and by his "care of the poor." He objected to the compulsory nature of Mussolini's "reforms" but found his approach unremarkable in light of Western society's general predilection for violence.[67] Gandhi nonetheless detected "behind Mussolini's implacability . . . a desire to serve his people" and a "passionate love" for them.[68]

Years later, he advised German Jews to stand up for their rights:

> If I were a Jew and were born in Germany . . . I would refuse to be expelled or to submit to discriminating treatment. And for doing this I should not wait for the fellow-Jews to join me in civil resistance, but would have confidence that in the end the rest were bound to follow my example. If one Jew or all the Jews were to accept the prescriptions here offered, he or they cannot be worse off than now. And suffering voluntarily undergone will bring

---

66 Bonhoeffer, *DBWE*, 4:144.

67 Bonhoeffer would almost certainly have agreed with Gandhi's judgment of Western society. In a 1932 lecture given in Berlin, Bonhoeffer described Western history as "a history of wars." Life, for Europeans and Americans, was essentially a fight for survival in which the "right to life" was earned in the struggle against nature and other human beings. In Bonhoeffer's peculiarly fecund vision of India, on the other hand, "the submerging soul recognizes itself again in all that lives, as if in thousands of mirrors. . . . It aches if nature suffers from violence; it is torn apart when living things are injured." Bonhoeffer, "Right to Self-Assertion," 250–52.

68 Gandhi, "Letter to Romain Rolland, December 20, 1931," in *CWMG*, 54:297, accessed June 23, 2020, https://www.gandhiashramsevagram.org/gandhi-literature/mahatma-gandhi-collected-works-volume-54.pdf. To Gandhi's credit, though, he also described Mussolini in this letter as "a riddle to [him]" and invited Rolland to "enlighten [him] on these matters." Lelyveld comments, "Appalled, Rolland wrote an emotional rebuttal, upbraiding [Gandhi] for passing such casual, ill-informed judgments." Before he could send the letter, however, he heard that Gandhi had been arrested in Bombay. Lelyveld, *Great Soul*, 223.

them an inner strength and joy which no number of resolutions passed in the world outside Germany can.[69]

Gandhi seems never fully to have understood the magnitude of the horrors unleashed in Hitler's Germany. As Lelyveld rightly remarks, "Gandhi, who'd tried writing to Hitler on the eve of world war in an attempt to soften his heart, never quite realized, or at least acknowledged, that the führer represented a destructive force beyond anything he'd experienced."[70]

Hitler, for his part, had a solution to Britain's problems in India. All you have to do, he once advised a British minister, is shoot Gandhi.[71] The fact that the British did not do this says much about the Indian situation—a situation that had no parallel in Germany. The British feared Gandhi's popularity and the potentially overwhelming power of the Indian masses. As Gandhi himself said, "We in India may in a moment realize that one hundred thousand Englishmen need not frighten three hundred million human beings."[72] Hitler had no such concerns. The Nazis were not an occupying power. They were fervent and ruthless nationalists who claimed the loyalty of a population that, in its eagerness to seek redress for the harsh terms of the settlement imposed on Germany after the First World War, was ripe for misdirection. If Bonhoeffer had tried to mobilize satyagraha in Nazi Germany, he would have been quickly silenced. Resistance was inevitably driven underground.

The question remains whether Bonhoeffer, under Gandhi's spell, may have warmed to the Mahatma's injunction to "melt Hitler's heart" with acts of nonviolent resistance, or whether he is more likely to have concluded that the surging tide of Nazism and a Raj on the ebb presented very different challenges, demanding very different solutions. If the latter, might he then perhaps have persuaded Gandhi of the difference in their situations and thereby saved him some (largely

69 Gandhi, Harijan, November 26, 1938, in Essential Gandhi, 287.
70 Lelyveld, Great Soul, 70.
71 Lelyveld, 281.
72 Gandhi, Young India, August 11, 1920, 137.

posthumous) embarrassment? I think this unlikely not least because, at the beginning of 1935, even Bonhoeffer could not have foreseen the full extent of the disaster that was unfolding in Nazi Germany. He had, though, already largely given up on trying to change Hitler's mind. In September 1934, he told Sutz, "Hitler has shown himself quite plainly for what he is, and the church ought to know with whom it has to reckon. . . . We have tried often enough—too often—to make Hitler aware of what is going on. . . . Hitler is not in a position to listen to us; he is *obdurate*, and as such he must compel *us* to listen—it's that way round. . . . *We* are the ones to be converted, not Hitler."[73] But Bonhoeffer would never be converted by this man. He was already firmly on the path that would lead to his murder in a German concentration camp in April 1945, just three weeks prior to Hitler's suicide and a little under three years before Gandhi's own violent death at the hands of a Hindu extremist in New Delhi.

Bibliography

Ambedkar, B. R. *Annihilation of Caste*. Edited by S. Anand. London: Verso, 2014.
Bethge, Eberhard. *Dietrich Bonhoeffer: A Biography*. Edited by Victoria J. Barnett. Rev. ed. Minneapolis: Fortress, 2000.
Bonhoeffer, Dietrich. *Dietrich Bonhoeffer Works*. Edited by Wayne Whitson Floyd Jr. Vol. 4, *Discipleship*, edited by Geffrey B. Kelly and John D. Godsey, translated by Barbara Green and Reinhard Krauss. Minneapolis: Fortress, 2003.
———. *Dietrich Bonhoeffer Works*. Edited by Wayne Whitson Floyd Jr. Vol. 6, *Ethics*, edited by Clifford J. Green, translated by Reinhard Krauss, Charles West, and Douglas W. Stott. Minneapolis: Fortress, 2005.
———. *Dietrich Bonhoeffer Works*. Edited by Victoria J. Barnett. Vol. 8, *Letters and Papers from Prison*, edited by John W. de Gruchy, translated by Isabel Best, Lisa E. Dahill, Reinhard Krauss, and Nancy Lukens. Minneapolis: Fortress, 2010.
———. *Dietrich Bonhoeffer Works*. Edited by Victoria J. Barnett. Vol. 10, *Barcelona, Berlin, New York: 1928–1931*, edited by Clifford J. Green, translated by Douglas W. Stott. Minneapolis: Fortress, 2008.
———. *Dietrich Bonhoeffer Works*. Edited by Victoria J. Barnett. Vol. 11, *Ecumenical, Academic, and Pastoral Work: 1931–1932*, edited by Victoria J. Barnett, Mark S. Brocker, and Michael B. Lukens, translated by Anne Schmidt-Lange, Isabel

---

73 Bonhoeffer, "From a Letter to Erwin Sutz," in *DBWE*, 13:217–18.

Best, Nicolas S. Humphrey, Marion Pauck, and Douglas W. Stott. Minneapolis: Fortress, 2012.

———. *Dietrich Bonhoeffer Works*. Edited by Victoria J. Barnett. Vol. 12, *Berlin: 1932–1933*, edited by Larry L. Rasmussen, translated by Isabel Best, David Higgins, and Douglas W. Stott. Minneapolis: Fortress, 2009.

———. *Dietrich Bonhoeffer Works*. Edited by Victoria J. Barnett. Vol. 13, *London: 1933–1935*, edited by Keith Clements, translated by Isabel Best. Minneapolis: Fortress, 2007.

———. *Dietrich Bonhoeffer Works*. Edited by Victoria J. Barnett. Vol. 14, *Theological Education at Finkenwalde: 1935–1937*, edited by H. Gaylon Barker and Mark S. Brocker, translated by Douglas W. Stott. Minneapolis: Fortress, 2013.

Gandhi, M. K. *The Collected Works of Mahatma Gandhi*. 98 vols. New Delhi: Publication Division, Government of India, 1999. https://www.gandhiashramsevagram .org/gandhi-literature/collected-works-of-mahatma-gandhi-volume-1-to-98.php.

———. *The Essential Gandhi: An Anthology of His Writings on His Life, Work, and Ideas.* Edited by Louis Fischer. 2nd ed. New York: Vintage Spiritual Classics, 2002.

———. *"Hind Swaraj" and Other Writings*. Edited by Anthony J. Parel. Cambridge: Cambridge University Press, 2009.

Green, Clifford. "Dietrich Bonhoeffer's Letter to Mahatma Gandhi." *Journal of Ecclesiastical History* 72, no. 1 (2021): 113–121. doi: 10.1017/S0022046920000093.

Kelly, Geffrey B., and C. John Weborg, eds. *Reflections on Bonhoeffer: Essays in Honor of F. Burton Nelson*. Chicago: Covenant, 1999.

Lelyveld, Joseph. *Great Soul: Mahatma Gandhi and His Struggle with India*. New York: Vintage, 2011.

Marsh, Charles. *Strange Glory: A Life of Dietrich Bonhoeffer*. New York: Vintage, 2015.

Rasmussen, Larry L. "Bonhoeffer, Gandhi, and Resistance." In *Reflections on Bonhoeffer: Essays in Honor of F. Burton Nelson*, edited by Geffrey B. Kelly and John Weborg, 50–55. Chicago: Covenant, 1999.

Roy, Arundhati. "The Doctor and the Saint." In *Annihilation of Caste*, by B. R. Ambedkar, edited by S. Anand, 15–170. London: Verso, 2014.

Schlingensiepen, Ferdinand. *Dietrich Bonhoeffer 1906–1945: Martyr, Thinker, Man of Resistance*. Translated by Isabel Best. London: T&T Clark, 2012.

CHAPTER 8

Led by the Kindly Light of Truth

Gandhi, Nonviolence, and the Renewal of Sociality

Stephen Pickard

Abstract: This essay focuses on Gandhi's humble pursuit of truth and nonviolence as a strategy and way of life orientated toward the common good and a renewed sociality. It argues that Gandhi's engagement with these fundamental themes within the context of an emergent Indian nationalism provides some important markers for contemporary society regarding notions of the common good, social wisdom, and leadership. I argue that Gandhi offers a deeper and critical wisdom that has the power to bind, heal, and make for the flourishing of a people. In an age of self-interest, Gandhi offers a radical self in the service of others for a greater common good. I examine one source for Gandhi's remarkable energy and resilience encapsulated in John Henry Newman's famous nineteenth-century hymn "Lead Kindly Light." Gandhi believed this hymn contained the "quintessence of all philosophy." It offers a clue for the spiritual energies required for the pursuit of truth, peace, and the renewal of social and political landscapes in our contemporary world.

"Truth Is Shy and Hard to Woo": A Personal Note

Mohandas Gandhi had both a remarkable impact and a continuing legacy not only for the people of India but for the world. Gandhi galvanized the Indian nationalist movement through the force of his life and practical nonviolent resistance to British rule. He left a legacy not only as a political figure but also as a writer, with over one hundred volumes of collected writings and an influence that touched one of Australia's great writers, Patrick White.[1]

---

1 Professor Satendra Nandan, in his Gandhi Oration to mark the International Day of Non-violence in October 2017 delivered at the National Press Club in Canberra, referred to the comment of the Australian writer and recipient of the Nobel Prize for

In July 2017, I had occasion to visit Parliament Square in London, and the statue that captured my attention was that of Mahatma Gandhi.[2] It had been unveiled in March 2015 to mark the hundredth anniversary of Gandhi's return to India to begin the struggle for independence from British rule. The unveiling had been conducted in the presence of Gandhi's grandson as well as the then prime minister, David Cameron. At the time, Cameron described Gandhi as "one of the most towering figures" in political history. He said, "By putting Gandhi in this famous square we are giving him an eternal home in our country. This statue celebrates the incredibly special friendship between the world's oldest democracy and its largest, as well as the universal power of Gandhi's message."[3] That's all undoubtedly true, though one hundred years ago, I doubt that the British government could have imagined the impact of Gandhi on the Indian nationalist movement of the day.

The film *The Viceroy's House* portrays (accurately I believe) Gandhi as cutting a lone figure in his protest against partition in that tumultuous and brutal period.

Gandhi did indeed galvanize a nation. He became the focus and the glue for an emergent sense of nationhood. He achieved this through a creative and powerful synthesis of national identity. The twin elements of unity in India in Gandhi's day were the British Raj (a somewhat artificial overlay of political authority) and a cultural religious caste system. Gandhi, through his time in South Africa and his experience

---

Literature, Patrick White, who said that "Gandhi achieved much with that quality of faith; we all in the nuclear age will have to call on our reserves of faith." "Humility and simplicity," said White, "are imperative for our survival and meaningful relationships." Professor Nandan's address was entitled "The Making of the Mahatma: An Australasian Perspective on Multiculturalism, Migration, Human Rights and Non-violence."

2   There is a similar statue in the national capital of Australia, Canberra. The monument was unveiled in 2002. The inscription reads, "Apostle of non-violence (Ahimsa) and truth (Satyagrah) October 2, 1869–30 January 1948. 'Generations to come, it may be, will scarce believe that such a one as this ever in flesh and blood walked upon the earth'—Albert Einstein."

3   "Unveiling Ceremony for the Gandhi Statue: David Cameron's Speech," Prime Minister's Office, March 14, 2015, https://www.gov.uk/government/speeches/unveiling -ceremony-for-the-gandhi-statue-david-camerons-speech.

as an outcast and exile, came to see that both of these elements of national unity were indeed dangerous and prevented the full flowering of a people's hopes and aspirations. His life and work were dedicated to finding a deeper unity—a stronger and more lasting social glue that would bind the people of India. That, it seems to me, was part of his great mission. Moreover, it was to be undertaken in a decidedly nonviolent manner that resonated with Gandhi's deepest convictions regarding the spiritual calling of humankind and the quest for truthful living through sacrifice and service.

In J. T. F. Jordens's *Gandhi's Religion*, the author offers a beautiful, homely image of Gandhi's capacity to harness and focus an Indian sense of oneness.[4] Likening Gandhi's synthesis to a "large, bulky homespun woollen shawl," Jordens remarks that "at first it looks very plain to the eye, but we can detect the beauty of the strong patterns and the contrasting shades of folk art. With its knots and unevenness, it feels at first rough to the touch; but soon we can experience how effective it is in warming cold and hungry limbs."[5]

Gandhi's unique way of drawing the people of India together provokes the question, What holds people and societies together? And perhaps more importantly, What are the conditions required for a flourishing human society? These questions underlie so much of contemporary political, cultural, and religious life across the globe. Various political, social, and economic management techniques are applied (in both liberal and illiberal forms) to create some kind of uniformity of purpose and vision. Efforts to generate a cohesive society often have the reverse effect of accentuating divisions. Of course, where there are increasing inequalities, it will always be an uphill struggle to grow strong, cohesive, caring communities. In this context, truth is soon reduced to matters of self-interest. Moreover, religion is always in danger of being captured by prevailing ideologies of power. The consequence is that neither the cause of truth nor that of religion is furthered, but rather, they undergo distortion and become tools in highly

---

4 J. T. F. Jordens, *Gandhi's Religion* (Oxford: Oxford University Press, 1998).

5 Jordens, 276.

conflictual and often violent societies. Modern Western societies feature two parallel developments: first, increasing cultural, religious, and
social diversity; and second, a tendency to become preoccupied with
one's own particular social, political, cultural, or religious group. The
disconnects here can be profound. They are exacerbated by those who
stand to benefit from promoting narratives of fear and anxiety.

However, the deeper truth is that we are connected to one another
and the blue planet. Environmental concerns, and recognition that our
lives are inextricably woven into the fabric of the planet and indeed
the cosmos, have reminded us that we are connected with one another
and the earth. People are migrating around the earth, and it will only
increase. In this process, the question of human rights cannot be
avoided or ignored. Nor can the truth question be consigned to the
interior dispositions of individuals on the assumption that any truth
will do and my truth is as good as yours. This was certainly antithetical
to Gandhi's way.

The deepest and most pressing issues of life raise the question of
truth and inevitably provoke controversy and conflict. In this respect,
I am reminded of the Australian Anglican bishop Ernest Burgmann's
final public words in 1960, broadcast nationally on ABC Radio: "My
conviction is that nothing is worth believing if it is not ready to be
subjected to repeated scrutiny. God does not want us to believe lies.
Truth is shy and hard to woo, but she is very lovely and worth a life's
devotion."[6] This was a sentiment that Gandhi embraced in his life and
work, and it proved extremely costly.

The point of foregoing somewhat personal reflections is to draw
attention to the importance of Gandhi for our contemporary context
and the questions that haunt us: How then shall we craft a future for
the common good? What kind of people do we need to become in
order to respond to such challenges, pressures, and anxieties? How
might Gandhi's way in truth contribute to a more peaceable society?
In what follows, I want to examine more closely Gandhi's approach

---

6 Peter Hempenstall, *The Meddlesome Priest: A Life of Ernest Burgmann* (Sydney: Allen &
Unwin, 1993), 339.

to truth (satya) and nonviolence (ahimsa) with particular attention to their outworking in his life of service, self-giving, and sacrifice. The work of René Girard will be particularly helpful in illuminating Gandhi's exemplary model of truth via self-giving as a circuit breaker in the cycle of societal violence. This is shown to have a strong resonance with the way of Jesus. The shy and kindly light of truth is manifested in a nonviolent sacrificial life. In so doing, it offers a window into a more hopeful path for a troubled and violent world. I briefly explore some of the implications of this in terms of a renewed sociality illuminated by faith in God in the final section of this chapter.

Performing the Truth

It is well known that Gandhi was a deeply religious and devout person in the Hindu tradition. However, his faith was anything but an orthodox or "high" Hinduism; rather, it was highly eclectic and individual. As one commentator notes, Gandhi's religion was "a maverick mix" that included Vaishnavism of a particular kind and ideas and ideals associated with Advaita Vedanta and Bhakti, Jainism, Buddhism, and Christianity.[7] And this was notwithstanding his own identification as a *sanatani*, or orthodox Hindu. His rejection of propositional and doctrinaire approaches to religion per se was the underside of his fundamental disposition toward religion—one of seeking the spirit of texts and traditions. This of course gave maximum scope for his eclectic probing and accumulation of a variety of sources of spiritual nourishment. However, what may appear entirely relativist, highly subjectivist, and unfocussed has in fact two powerful drivers: the tests of satya (truth) and ahimsa (nonviolence). Applying these two criteria to any and all religious texts provided Gandhi with a hermeneutic to uncover true spiritual wisdom. While adherence to these two criteria might not absolve Gandhi from his apparent "unblushing relativism," the clue

---

7 Akeel Bilgrami, "Gandhi's Religion and Its Relation to His Politics," in *The Cambridge Companion to Gandhi*, ed. Judith M. Brown and Anthony Parel (Cambridge: Cambridge University Press, 2011), 93.

to his somewhat unsystematic framework is located in his appeal to "experience." What impact did this have on Gandhi's religious and indeed political outlook and practice? First, in relation to the criterion of satya, the priority of experience over doctrinaire and/or propositional approaches involved a number of things. For one, "truth carries the conviction of those who experience it, and not for others."[8] Does this mean there is unbridled pluralism regarding the question of truth? In one sense, Gandhi insists that religious pluralism is the necessary corollary of his position regarding experience. On the other hand, this fact does not "dampen the confidence in his own convictions of the truth as he judges it."[9] Indeed, Gandhi intended his deeply held convictions regarding truth to be enacted and universalized, the implication being that such convictions were thus open to the world for interrogation and response. The obverse of this was to accept the trivial nature of belief—a mere matter of taste. The nexus between the logic of plurality, the inherent subjectivism of experience, and the universal trajectory of personally held belief requires some resolution. For Gandhi, satya is fundamentally experiential yet orientated beyond the self and involves a recommendation for a way of life for society.

On what authority does this universal claim for truth rest? The clue here seems to be captured in Gandhi's notion of satyagraha (force of truth to which one holds firm) for the public person. The confluence of personal religious conviction and universal intent amid an array of religious views devolved for Gandhi into a matter of performance. Gandhi's experiential way in truth involved being an exemplar of the kind of life that correlated with the kind of truth held to be of public and universal significance. The force of truth was not primarily (if at all) to be located in doctrines and principles, over which endless quarrels constantly erupted. Rather, the force of truth was the force of a true life. It was via performance that the force of truth proved persuasive. This was echoed in Gandhi's words addressed to certain Christian missionaries: "A rose does not need to preach. It simply spreads its

8 Bilgrami, 96.
9 Bilgrami, 97.

fragrance. The fragrance is its own sermon."[10] Such an attitude had a certain Franciscan resonance, as exemplified in Saint Francis's advice to "preach the gospel at all times; when necessary use words." Gandhi's approach was by necessity closely aligned with the virtues of tradition with a strong accent on humility and patience, even as one held resolutely to one's convictions.

The Way of Nonviolence

Gandhi's experiment with truth, as he called it, was correlated with his conviction regarding nonviolence, ahimsa. For example, the reason matters of truth could not be resolved into principles and/or doctrines was that such a reliance on a cognitive concept of truth was generative of discord and conflict. Inevitably, it resulted in the denial of the claims of one or another party, and such denials effectively discounted the authenticity of the other's experience. Propositional accounts of truth traded on a stubborn resistance to interrogation from an alternative position. The allure of certainty sacrificed openness to the possibility of learning from others. The way of nonviolence required a certain humility of practice. Only in this way might the possibility arise for the force of truth (satyagraha) to be received and transform.

The concept of ahimsa is complex, and its English rendering as "nonviolence" fails to capture its full meaning: "Ahimsa is a Sanskrit word which refers simply to the *absence* of any or all harmonious or helpful behavior; the prefix 'a' is a negation of this negation."[11] Thus ahimsa is more than mere nonviolence; rather, it is the absence of an absence. More akin to "a presence, an active reparation, it is restorative compassion; even redemptive action."[12] On this account, ahimsa is not the way of inaction and passivity but rather strong engagement

---

10 Gandhi quoted in S. J. Imam-Ud-Din, *Gandhi and Christianity* (Rawalpindi, India: Northern Indian Publishing, 1946), 134.

11 Edward Alam, "The Metaphysics of Violence: Comparative Reflections on the Thought of René Girard and Mahatma Gandhi," *Journal of Islamic Studies on Human Rights and Democracy* 1, no. 1 (Autumn 2017): 4.

12 Alam, 4.

of a particular kind with the processes and structures of violence. The way of ahimsa carries with it the intent of breaking the spiral of violence that is a fundamental feature of public actions and indeed movements that run counter to prevailing systemic structures of violence. Gandhi was acutely aware that violence was generative of further violence and of "how violence through mimesis easily escalates by turning adversaries into enemy twins. Mimicking violence easily equalizes all actors."[13] In this vein, Gandhi distanced himself from terrorist attacks upon British occupation, recognizing that "by violently fighting against the occupiers, India would become like the occupying power."[14] For this reason, "evil must not be imitated in any way because evil means lead to evil ends," whereas "if evil does not receive the corresponding response, it ceases to act, dies of want of nutrition."[15]

Nonviolent action constituted a response to evil with good. Such a positive engagement with the powers presumed an ontology of peace. Nonviolence functioned as a circuit breaker to the spiral of violence. To be effective, it required exemplars to model a different pattern of engagement—one not based on an imitation of the violence embodied in the system. Gandhi's way of nonviolence was constitutive of his commitment to satyagraha—the force of truth. In his autobiography Gandhi, clarified the relationship between the concepts thus: "Without ahimsa it is not possible to seek and find Truth. Ahimsa and Truth are so intertwined that it is practically impossible to disentangle and separate them. . . . Nevertheless, ahimsa is the means and Truth is the end. Means to be means must always be within our reach, and so ahimsa becomes our supreme duty and Truth becomes God for us. . . . We . . . should ever repeat one mantra: 'Truth exists, it alone exists. It is the only God and there is but one way of realising it.'"[16]

---

13 Wolfgang Palaver, "Sacrifice between East and West: René Girard, Simone Weil, and Mahatma Gandhi on Violence and Nonviolence," in _Mimesis and Sacrifice: Applying Girard's Mimetic Theory across the Disciplines_, ed. Marcia Pally (London: Bloomsbury Academic, 2019), 58.

14 Palaver, 58.

15 Palaver, 58.

16 Jordens, _Gandhi's Religion_, 252.

The concepts were correlated and mutually determining. And the practice of these twin convictions was a direct challenge to the dynamic of structural violence and oppression. Ahimsa had echoes of Jesus's radical injunction in Luke's Gospel to love the enemy and do good to those who hate you: "But I say to you that listen, Love your enemies, do good to those who hate you, bless those who curse you, pray for those who abuse you. If anyone strikes you on the cheek, offer the other also; and from anyone who takes away your coat do not withhold even your shirt. Give to everyone who begs from you; and if anyone takes away your goods, do not ask for them again. Do to others as you would have them do to you" (Luke 6:27–31).

This radical Christian ethic reappears in the apostle Paul's letter to the Church at Rome:

> Do not repay anyone evil for evil, but take thought for what is noble in the sight of all. If it is possible, so far as it depends on you, live peaceably with all. Beloved, never avenge yourselves, but leave room for the wrath of God; for it is written, "Vengeance is mine, I will repay, says the Lord." No, "if your enemies are hungry, feed them; if they are thirsty, give them something to drink; for by doing this you will heap burning coals on their heads." Do not be overcome by evil, but overcome evil with good. (Rom 12:17–21; cf. 1 Pet 3:9–11)

In the 1930s, Gandhi established a new ashram on the outskirts of Ahmedabad called Satyagraha Ashram. This ashram "was intended to nurture and train a new kind of person, a *satyagrahi* . . . a person totally dedicated to the good and the freedom of the country, and prepared to put his life on the line . . . a *sannyasi*, a social reformer and political activist all in one."[17] Social reform and political activism, in keeping with the twin criteria of satyagraha and ahimsa, required active peaceful engagement with the powers. They necessarily entailed a refusal to become enmeshed in patterns of relating that maintained the status quo and led to further repression and violence. A good example of this active peaceful engagement is Gandhi's famous Salt Satyagraha march

---

17 Jordens, *Gandhi's Religion*, 176.

of 1930. Approximately eighty people who embodied the new kind of nonviolent activist (satyagrahi) and were chosen from the Sabarmati Ashram walked 240 miles to the seashore of Dandi to collect salt. William Connolly, in his reflections on the possibilities for a nonviolent militarism, notes, "This march was in direct disobedience of English law that required salt to be bought from the empire. Gandhi carried his handful of salt to the authorities to demand arrest for having broken the law. Brilliant."[18] Although it may have violated the law (itself designed to maintain systemic power over the population), this civil disobedience protest was nonviolent. It was met with British police beating hundreds of nonviolent protesters in Dharasana and Gandhi being jailed.

Suffering, Service, and Sacrifice

The Girardian scholar Wolfgang Palaver comments that "despite the West's admiration for Gandhi, it often overlooks how strongly he emphasised that the nonviolent struggle against injustice presupposes a readiness to suffer and to sacrifice oneself."[19] Gandhi found in the ancient Indian traditions of sacrifice clues to suffering as a way of overcoming violence. In this sense, satyagraha "was simply a new name for 'the ancient law of self-sacrifice' or 'the law of suffering.'" Jordens draws attention to Gandhi's comment that the notion of passive resistance associated with ahimsa "is not really resistance but a policy of communal suffering."[20] In a similar vein, the related concept of satyagraha, which Gandhi could also refer to as "love-force" or "soul-force," meant that pursuit of truth "did not admit of violence being inflicted on one's opponent but that he must be weaned from error by patience and sympathy. . . . And patience means suffering. So, the doctrine came to mean vindication of truth, not by infliction of suffering on the opponent but on one's self."[21]

---

18 William Connolly, *Facing the Planetary: Entangled Humanism and the Politics of Swarming* (Durham, NC: Duke University Press, 2017), 133.

19 Palaver, "Sacrifice between East and West," 58.

20 Jordens, *Gandhi's Religion*, 41.

21 Mohandas Gandhi, *Non-violent Resistance (Satyagraha)* (Mineola, NY: Dover, 2001), 6. Quoted in Palaver, "Sacrifice between East and West," 58.

Self-suffering was, for Gandhi, bound up with service, the roots of which were in his early upbringing and indeed "consistently pervaded the development of Gandhi's religious endeavour."[22] Service involved renunciation of prestige, money, caste, wife, family, and even life itself. And while service was fundamentally orientated toward the well-being of a country and its peoples, it was at the same time undertaken as an expression of his desire for self-realization and the attainment of *moksha*—ultimate end of life. In short, public service (Gandhi used the term *seva*) was the means to a higher end, an entirely novel association in Hinduism.[23] Gandhi later wrote that "it is the universal experience that God always saves the man [*sic*] who whole-heartedly devotes himself to the service of others."[24]

While Gandhi's concept of service had its roots in both familial contexts and deeply held religious convictions concerning the purpose of life, it was at the same time always public and necessarily political. It could not be otherwise given the link for Gandhi between his religious sensibilities—which were at once personal and public and embodied in a life of public service—and political action. Religion was ethical and public precisely because the religious life was encompassing of all life and could not be bracketed out from the concerns and activities of society. Religion, ethics, and politics were a threefold cord that could not be and should not have been broken.

Self-suffering through service constituted for Gandhi a sacrifice. At this point, Gandhi takes an entirely different course from the Hindu traditions regarding sacrifice. The ancient concept of sacrifice (*yajna*) in the Vedas involved sacrifices to the gods in order to appease and secure favors. In the Brahmanas, this concept of sacrifice was transformed into sacrificial formulas and rituals to access cosmic powers.

---

22 Jordens, *Gandhi's Religion*, 34.

23 Jordens notes the link between moksha and the duty of nonviolence, mercy, and kindness, which belong to the preparatory work of the seeker after moksha. Jordens identifies the origins of the link between service and moksha in Gandhi's early childhood but also recognizes the influence of Tolstoy's *The Kingdom of God Is within You*, trans. Constance Garnett (New York: Cassell, 1894). Jordens, *Gandhi's Religion*, 35.

24 Gandhi quoted in Jordens, *Gandhi's Religion*, 37. Originally from *Indian Opinion*, 1907.

Gandhi eschewed this sacrificial system and reinterpreted yajna as "the offering, the dedication of an action in devotion to Lord Krishna."[25] For Gandhi, this self-offering resolved itself into service: "If we aspire to be good, we must ceaselessly work to serve others, serve them in a perfectly disinterested spirit. . . . We may serve . . . because the Lord dwells in him and we serve that Lord."[26] Hence for Gandhi, service was a yajna, a sacrifice, "because the action is not performed for selfish purposes, but for the sake of others. Because the Lord dwells in them, the act of offering becomes a sacred act, a liberating act consecrated to the divine."[27] In this way, Gandhi cemented the nexus between the religious quest for realization of the Truth and selfless service of "the others"—that is, all people of the world, the lame and the afflicted, the country—indeed a universal service. Sacrifice assumes a decidedly outer-directed, compassionate, and nonviolent orientation.

Breaking the Cycle of Violence

Gandhi's nonviolent militancy, with its deep religious roots and embodiment in political action, proved a disturbing challenge to British imperialism. The dynamics of this broader context can be usefully interpreted through the lens of René Girard's insights into the structure of violence, mimesis and scapegoating, and the role of the exemplar in breaking the cycle of violence. What soon becomes apparent is the genius and radical challenge Gandhi's mission represented to British rule in India. A number of issues arise.

First, for a number of postcolonial commentators, the colony is the place where the violence of the home society is exported, and scapegoat victims are chosen to keep the peace there. The Girardian scholar Scott Cowdell observes in his discussion of "foreignness" and the construction of "the other" or "alien" that "the other has been cast out of

---

25 Jordens, 261.
26 Gandhi as quoted in Jordens, 261.
27 Jordens, 261.

the Western self and positioned abroad."[28] Thus for the sake of the mother country—its growth, wealth, and power—the colony, in this case India, is bled economically and subject to an oppressive military rule and control. As Cowdell notes, in this way, the colonial "is certainly scapegoated, providing a safe outlet for a lot of violence brewing at home, also by being excluded and programmed for failure as a self-definitional imperative of the successful and superior colonial master."[29] This involves "creating in the colony the same suppression of otherness that exists at home in other forms."[30] This dynamic is a feature of George Orwell's essay "Shooting an Elephant," in which the colonizers play the role of the "hard man" and rule through systemic violence. Orwell's point is that this role was expected of him as British policeman in the colony.[31] In this way, "the violent victim mechanism of modernity now oppresses the colonial, who must live in the colonizer's imagination as a delinquent failure in perpetual need of being 'whipped into shape.'"[32]

Second, as a consequence of this dynamic, "the colonial subject comes to ingest the psychic violence that has led the colonial master to reject part of himself in the first place, coming to believe that 'I am the failed other.'"[33] This is the conditioning to which the colonized are subjected, and as a result, "desire for what the master has—power and self-determination, in effect for superior being—requires the violent rejection of everything the master is."[34] In Girardian terms, violence against the colonial oppressor is just what you'd expect from internal mediation. The model of authority and power becomes the rival, and vice versa, so an escalation of violence develops. No sacrifice serves to unify the rivals, so the thing escalates into civil war. The masters

---

28 Scott Cowdell, *Abiding Faith: Christianity beyond Certainty, Anxiety, and Violence* (Eugene, OR: Cascade, 2009), 89.

29 Cowdell, 89.

30 Cowdell, 90.

31 For a discussion of Orwell's essay, see Ashis Nandy, *The Intimate Enemy: Loss and Recovery of Self under Colonialism* (New Delhi: Oxford University Press, 1983), 40–42.

32 Cowdell, *Abiding Faith*, 90.

33 Cowdell, 89.

34 Cowdell, 90.

punish the colonials, and this can serve a scapegoating function for keeping peace at home (rather like the way the Australian government punishes asylum seekers in detention). The colonials will also scapegoat turncoats and informers to keep themselves united. But no sacrifice seems to unify the master and the slave (except the distraction of a world war, perhaps). This dynamic underlies the emergence of the violent revolutionaries "from below," "transposing the desire of those dominating them 'from above.'"[35] Girard's comment on this dynamic is apposite: "Only someone who prevents us from satisfying a desire which he has inspired in us is truly an object of hatred."[36] Frantz Fanon, a psychoanalyst of colonialism, states it thus: "The settler's work is to make even dreams of liberty impossible for the native. The native's work is to imagine all possible methods for destroying the settler. On the logical plane, the Manicheism of the settler produces a Manicheism of the native. To the theory of the 'absolute evil of the native' the theory of the 'absolute evil of the settler' replies."[37] In this vicious scenario, the suffering victim becomes a violent hater, a mimetic double of the colonial oppressor. This arises because the rivals desire the same object—in this case rule of the Indian nation, either colonial or self-rule—and continually thwart and/or subvert each other and desire the object all the more. In this sense, as Girard notes, "violence is supremely mimetic," arising out of spiraling mimetic rivalry.[38]

Third, it is precisely at this point that Gandhi's nonviolent militancy constituted a radical response to the violent dynamic of colonial rulers and colonized peoples. Gandhi did not engage in rivalrous behavior that fed into the spiral of violence. This, of course, invites the question of whether and in what sense there might be a positive form

---

35 Cowdell, 90.

36 René Girard, *Deceit, Desire, and the Novel: Self and Other in Literary Structure*, trans. Yvonne Freccero (Baltimore: Johns Hopkins University Press, 1965), 9–10. Quoted in Cowdell, *Abiding Faith*, 90.

37 Frantz Fanon, *The Wretched of the Earth*, trans. Constance Farrington (New York: Grove, 1963), 63.

38 Scott Cowdell, *René Girard and the Non-violent God* (Notre Dame, IN: University of Note Dame Press, 2018), 151, quoting Girard, "Mimesis and Violence" (1979), in *The Girard Reader*, ed. James G. Williams (New York: Crossroad, 1996), 9–19, on 12–13.

of rivalry in which, for example, "the goal is to outdo a saintly model, or indeed Christ himself, in showing respectful, nonrivalrous regard for others."[39] Indeed, Gandhi offered precisely such an example of positive rivalry with distinct echoes of Jesus's Sermon on the Mount. He referred to nonviolent noncooperation with British rule as arising not from hatred but from friendship with and love of the oppressor. Hence he can state in 1925, "My attitude towards the English is one of utter friendliness and respect. I claim to be their friend. . . . A time is coming when England will be glad of India's friendship, and India will disdain to reject the proffered hand because it has once despoiled her."[40] In the same year, he writes, "My non-cooperation has its roots not in hatred, but in love."[41]

This fundamental attitude toward the English did not negate Gandhi's hatred of the oppressive yoke of the British occupation of India and its exploitative operations. Yet he was clear that the love he had for the English was based not on their goodness but on a higher calling of love for all. For if it was otherwise, then he would have "soon [begun] to hate them when their ways displease[d] [him]. A love that is based on the goodness of those whom you love is a mercenary affair."[42] Gandhi appeared to look beyond the oppressive nature of British imperial rule to the "other" West, the repressed shadow. In this respect, Ashis Nandy observes that the most creative response to the perversion of Western culture, typified by British imperial rule in India, came from its victims: "It was colonial India, still preserving something of its androgynous cosmology and style, which ultimately produced a transcultural protest against hyper-masculine world view of colonialism, in the form of Gandhi."[43] Nandy comments that Gandhi "always tried to be a living symbol of the other West. . . . He implicitly defined his ultimate goal as the liberation of the British from the psychology of British

39 Cowdell, 142.
40 M. K. Gandhi, *The Essential Gandhi: His Life, Work, and Ideas*, ed. Louis Fischer (New York: Vintage, 1962), 192. Originally from *Young India*, January 29, 1925.
41 Gandhi, 193.
42 Gandhi, 193.
43 Nandy, *Intimate Enemy*, 48.

colonialism."[44] Hence his search for the "salvation" of India included a hope for Britain's liberation.

Thus Gandhi does not become the "enemy twin" because he eschews violence even as he engages in civil disobedience. He desires to "blunt the edge of the tyrant's sword not by putting up against it a sharper-edged weapon, but by disappointing his expectation that I would be offering physical resistance. The resistance of the soul that I should offer instead would elude him."[45] This mode of resistance was more than simply a personal matter of interior disposition; it was deeply political and foundational for the kind of nation Gandhi imagined for India. To resist colonial rule with physical force would set him on a path of spiraling violence. If, on the other hand, "India succeeds in making British Rule impossible without matching the British bayonet with another bayonet, she will rule herself too with the same means."[46] One consequence of Gandhi's nonviolent resistance was that the British couldn't make a monster out of him. The way of ahimsa disrupts the usual pattern of violence associated with the colonizer and colonized. Yet as Erikson observes in relation to the protest at the Dharasana salt works not far from Dandi during the Salt March, "The very absence of violence, however, again aroused the police to pointless viciousness."[47] The loss of moral prestige cannot be disguised by the attempt to transpose nonviolent action of peaceful protest into violent attack. The oppressor, of necessity, is welded to a violent system of rivalry even in the face of a countermovement of peaceful militancy. Yet Gandhi's way of nonviolence was not absolute. If, for example, there was a choice between cowardice and violence, he advised violence: "I would rather have India resort to arms in order to defend her honour than that she should in a cowardly manner become or remain a helpless witness to her own dishonour."[48] Nonetheless, he believed nonviolence to

---

44 Nandy, 48–49.
45 Gandhi, *Essential Gandhi*, 188.
46 Gandhi, 191.
47 Erik Erikson, *Gandhi's Truth: On the Origins of Militant Nonviolence* (Toronto, Canada: W. W. Norton, 1969), 446.
48 Gandhi, *Essential Gandhi*, 157.

be "infinitely superior to violence, forgiveness is more manly than punishment. . . . But . . . forgiveness only when there is the power to punish."[49] In Gandhi's mind, the capacity to forgive was associated with "a definite recognition of our [Indian] strength."[50]

Gandhi's method was nonviolent sacrifice: "My method is conversion, not coercion, it is self-suffering, not the suffering of a tyrant."[51] Yet given the power and inherent violence of the colonial system, Gandhi was well aware that his method would not put an end to violence. In this sense, his way of peace came with a barb in the tail. It had echoes of Jesus's controversial statement in the Gospels: "Do not think that I have come to bring peace to the earth; I have not come to bring peace, but a sword" (Matt 10:34). This controversial text of Matthew's Jesus assumes great significance from a Girardian point of view. In it, Jesus exposes the easy peace that comes from the scapegoating of victims. Unless this mechanism, which is woven into the colonial narrative, is met with a counternarrative of nonviolent and hence positive sacrifice, real peace remains elusive. Gandhi's way has resonance with the Christian disciple who follows Jesus into a world without rivalry. While the way of nonviolence would not end violence, it offered Gandhi, among other things, a method of (a) undermining the cycle of violence encoded into the dynamic of British rule in India and (b) showing an alternative and genuine way of liberation which remains as relevant in the twenty-first century as it did in Gandhi's time.

Led by the Kindly Light of Truth

Gandhi's "method" of nonviolent militancy was never an abstract principle as such. It represented a hard won personal and religious journey, and it was in fact sustained by the deeply religious sensibility in which it had been nurtured. This points to a fundamental issue concerning

---

49 Gandhi, 157.
50 Nandy comments that "Gandhi's non-violence was probably not a one-sided morality play" in which humane Hindus were pitted against inhuman British. Nandy, *Intimate Enemy*, 49. It was of course more complex.
51 Gandhi, *Essential Gandhi*, 189.

the whence of the inner strength to continue the pursuit of truth and commitment to nonviolence. Sustained engagement of the kind Gandhi exemplified requires an inner composure and deep faith. Gandhi gave a clue at the end of his life: "In my daily prayers I earnestly pray to God to lead me from untruth to truth. Isn't the same idea conveyed in 'lead kindly light'"?[52] This hymn, composed by John Henry Newman at a period of intense personal trauma as he left the Church of England for Rome in the mid-nineteenth century, was well known to Gandhi from his years in England. This was the hymn that spoke to Gandhi more than any others that he knew and sang. The hymn contained, Gandhi believed, the "quintessence of all philosophy."[53] He meditated daily upon it's words, encouraged his supporters to do the same, broke fasts with it, chastised the press with it, quoted it to the British in difficult conversations, had it translated so it could be sung at daily meetings, and closed many writings and speeches with the distinctive call of the hymn, "one step enough for me." He considered that the hymn applied to organizations as much as individuals; it was for Gandhi (perhaps not for the nationalist movement as a whole) a fine representation of the spirit of his satyagraha campaigns.[54] The words that captured Gandhi were these:

> Lead, kindly light, amid the encircling gloom,
> Lead Thou me on,
> The night is dark and I am far from home,
> lead Thou me on;
> Keep thou my feet, I do not ask to see
> The distant scene—one step enough for me.[55]

---

52 William Emilsen, "Gandhi and 'Lead, Kindly Light,'" in *This Immense Panorama: Studies in Honour of Eric J. Sharpe*, ed. Carole M. Cusack and Peter Oldmeadow, Sydney Studies in Religion 2 (Sydney: School of Studies in Religion, University of Sydney, 1999), 230.

53 Emilsen, 230.

54 Emilsen, 231.

55 First stanza of Newman's poem, "The Pillar and the Cloud," composed in 1833. Subsequently, the whole poem was published as a hymn with the title "Lead, Kindly Light," in *Hymns Ancient and Modern*, Church of England (London: Novello, 1868).

The thought that sufficient light was given to take the next step was crucial to Gandhi. This so infused Gandhi's soul that eventually it became the song of the ashrams. Hindu, Muslim, and Christian supporters of Indian independence sang it every Friday evening, as Gandhi said, on "the day of Jesus' crucifixion." In this respect, Nandy comments that "Gandhi's partiality for some of the Christian hymns and Biblical texts was more than the symbolic gesture of a Hindu towards a minority religion in India. It was also an affirmation that, at one plane, some of the recessive elements of Christianity were perfectly congruent with elements of Hindu and Buddhist world views and that the battle he was fighting for the minds of men [sic] was actually a universal battle to rediscover the softer side of human nature, the so-called non-masculine self of man relegated to the forgotten zones of the Western self-concept."[56] This is an interesting and important observation from a Gandhian scholar. In a curious way, it returns us to some questions posed at the outset of this chapter: What holds us together? Is it a common purpose, the common good, a common spirit, a new song? In the fake news and "alternative facts" environment of today, do we believe in the force of truth? Gandhi offers us a deeper wisdom that has the power to bind and repair the rich and complex dimensions of the human spirit.

A Nonviolent Sociality

It is precisely at this point that Gandhi's method of nonviolence opens up possibilities for a new sociality through which people and communities might be drawn more deeply into the purposes of a peaceful God. This statement needs teasing out in the closing section of this chapter. To do so, I make the following points.

First, I want to return to an earlier remark in this chapter wherein I suggested that the metaphysical foundation for Gandhi's way of nonviolence was nothing less than an ontology of peace. In the Christian and Jewish theological traditions, such an ontology is embedded in

56 Nandy, *Intimate Enemy*, 49.

creation as such. Peace, and its correlate justice, constitutes the shalom of God as unfolded in the priestly account of creation in Genesis 1. As such, peace is an originative bestowal of God. This of course does not mean that harmony is a permanent feature of life in society. Indeed, the history of the world and its peoples is marked by conflict, rivalry, violence, and fragmentation. The early chapters of Genesis, and in particular the Cain and Abel story, exemplify this. A realistic account of life together points to continuing disturbance and the interplay of competing powers. This is what makes René Girard's analysis of this dynamic so important and useful in understanding Gandhi's counter-movement of nonviolence. Gandhi's pursuit of truth entailed the practice of nonviolence. It was his method to break the cycle of violence embedded in a rivalrous culture and empire. He hoped for a new day, a new Indian society in which peace would rule the hearts and minds—indeed, the nation. It was an ideal most certainly, but the force of this ideal was to be observed through performance. Gandhi becomes the exemplar to inspire people to a different way of life in society. To be led by the kindly light of truth involved immense personal and communal sacrifice of service and suffering. It was indeed the road less traveled.

Second, the Christian ethicist Stanley Hauerwas noted almost four decades ago that "the question of violence is the central issue for any Christian social ethic."[57] His comment was made in the context of the pursuit of justice in public life and social repair. He noted that the resort to violence as a means to achieve justice "stills the imaginative search for non-violent ways of resistance to injustice."[58] Hauerwas was clear that the quest for justice was based on truth "which has no need to resort to violence to secure its own existence."[59] While this has a distinct idealist tone to it, Hauerwas, echoing Gandhi's own experience, was equally clear that justice based on truth "comes at best fitfully to nation states" given that people prefer order based on lies, hate, fear,

57 Stanley Hauerwas, *The Peaceable Kingdom: A Primer in Christian Social Ethics* (London: SCM, 1983), 114.
58 Hauerwas, 114.
59 Hauerwas, 115.

and resentment to the claims of truth. As a Christian social ethicist, Hauerwas argued that the church, being a "community based on God's kingdom of truth," had a particular vocation amid a world of violence to inculcate habits of peace and bear witness to such a new way of life in its multiple engagements.[60]

Third, Hauerwas proposed that the peaceful path of truth and justice is exceedingly fraught. For a start, "the very idea of renouncing all possibilities of violence from our lives frightens us."[61] Why? Because it entails surrender of control, of our very selves. This has strong affinities with Gandhi's advocacy of sacrifice and surrender. It has been more recently identified in Christian theology as the "dispossession of the self" entailed in compassionate acts.[62] Hauerwas drew attention to the fact that the way of violence and power over others seems to be encoded into any efforts to harness resources to alleviate serious world problems: "The violence that provides the resources for the powers of the world to do their work lies in each of our souls."[63] Yet this does not mean the way forward is to first change the individual's heart and then look at the wider structural and systemic issues. That simply generates a false dichotomy, "since our hearts are also within the wider structures."[64] Hauerwas calls for a new imagination as a way toward a new kind of sociality: "To be lured into the world of non-violence requires a transformation of our imaginations."[65] Such a renewed imagination entails grasping a measure of God's peace and its reality in the present through the spirit of peace. Only then might we be able to begin where we are, to do the one thing needful, to participate in the purposes of

60 Hauerwas, 115.
61 Hauerwas, 149.
62 Oliver Davies, *Theology of Compassion: Metaphysics of Difference and the Renewal of Tradition* (Grand Rapids, MI: Eerdmans, 2001). For Davies, the activation of the image of the triune God is intimately and powerful related to compassion such that "to speak of God as compassion is to accept his injunction that we ourselves should be compassionate, and it is to understand that undergoing the dispossession of the self-entailed in compassion is to align our own 'being' with God's 'being,' and thus performatively, to participate in the ecstatic ground of the Holy Trinity itself" (252).
63 Hauerwas, *Peaceable Kingdom*, 150.
64 Hauerwas, 150.
65 Hauerwas, 151.

God to generate a new more inclusive unity ("God's international") that transcends loyalty to nation and class but yet begins in our own localities and nations. Hauerwas, in many ways echoing Gandhi's method, suggests some critical components in the pursuit of a new sociality energized and shaped by an ontology of peace.

Fourth, the theme of a renewed sociality has been taken up by Daniel Hardy in a programmatic essay.[66] Hardy locates the impetus for sociality in God's creative purposes for the world, "traced to the *logos* God operative in creation."[67] On this account, sociality belongs to those "necessary notes of being": unity, truth, goodness, and beauty. However, the reality of broken communities, violence, and dysfunction subverts what is natural to human life together. In this context, the story of Jesus Christ and the ongoing work of the Spirit of the risen Christ is the definitive story of the Christian community. Central to this is the account of the way in which people and all creation are drawn into the fulfillment of the originative gift of true sociality. This story becomes the life spring of Christian witness to God's peaceable kingdom. In space and time, this ongoing work has been a fundamental purpose of the ecclesia of God. Unsurprisingly, it has a decidedly communal and political dimension, not simply a pious ideal.[68]

To be led by the kindly light of truth is a profoundly communitarian and prophetic activity characterized by suffering. Gandhi's spiritual and practical intuition knew this well. It was one reason he was so attracted to the Gospel accounts of the life of Jesus and the Sermon on the Mount. It is precisely at this point that Gandhi's method of nonviolence and performative notion of truth is in keeping with all movements, aspirations, and concrete actions for social renewal. Gandhi's method has universal import, for it is the power that connects peoples of the world, their religious traditions, and all who share such spiritual affinities for a better future. It is also the reason the ecclesia of

---

66 Daniel Hardy, "Created and Redeemed Sociality," chap. 11 in *God's Ways with the World* (Edinburgh: T&T Clark, 1996).

67 Hardy, 42.

68 For my own attempt to trace this movement, see "A Renewed Sociality," chap. 4 in *Seeking the Church: An Introduction to Ecclesiology* (London: SCM, 2012).

God finds such a resonance between the way of Gandhi and the way the kindly light of truth shines forth in Jesus Christ.

Bibliography

Alam, Edward. "The Metaphysics of Violence: Comparative Reflections on the Thought of René Girard and Mahatma Gandhi." *Journal of Islamic Studies on Human Rights and Democracy* 1, no. 1 (Autumn 2017): 1–14.

Bilgrami, Akeel. "Gandhi's Religion and Its Relation to His Politics." In *The Cambridge Companion to Gandhi*, edited by Judith M. Brown and Anthony Parel, 93–116. Cambridge: Cambridge University Press, 2011.

Cameron, David. "Unveiling Ceremony for the Gandhi Statue: David Cameron's Speech." Prime Minister's Office, March 14, 2015. https://www.gov.uk/government/speeches/unveiling-ceremony-for-the-gandhi-statue-david-camerons-speech.

Connolly, William. *Facing the Planetary: Entangled Humanism and the Politics of Swarming*. Durham, NC: Duke University Press, 2017.

Cowdell, Scott. *Abiding Faith: Christianity beyond Certainty, Anxiety, and Violence*. Eugene, OR: Cascade, 2009.

———. *René Girard and the Non-violent God*. Notre Dame, IN: University of Notre Dame Press, 2018.

Davies, Oliver. *Theology of Compassion: Metaphysics of Difference and the Renewal of Tradition*. Grand Rapids, MI: Eerdmans, 2001.

Emilsen, William. "Gandhi and 'Lead, Kindly Light.'" In *This Immense Panorama: Studies in Honour of Eric J. Sharpe*, edited by Carole M. Cusack and Peter Oldmeadow, Sydney Studies in Religion 2, 227–237. Sydney: School of Studies in Religion, University of Sydney, 1999.

Erikson, Erik. *Gandhi's Truth: On the Origins of Militant Nonviolence*. Toronto, Canada: W. W. Norton, 1969.

Fanon, Frantz. *The Wretched of the Earth*. Translated by Constance Farrington. New York: Grove, 1963.

Gandhi, Mahatma. *The Essential Gandhi: His Life, Work, and Ideas*. Edited by Louis Fischer. New York: Vintage, 1962.

———. *Non-violent Resistance (Satyagraha)*. Mineola, NY: Dover, 2001.

Girard, René. *Deceit, Desire, and the Novel: Self and Other in Literary Structure*. Translated by Yvonne Freccero. Baltimore: Johns Hopkins University Press, 1965.

———. "Mimesis and Violence." In *The Girard Reader*, edited by James G. Williams, 9–19. New York: Crossroad, 1996.

Hardy, Daniel. *God's Ways with the World*. Edinburgh: T&T Clark, 1996.

Hauerwas, Stanley. *The Peaceable Kingdom: A Primer in Christian Social Ethics*. London: SCM, 1983.

Hempenstall, Peter. *The Meddlesome Priest: A Life of Ernest Burgmann*. Sydney: Allen & Unwin, 1993.

Imam-Ud-Din, S. J. *Gandhi and Christianity*. Rawalpindi, India: Northern Indian Publishing, 1946.

Jordens, J. T. F. *Gandhi's Religion*. Oxford: Oxford University Press, 1998.

Nandan, Satendra. "The Making of the Mahatma: An Australasian Perspective on Multiculturalism, Migration, Human Rights and Non-violence." Gandhi Oration, International Day of Non-violence at the National Press Club, Canberra, October 2, 2017.

Nandy, Ashis. *The Intimate Enemy: Loss and Recovery of Self under Colonialism*. New Delhi: Oxford University Press, 1983.

Newman, John Henry. "Lead, Kindly Light." In *Hymns Ancient and Modern*, Church of England, 198. London: Novello, 1868.

Palaver, Wolfgang. "Sacrifice between East and West: René Girard, Simone Weil, and Mahatma Gandhi on Violence and Nonviolence." In *Mimesis and Sacrifice: Applying Girard's Mimetic Theory across the Disciplines*, edited by Marcia Pally, 51–63. London: Bloomsbury Academic, 2019.

Pickard, Stephen. *Seeking the Church: An Introduction to Ecclesiology*. London: SCM, 2012.

CHAPTER 9

Swadeshi and the Self-Sufficiency of Religions

GANDHI'S THOUGHTS ON CONVERSION AND NICHOLAS OF CUSA'S DIALOGUE OF PERSPECTIVES

Peter Walker

Abstract: Nicholas of Cusa (1401–1464) and Mohandas Gandhi (1869–1948) stand a world apart, yet a common feature of their distant lives was the desire to reconcile differences into unity. This is especially evident in their ideas about relations among the religions. Cusa's pioneering work on interreligious dialogue, *On the Peace of Faith*, and his mystical masterwork, *On the Vision of God*, center upon his signature concept that the knowledge of God comes only at the coincidence of opposites. This *coincidence* establishes the value of different religious perspectives when seeking the presence of the Infinite. In Gandhi's ideas about religious conversion, we encounter an intriguingly complementary proposal. Gandhi argued for the spirit of swadeshi, or self-sufficiency, in matters of religion. Originally, swadeshi was a popular strategy to reduce India's dependence on British products and promote domestic production—Indian self-sufficiency. Gandhi extended this notion to the religious "market" by promoting the self-sufficiency of each religion and arguing against proselytizing for conversion. If one's ancestral religion is found to be defective, it is to be reformed rather than abandoned. Gandhi believed that each religion contains both truth and error, each may learn from the other, and none may claim superiority. This essay will examine and compare Gandhi and Cusa as exemplars of the search for interreligious reconciliation and unity.

Introduction

Nicholas of Cusa and Mohandas Gandhi stand a world apart, both historically and religiously. On the one hand, we find a fifteenth-century German Christian theologian and cardinal of the Catholic Church and, on the other, the father of modern India, a Hindu with broad religious interests. Yet one common feature of these two distant lives was the desire Nicholas and Gandhi both held to foster understanding and respect among the peoples of the world's religions. Nicholas's pioneering work on interreligious dialogue, *De pace fidei* (*On the Peace of Faith*, 1453), and his mystical masterwork, *De visione Dei* (*On the Vision of God*, 1453), both promote the value of engaging many perspectives when seeking an understanding of God. Gandhi advocated for the spirit of swadeshi, or self-sufficiency, in matters of religion. Swadeshi had been a rallying cry to promote support for domestic Indian goods over dependence on British supplies. Gandhi expanded the idea to the religious marketplace. Proselytizing should be abandoned, he argued, and the self-sufficiency and integrity of each religion should be honored. This essay will explore Gandhi's ideas about religious conversion and Nicholas's concept that knowledge of God is deepened by a dialogue of perspectives in order to propose that interreligious dialogue is a valuable tool for religious conversion—yet *not* the form of religious conversion that those words commonly bring to mind. First, let us go back to the fifteenth century.

Nicholas of Cusa

Unlike Gandhi, Nicholas of Cusa is not well known beyond a small number of academics, a devoted group of "Cusa specialists," and so a brief introduction to his life and writings may be helpful. Nicholas was born in 1401 beside the Mosel River, upon which his father was a boatman. His powerful curiosity soon led Nicholas well beyond the life into which he was born. He studied liberal arts at the University of Heidelberg, graduated with a doctorate in canon law from the University of Padua, and studied theology and philosophy at the University of Cologne.[1]

1 Prasad J. N. Theruvathu, *Ineffabilis in the Thought of Nicholas of Cusa* (Münster, Germany: Aschendorff, 2010), 3.

Nicholas was an eclectic thinker, and so alongside these formal studies, he developed interest in art, architecture, mathematics, and philosophy.[2] He was among the first to speculate that the universe may be infinite, and thus, given the impossibility of locating the center of that which is infinite, he also proposed that it was not possible to say with certainty that the earth is the center of the universe. He invented the concave lens, along with various instruments for measuring the level of moisture in the air, and the second-oldest-known map of Europe is thought to be the work of his hand. His brilliance was recognized early, and upon graduating in canon law, Nicholas was offered a professorship at the University of Leuven,[3] which he nevertheless declined in order to become an advisor to the archbishop of Trier. From that post, he found himself a key player at the Council of Basel in the 1430s, an experience that provoked his first major writings, *De concordanta catholica* (*The Catholic Concordance*, 1433) and *De docta ignorantia* (*On Learned Ignorance*, 1440).

Occupying a pivotal position in Nicholas's writings from Basel onward was the concept of *coincidentia oppositorum*, the coincidence of opposites.[4] His signature variation on that concept—namely, that the path to the knowledge of God reaches its destination only at the point where opposites coincide—is emblematic of his quest for religious unity. In grasping this idea, we grasp much about the way Nicholas's mind worked.

The principles of reason call on us to distinguish between opposites. For example, a red light is not a green light, a circle is not a square, a liquid is not a solid, and so on. In this way, we delineate between one thing and another in order to define it and, thereby, *know* what the thing is (and what it is not). To define is to make finite (*de fine*), a process in which we discriminate between one thing and another by comparing, contrasting, distinguishing, and ultimately, defining the

2 Erich Meuthen, *Nicholas of Cusa: A Sketch for a Biography*, trans. David Crowner and Gerald Christianson (Washington, DC: Catholic University Press, 2010), 15–21.
3 Theruvathu, *Ineffabilis*, 4.
4 Jasper Hopkins, *Nicholas of Cusa's Dialectical Mysticism: Text, Translation and Interpretive Study*, 3rd ed. (Minneapolis: Arthur J. Banning, 1996), 67.

world around us. Yet Nicholas argued that this method of comparing and distinguishing in order to define breaks down in the course of any attempt to attain knowledge of that which cannot be made finite, that which we cannot de-fine—namely, that which is infinite.[5] Given it was fundamental to Nicholas's Christian faith that God is infinite,[6] he taught that knowledge of God is attained when we apprehend that God, who is beyond de-fining, is encountered only as we transcend this process of distinction and definition, only as we transcend the notion that knowledge of God can be achieved via a series of con-tradictions and oppositions. When the limitations of reason are rec-ognized, we begin to perceive that the infinite God is ahead of us, at a place of mystery within which all rational distinctions coincide. In apprehending this path, which Nicholas likened to entering a cloud or mist, we start to move toward an understanding of God as the One in whom all oppositions are enfolded—the *coincidentia oppositorum.*[7]

For this style of epistemological wrestling with the knowledge of God, and his other contributions to the intellectual history of Chris-tianity in Europe, Nicholas has been described as Germany's finest

---

5 We should note that Nicholas's idea is not that *God* is the coincidence of opposites. Rather, his proposal is that knowledge of God comes as we enter the darkness and the *paradise* of knowing that is encountered beyond the contradictories of reason—a par-adise in which there is the coincidence of opposition. We should also note that this knowledge of God does indeed pass through reason. It does not neglect reason. Yet nonetheless, the knowledge of God transcends reason.

6 "The concept of *infinitas absoluta* is the primary perspective of all Cusanus' decisions attempting to express God's being as an absolute." Davide Monaco, *Nicholas of Cusa: Trinity, Freedom and Dialogue* (Münster, Germany: Aschendorff, 2016), 121.

7 Here, where the mystery of God seems most impenetrable, at a place Nicholas describes as "beyond the wall of Paradise," we approach God. Nicholas writes, "Hence, I experi-ence the necessity for me to enter into obscuring mist and to admit the coincidence of opposites, beyond all capacity of reason, and to seek truth where impossibility appears. And when—beyond that [rational capacity] and beyond every most lofty intellectual ascent as well—I come to that which is unknown to every intellect and which every intellect judges to be very far removed from the truth, *there* You are present, my God, You who are Absolute Necessity." Nicholas of Cusa, *De visione Dei* (1453), chap. 9, paras. 38–39, trans. Jasper Hopkins, in Hopkins, *Nicholas.* Hereafter all references to *De visione Dei* will be from the Hopkins translation.

fifteenth-century philosopher.[8] One of the most apposite descriptions of Nicholas was offered by George Sarton in his study of the early scientists of the Renaissance: "A Prince of the church but also a philosopher; a man of science with bold ideas, a forerunner of Erasmus."[9] Nicholas was made bishop and then cardinal in the 1450s and concluded his ecclesial career as the vicar-general of Rome. He died in 1464.

Of special interest for this inquiry is the fact that Nicholas was among the first Christian thinkers to advocate for dialogue as a means of achieving peace among the religions. Within months of the fall of Constantinople in 1453, while Europe was mired in fear and showered with anti-Muslim polemic, he wrote *On the Peace of Faith* and, soon after, *On the Vision of God*. Both books stood in irenic contrast to the prevailing mood of interreligious suspicion. Michel de Certeau sets the scene by observing that, in 1453, the "world [was] coming apart":

> To the West, the Hundred Year's War (1337–1453) between France and England has ended. A period of nations is beginning. To the East, the Eastern Roman Empire is collapsing as Constantinople is taken by the Turks (1453). Nicholas of Cusa, who had been there in 1437, had just brought the frightful news back from Rome, and amidst the rumours of horrors, violence and blood everywhere, he wrote, one month before *On the Vision of God*, his *On the Peace of Faith*, an anti-Babelian vision of a heavenly theatre in which, one after another, a delegate from each nation gets up to bear witness to the movement which supports it. Greek, Italian, Arab, Indian, Chaldean, Jew, Scythian, Gaul, Persian, Syrian, Turk, Spaniard, German, Tartar, Armenian, and so forth, each one comes to attest in the language of his own tradition to the truth which is one: this harmony of "free spirits" answers the furies of fanaticism.[10]

It is this *Vision of God* to which de Certeau refers, widely considered Nicholas's literary masterpiece,[11] that will draw our attention here. In my

---

8 Donald Duclow, "Life and Work," in *Introducing Nicholas of Cusa: A Guide to a Renaissance Man*, ed. Christopher M. Bellitto et al. (Mahwah, NJ: Paulist, 2004), 26.

9 George Sarton, *Six Wings: Men of Science in the Renaissance* (Madison: University of Wisconsin Press, 1959), 97.

10 Michel de Certeau, "The Gaze of Nicholas of Cusa," *Diacritics* 17, no. 3 (1987): 3.

11 Hopkins, *Nicholas*, 44.

mind's eye, I can imagine Nicholas and Gandhi holding an engaging conversation about peace among the religions, and so we will come to some possible connections shortly. First, we turn our attention to Gandhi's thoughts on the spirit of swadeshi and religious conversion so that we may have them in mind when we reengage Nicholas.

Gandhi and the Spirit of Swadeshi

Gandhi's writings on religion exhibit an intriguing and confounding blend of concepts. For example, he said that he detests conversion yet finds it highly desirable. Perhaps we need to get to the bottom of what Gandhi meant by conversion. Elsewhere, he declares that Christianity and his own Hindu faith are equally true, yet also that he does "not accept the orthodox teaching that Jesus was or is God incarnate."[12] Given this particular teaching about Jesus sits at the heart of Christianity, Gandhi's inability to accept Christianity's doctrine of the incarnation is difficult to reconcile with his statement that Christianity and Hinduism are equally true. Of course, his writings about religion, spanning many decades and circumstances, were not planned as a systematic offering, and so an element of incoherence is understandable. Our aim here is to untangle Gandhi's views on conversion, for in doing so, we find that Gandhi articulates a constructive view of religious conversion yet objects to the way conversion is ordinarily understood. His extension of the concept of the swadeshi spirit of self-sufficiency to matters of religion is the key.

Gandhi introduced the term *swadeshi* into anticolonial discourse in India as a call for Indian self-sufficiency (*swa* = self, *deshi* = sufficiency). As Bhushan and Garfield explain, "Its obvious primary sense involves the products of one's own land—a kind of 'buy Indian' campaign—and indeed, that was a large component of swadeshi. The most prominent example concerns the campaign to buy Indian khaki (cotton clothing)

---

12 Sarah Claerhout, "Gandhi, Conversion, and the Equality of Religions: More Experiments with Truth," *Numen* 61, no. 1 (2014): 56–57.

instead of cloth from Manchester."[13] Yet Gandhi extended the application of swadeshi beyond "buy Indian." Gandhi's advocacy for swadeshi was a commitment to buy Indian cloth, yes, but also to upholding local forms of language, tradition, belief, handicraft production, and community life. Swadeshi had a societal and spiritual meaning beyond the economic. Self-sufficiency was the best means of sustaining a meaningful life and harmonious communities. Further, commitment to swadeshi extended to resistance. As Bhushan and Garfield have observed, "For Gandhi, this commitment to valorize [the local and ancestral] also entails a commitment to resist—to resist traditions, languages, ideologies, and forms of life alien to one's own culture. Resistance becomes a way of preserving one's own culture."[14]

While British rule was Gandhi's target, his real foe was modernity. Modernization appeared like a path to liberation to some in colonial India, but Gandhi thought otherwise. He saw modernity as a political, industrial, and social web that strangled unwitting nations and individuals. Others of his day, including Jawaharlal Nehru, thought modernization held the promise of an independent and prosperous India. Gandhi thought this to be a deception. Modernization was not the road to freedom but the dead end of freedom. He believed modernity eroded national and individual freedom by superimposing a homogenous set of social institutions, markets, values, and even modes of conduct upon local traditions that had been meaningful, respected, and sustaining for generations. Modernity's promise of profit and progress eroded individual liberty and local community by imposing homogeneity upon a myriad of formerly heteronomous cultures. Thus there was a moral element, above the economic, to Gandhi's commitment to self-sufficiency. We must also note that Gandhi was not closed to engaging different traditions and modern ideas. Rather, he was concerned that the foreign and new would dominate and disintegrate the

---

13 Nalini Bhushan and Jay L. Garfield, "Swaraj and Swadeshi: Gandhi and Tagore on Ethics, Development, and Freedom," in *Value and Values: Economics and Justice in the Age of Global Interdependence*, edited by Roger T. Ames and Peter D. Hershock (Honolulu: University of Hawai'i Press, 2015), 259, 263.

14 Bhushan and Garfield, 263–64.

local and traditional. Thus it is on this broad map of the meaning of the swadeshi spirit of self-sufficiency that we may locate the way Gandhi applied the idea to religious conversion.

Gandhi and Religious Conversion

"I cannot understand a man changing the religion of his forefathers at the insistence of another," Gandhi once wrote.[15] In fact, Gandhi frequently wrote of his incomprehension at the thought of replacing one religion with another. He objected, for example, to the practices of *shuddhi* promoted by nineteenth-century Hindu reform movements as a means of converting Muslims and Christians to Hinduism.[16] This is evident when Gandhi writes of conversion being a process that leads to a better practice of one's own faith: "My instinct tells me that all religions are more or less true. All proceed from the same God, but all are imperfect because they come down to us through imperfect human instrumentality. The real *shuddhi* movement should consist of each one trying to arrive at perfection in his or her own faith. In such a plan character would be the only test. What is the use of crossing from one compartment to another, if it does not mean a moral rise?"[17]

Religious conversion is a perennially contentious issue in India, rarely absent from political agendas or national debate. While the objection to conversion is often linked to Hindu nationalism, this was not Gandhi's perspective. His desire for harmony among Hindus and Muslims was widely known, as was his regard for Christianity. Gandhi's strong opposition to proselytizing rested not in Hindu nationalism but in the extension of the spirit of swadeshi to the domain of religion.[18]

Gandhi considered his Hindu tradition, for example, to have a strong swadeshi spirit. It was this spirit that explained the absence

---

15 Mohandas Karamchand Gandhi, *The Collected Works of Mahatma Gandhi* (Delhi: Ministry of Information and Broadcasting, Government of India, 1964–94), 33:100–101.

16 Claerhout, "Gandhi," 63.

17 Gandhi, *Collected Works*, 24:148–49.

18 Claerhout, "Gandhi," 54–55.

of a proselytizing impulse among Hindus. A Hindu refuses to change religion not necessarily because he considers it superior but because it is the faith of his ancestors, is sufficient for his needs, and can be reformed when and where error is found. For Gandhi, the proper response to deficiency in religion is to reform rather than abandon it. We have noted swadeshi was originally and primarily a rallying cry to reduce India's dependence on British products and promote, instead, the sufficiency of Indian goods. Gandhi's perspective on conversion is an extension of this economic strategy to the religious market. By suggesting that people of faith be committed to their ancestral religion, he is making a stand for the same principle of self-sufficiency.

Gandhi called for all religions to respect this swadeshi spirit. For example, if Christians would recognize the integrity of other religions, and that genuine conversion takes place within one's own tradition rather than by moving from one religion to another, missionaries would cease to be driven by proselytizing and focus on charity and service instead. It is because Christian humanitarian work ultimately aims at converting people that the work of the missionary suffers. Instead of convincing others that their religion is superior, it is the responsibility of all people of faith to be committed to their tradition and then work for its improvement, for its *conversion*.[19]

What, then, shall we conclude about Gandhi's ideas on religious conversion before reengaging Nicholas in this conversation? First, the concept of conversion is important to Gandhi, but he seems to have understood conversion to mean an ongoing cycle of spiritual and moral growth, both of individual believers and of religious traditions as a whole. Second, Gandhi understood that all believers have a responsibility for their ongoing personal conversions, their own spiritual and moral growth, as well as the ongoing conversion of their particular religious traditions. A Christian, for example, should attend to his or her personal spiritual and moral growth and the ongoing reform of the Christian church. And a third and final observation about Gandhi's

---

19 I am indebted here again, as I am throughout this discussion, to Sarah Claerhout's "Gandhi," 62–63.

view of conversion follows from these two—namely, conversion should not be understood as a conscious campaign to persuade others of the superiority of one's own religion and the inferiority of theirs. We catch a glimpse of Gandhi's extension of the spirit of swadeshi to religious conversion in this frequently quoted portion of his 1928 discussion of "fellowship":

> I came to the conclusion long ago, after prayerful search and study and discussion with as many people as I could meet, that all religions were true and also that all had some error in them. And that whilst I hold my own, I should hold others as dear as Hinduism, from which it logically follows that we should hold all as dear as our nearest kith and kin and that we should make no distinction between them. So we can only pray, if we are Hindus, not that a Christian should become a Hindu, or if we are Mussalmans, not that a Hindu or Christian should become a Mussalman, nor should we even secretly pray that anyone should be converted. But our inmost prayer should be that a Hindu should be a better Hindu, a Muslim a better Muslim, and a Christian a better Christian.[20]

Nicholas of Cusa's Vision of God

With Gandhi's perspective on conversion in mind, we depart the twentieth century and return to the mid-fifteenth century, where we again locate Nicholas of Cusa. Are there connections to make between Gandhi's spirit of swadeshi and Nicholas's ideas about the knowledge of God as *coincidentia oppositorum*? Exploring an exercise Nicholas designed to give practical expression to his idea—an exercise about gaining a vision of God at the point where different perspectives coincide—may help us here.

Nicholas corresponded frequently with a community of Christian monks at Saint Quirin's Monastery in Tegernsee, which fell within his bishopric of Brixen. The monks wrote in 1453 to ask Cardinal Cusa for help in answering a question that had been troubling them: How

---

20 Gandhi, *Collected Works*, 35:461–64. I note also that Claerhout observes, "Gandhi appears to have another conception of truth in mind than truth as a property of propositions, doctrines, or beliefs. . . . The ambiguity about the meaning of 'truth' in religion is common in Gandhi's writings," 66–67.

may we know God? Behind the question lay a debate about mystical theology: Is it our hearts or is it our minds that enable knowledge of God? Put another way, Is it the affections or intellect where we are open or opened to an understanding of God? It is hard to miss the fact that both options, heart or mind—and a third option, heart and mind, if we choose to see it—are focused on the individual. So Nicholas decided that he would offer the monks a lesson on the importance of appreciating multiple perspectives and answered their question with a small book, which he titled *On the Vision of God*. Nicholas also designed an exercise for the monks to undertake together before reading the book. The centerpiece of the exercise was an image of an all-seeing face.

"How can we truly know God?" the monks had asked. Nicholas instructed them to set the image of the all-seeing face against a wall in their monastery, form a semicircle around it, and look upon the image in silence, as if looking into the very face of God. In this first moment, he hoped that each monk would perceive "how diligently [the gaze] is concerned for each one of them, as if it were concerned for no one else; but only for him who experiences that he is seen. . . . To the brother who is situated in the east, it will seem as if the face is looking to the east; to the brother in the south, that the face is looking to the south."[21]

Next, Nicholas asked the monks to walk from one side of the image to the other, still in silence, and keeping their eyes fixed at all times on the face. In this second moment, he hoped that each monk would perceive that the gaze never left him, not even while he was moving: "Let the brother who was in the east situate himself in the west, and he will experience the gaze fixed on him in the west, just as it had previously been in the east."[22]

As affecting as those first two stages might have been, it is with the third stage of the exercise that Nicholas hoped the monks would perceive an even more striking discovery, one they could not make by themselves. In their third and final act around the icon, Nicholas asked the monks to break their silence and speak with one another about

21 Nicholas of Cusa, preface to *De visione Dei*, paras. 3–4.
22 Nicholas of Cusa, para. 3.

what they had experienced. In this moment, as they entered dialogue, Nicholas hoped the monks would learn that the all-seeing gaze had followed every one of them, even those who had been moving in opposite directions. Nicholas wrote, "Through the disclosure of [his fellow brothers], each monk will come to know that the gaze does not desert anyone—not even those who are moving in contrary directions."[23]

Nicholas's exercise is only that—a staged event in which *seeing* is an analogy for *knowing*. Yet there is something in this paraliturgy. Whereas the monks could see while standing in silence or silently moving from side to side that the all-seeing gaze was always resting upon them personally, the insight that the gaze was resting simultaneously upon them all was dependent on listening to one another and trusting what was heard from different perspectives. How may we know God? Yes, we may know something of God on our own. However, the third stage of this little play releases its simple yet profound insight. The gaze of God can feel so generous upon us that we might mistakenly assume we are its sole recipients, or that ours is the single point from which to gain a correct perspective. Yet as we listen with trust to those who gain their perspective from other places, we begin to attain an even fuller vision of the One who sees us all. Only by listening to the perspective of those who stand in a different place do we begin to perceive that there are things invisible to us that are yet visible to them. Taking this observation one step further, our very awareness of the possibility of the presence of that which is invisible comes only if we are willing to trust those who speak from different perspectives.

The Tegernsee monks were invited to trust that the path to the knowledge of God is a mystery analogous to their experience around the image of God. There, each brother comes to the realization that he sees and is seen by the gaze regardless of where he stands. Further, on hearing his fellow monks declare that they too have been held by the gaze, regardless of where they stood, he also begins to perceive that there is a deeper wisdom available than he had initially been able to comprehend. The gaze in which they all feel held is one and the same

---

23 Nicholas of Cusa, para. 4.

gaze. It sees them all, regardless of their location. And so, although all see the face, and all feel themselves seen, the vision of God they each obtain is a contraction of the whole, a limited perspective. As the monks begin speaking with one another, and only in that moment, they come to realize there is an *excess*—an excess that, by his sight alone, no single monk can comprehend. The valuable heuristic insight follows. Only dialogue allows each participant to understand that he sees merely a part of the whole; God is greater than any single perspective can encompass. Hearing from many perspectives will allow the knowledge of God to deepen.

Gandhi and Nicholas: Religious Conversion and Perspectives in Dialogue

We have been exploring Gandhi's thoughts on religious conversion and Nicholas of Cusa's ideas about how to obtain knowledge of God. The differences between the two men and their ideas are obvious, significant, and must not be understated. Gandhi is encouraging respect and peace among India's great variety of religions by arguing that conversion should be understood as an internal spiritual reform—an ongoing process taking place within each believer and each religious tradition— rather than an external campaign focused on recruiting "converts" from other traditions. Nicholas, on the other hand, is hoping to teach a group of Christian monks how to deepen their knowledge of God. He does that via an exercise that demonstrates the value of engaging with different points of view. Yet amid the clear differences between Nicholas and Gandhi, some common ground does come into view: respect for the integrity of particularity and the importance of diversity, recognition that every perspective contains some truth and some error, and the commitment to an ongoing process of reform and refinement. Both Gandhi's extension of the swadeshi spirit to religious conversion and Nicholas's application of *coincidentia oppositorum* to the dialogue around the all-seeing icon seek to uphold the value of heteronomy over the homogenization of ideologies of the universal. And so, arising from these points of connection, we will venture to join one key idea from Nicholas to Gandhi's reading of conversion in a way that, hopefully, enriches our perspective on both conversion and interreligious dialogue.

Among the most helpful aspects of Nicholas's exercise around the image of an all-seeing face is its demonstration of the epistemological significance of the other.[24] We learn from difference. We learn from that which is other*wise* to our current perspective. What we learn may serve to confirm or contradict our current perspective, yet either way, we learn. Knowledge is reformed and refined by the encounter. Each monk in the exercise is drawn to reflect on the part played by his fellow monks in deepening his knowledge of God. And having established an awareness of the epistemological significance of the other, Nicholas also demonstrates the epistemological significance of dialogue, the value of listening to diverse points of view. In becoming aware of the different perspectives held by those who see (and are seen) by the all-seeing face, each participant becomes aware of the merit in establishing a habit of dialogue. The search by those who are finite for an understanding of the One who is infinite is never-ending. The Infinite is inexhaustible. Yet moments of insight, sometimes affirming our point of view and sometimes calling it into question, come in the experience of dialogue. To assume our perspective is the only reservoir of truth not only impedes our search for an understanding of God; it jeopardizes that search altogether. For by placing our trust in a single point of view, we assume an absolute status for a posture that is finite and, therefore, inherently and always limited. That the human search for knowledge of God is enhanced by drawing differing perspectives into conversation is perhaps the central lesson of Nicholas's experiment.

---

24 My use of the term *the other* is more pragmatic than the occasionally obsessive engagement with alterity. Rather, my use of the term is simply to acknowledge that, in the face of the other, we become relational and responsible, are made aware of our contracted place and of the risk of betraying our perspective, along with that of others, should we pretend to have a totality of vision or knowledge and, finally, it is also in the face of another that we become open to the possibilities vested in the idea of infinity. See Michael Barnes, "Facing the Other," in *Theology and the Dialogue of Religions* (Cambridge: Cambridge University Press, 2002), 65–96.

This is where we might join the insights around the icon with Gandhi's concept of conversion. Gandhi saw conversion as a process of internal spiritual reform for individual believers and each religion. Conversion was not about interreligious proclamation, or spiritual imperialism. Yet Gandhi's concept of conversion might be enhanced by encouraging a different form of engagement between religions— engagement by dialogue—because of its potential benefit to that very process of internal spiritual reform. By advocating for a spirit of self-sufficiency within religions, did Gandhi unwittingly impede one practice that may enrich our ongoing spiritual reform? Can we say that interreligious dialogue has an important place, and perhaps an essential place, in the spiritual practices of intrareligious conversion? Or, put another way, that developing the habit of learning from the religious *other* is valuable to our personal spiritual reform and the reform of our particular religious tradition? To our conversion?

Nicholas crafted an exercise to provoke a dialogue among the Tegernsee monks. They were all Christian, and so we might call that an intrareligious dialogue. Through that dialogue, Nicholas sought to lead his fellow Christians to appreciate that their understanding of God is always limited by their finitude, yet their understanding may expand by listening to one another. With that epistemological framework established, we might also propose that every religion understands the divine in ways that are inevitably limited, and so each religion's understanding may be expanded by listening to the witness of other religious traditions.

Nicholas would very likely have sympathized with Gandhi's view that there is truth in all religions, but he would have balked at the idea that all religions are equally true. Nevertheless, the two men may well have held an engaging, if robust, conversation about their respective ideas. Nicholas's epistemological framework of a dialogue of perspectives calls for an ongoing interrogation of our personal and collective religious vision. That is to say, Nicholas's *visio* seeks to provoke a continuous questioning of our finite understanding of God, and the manner in which that finite understanding is expressed in personal faith, as well as the collective witness of religious traditions. There is much here that resonates with Gandhi's thoughts on religious conversion. Placing a prominent commitment to interreligious dialogue alongside Gandhi's perspective might provide even greater means and motivation to revisit and refine our knowledge of God, doing so respectfully and without the spiritual imperialism so often found in proselytism. Dialogue leads us to acknowledge where our vision is incomplete or wanting. Or, to employ the same analogy as Nicholas, to acknowledge where we have not *seen* the divine as clearly as others. The dialogue of perspectives is not an epistemological framework that advocates "your vision and my vison are equally true." Yet it is an epistemological framework that may be summarized as "I need your vision, as indeed you need mine, in order that we may focus more clearly on the presence of the sacred."[25] It is tempting to suggest that, were Gandhi and Nicholas ever to have had an opportunity to speak with one another, they might both have agreed that the process of spiritual reform and refinement, the process of conversion, is enriched by interreligious dialogue.

Bibliography

Barnes, Michael. *Theology and the Dialogue of Religions.* Cambridge: Cambridge University Press, 2002.

Bhushan, Nalini, and Jay L. Garfield. "Swaraj and Swadeshi: Gandhi and Tagore on Ethics, Development, and Freedom." In *Value and Values: Economics and Justice in the Age of Global Interdependence,* edited by Roger T. Ames and Peter D. Hershock, 259–271. Honolulu: University of Hawai'i Press, 2015.

Claerhout, Sarah. "Gandhi, Conversion, and the Equality of Religions: More Experiments with Truth." *Numen* 61, no. 1 (2014): 53–82.

de Certeau, Michel. "The Gaze of Nicholas of Cusa." *Diacritics* 17, no. 3 (1987): 2–38.

Duclow, Donald. "Life and Work." In *Introducing Nicholas of Cusa: A Guide to a Renaissance Man,* edited by Christopher M. Bellitto, 25–47. Mahwah, NJ: Paulist, 2004.

Gandhi, Mohandas Karamchand. *The Collected Works of Mahatma Gandhi.* Delhi: Ministry of Information and Broadcasting, Government of India, 1964–1994.

---

25 Monaco, *Nicholas,* 94–95.

Hopkins, Jasper. *Nicholas of Cusa's Dialectical Mysticism: Text, Translation and Interpretive Study.* 3rd ed. Minneapolis: Arthur J. Banning, 1996.

Meuthen, Erich. *Nicholas of Cusa: A Sketch for a Biography.* Translated by David Crowner and Gerald Christianson. Washington, DC: Catholic University Press, 2010.

Monaco, Davide. *Nicholas of Cusa: Trinity, Freedom and Dialogue.* Münster, Germany: Aschendorff, 2016.

Sarton, George. *Six Wings: Men of Science in the Renaissance.* Madison: University of Wisconsin Press, 1959.

Theruvathu, Prasad J. N. *Ineffabilis in the Thought of Nicholas of Cusa.* Münster, Germany: Aschendorff, 2010.

CHAPTER 10

Gandhi and Thurman

RELIGION, RESISTANCE, AND THE
TWENTY-FIRST-CENTURY QUEST FOR PEACE

C. Anthony Hunt

Abstract: Howard Thurman's encounter with Mohandas Gandhi helped Thurman shape a philosophy of nonviolence as an active force of resistance. Thurman was among the leading African American Christian religious figures attracted to the thinking and praxis of Gandhi. Thurman's contact with Gandhi would serve to codify his thinking with regard to nonviolence while also serving as an impetus for his ongoing search for the realization of what Thurman deemed to be "common ground" in the striving for authentic community. Certainly, Gandhi's success with social and political reform in India was solid evidence for nonviolence, a praxis of resistance and just peacemaking, and served as a model for the likes of not only Thurman but African American religious leaders like Benjamin Mays, William Stuart Nelson, Mordecai Johnson, Edward Carroll and Martin Luther King Jr. This chapter will explore the ways in which Howard Thurman's engagement with Gandhi served to reinforce, confirm, and provide deeper insights as to the efficacy of nonviolence—as expressed in Gandhian satyagraha and ahimsa and the Christian love-ethic—in resistance to racial and social oppression and in the ongoing search for common ground and quest for peace in the churches and society today.

Howard Thurman's encounters with Mohandas Gandhi and Gandhi's thinking were critical in helping shape Thurman's understanding and philosophy of nonviolence as an active force of resistance. He was among the leading American Christian religious figures attracted to the thinking and praxis of Gandhi and was impressed with Gandhi's ideas on the power of nonviolence as a method that positively responds to the spiritual needs of humanity while at the same time accomplishing the necessary political transformation of the social order.[1]

Gandhi provided a deep field of ideas from which Thurman gleaned. His contact with Gandhi served to codify Thurman's thinking with regard to nonviolence while also serving as an impetus for Thurman's ongoing search for the realization of what he deemed to be "common ground."

This chapter will explore ways in which Howard Thurman's engagement with Mohandas Gandhi served to reinforce, confirm, and provide deeper insights as to the efficacy of nonviolence—as expressed in Gandhian satyagraha and ahimsa as means of resistance to racial and social oppression—and how these ideals served as tools in the ongoing search for common ground and peace in the churches and society.

Thurman, Gandhi, and the Making of Radical Resisters

Howard Thurman is considered by many to have been one of the seminal American religious figures of the twentieth century. Recognized in 1953 by *Life* magazine as one of the twelve greatest preachers in America, he was variously described as a pastor, theologian, philosopher, mystic, and prophet. Throughout his ministry, he sought to draw on the raw materials of life as critical resources of Christian faith in ways that would address his overarching theological concern for the articulation and appropriation of a Christian witness that would give impetus to personal spiritual growth while ultimately actualizing social transformation, peacemaking, and inclusive community.

Thurman was the grandson of slaves, and his faith was formed within the context of the southern Black Baptist tradition. Born in segregated Daytona, Florida, on November 18, 1899, he stayed in that city until the absence of educational opportunities for Blacks forced him to go to Jacksonville for a high school education. He completed undergraduate studies at Morehouse College in Atlanta, Georgia, in 1923 and

---

1 Elizabeth Yates, *Howard Thurman: Portrait of a Practical Dreamer* (New York: John Day, 1964), 104–9.

graduate theological studies at Rochester Divinity School in Rochester, New York, in 1926.

Thurman's ministerial career formally began in Oberlin, Ohio, where, from 1926 to 1928, he pastored an African American Baptist congregation. From 1932 to 1944, he served as dean of the Andrew Rankin Memorial Chapel and professor of religion at Howard University, and in 1953, he became the first African American dean at a majority white university as dean of Marsh Chapel and professor of spiritual resources and disciplines at Boston University. During this same period, he formed the Howard Thurman Educational Trust, which continues to disburse funds for various humanitarian endeavors, most notably scholarships for African American students in the South. Prominent among Thurman's many involvements was the San Francisco–based church that he cofounded and copastored from 1944 to 1953 with Alfred Fisk—the Church for the Fellowship of All Peoples—heralded as the first authentically racially inclusive model of institutional religion in the United States.[2]

He was a multidimensional person who lived on all levels of existence—physical, emotional, and spiritual. Describing his attributes is like constructing a bridge. To be effective, the bridge must reach both sides, or the traveler will fall.[3] Vincent Harding captured the essence of Thurman as a "God-intoxicated" man when he wrote about him in the introduction to Thurman's *For the Inward Journey*. Harding observed that Thurman was a person who was constantly moving toward the source of all human life and truth via the concrete beauty and terror of the Black experience in the United States.[4] Thurman as a "God-intoxicated" man offered a paradigm of God-centered and God-inspired ministry. The effectiveness of Thurman's Christian witness is to be viewed in light of this connectedness with God. With Christ as the center of his word

---

2 Alton Pollard, *Mysticism and Social Change: The Social Witness of Howard Thurman* (New York: Peter Lang, 1992), 3.

3 Michael I. N. Dash, Jonathan Jackson, and Stephen C. Rasor, *Hidden Wholeness: An African American Spirituality for Individuals and Communities* (Cleveland: United Church, 1997), 1.

4 Howard Thurman, *For the Inward Journey* (Richmond, IN: Friends United, 1984), x.

and witness, Thurman remained inspired to prophetically challenge principalities and the powers of the church and society to work for peace with justice.

Lerone Bennett Jr., in his eulogy of Thurman in 1981, pointed to Thurman's perspective on life: "A man cannot be at home everywhere, unless he is at home somewhere."[5] One has to know from whence they have come in order to understand how they will operate within the context of present reality and future possibility. Thurman seemed to be at home with his roots in southern Black culture and was also able to practice ministry, teach, and live in ways that crossed cultural and theological perspectives.

Walter Fluker asserts that Thurman's life and work provide excellent insights into his generation of nonviolence and Black leadership in the South. Thurman is properly located within the context of the struggle for liberation from Black oppression. His vision of community was significantly shaped by his encounters with the extremes of race and class domination in America's Deep South at the turn of the twentieth century.[6]

As early as 1928 in his article "Peace Tactics and a Racial Minority," Thurman began to outline how a "philosophy of pacifism" could begin to eliminate whites' will to control and Blacks' will to hate. His primary concern was to call a truce to attitudes that promoted separation.[7]

Mohandas Gandhi's title, "mahatma"—literally translated as "whose essence of being is great"—was befitting his life's achievements. Huston Smith asserted that the most notable achievement for which the world credited Gandhi was the peaceful British withdrawal from India.

---

5 Lerone Bennett Jr., "Eulogy of Howard Thurman: Tributes to Genius," *African American Pulpit* (Winter 1981): 63. Bennett made reference to Thurman's perspective on life and personal identity at Thurman's funeral in 1981.

6 Walter Fluker, "Dangerous Memories and Redemptive Possibilities: Reflections on the Life and Work of Howard Thurman," in *Black Leaders and Ideologies in the South: Resistance and Nonviolence,* ed. Preston King and Walter E. Fluker (New York: Routledge, 2005), 148.

7 Luther E. Smith, *Howard Thurman: The Mystic as Prophet* (Richmond, IN: Friends United, 2007), 133. Luther Smith makes reference to Thurman's "Peace Tactics and a Racial Minority," *World Tomorrow,* December 1928, 505–7.

What is not as well known is that among his own people, he lowered a barrier thought by many to be much more formidable than that of British colonialism in India, racism in the United States, or apartheid in South Africa—renaming and redefining the lowest caste of Dalits and "untouchables" in India as "harijans," God's children, and raising them to human status.[8]

The formative ideas of Gandhi's philosophy of nonviolence began to take shape in the years he worked to better the social and economic conditions of Indians in South Africa. He spent twenty years in South Africa as an acknowledged leader of the Indian people.[9] Rajmohan Gandhi, research professor at the Center for South Asian and Middle Eastern Studies at the University of Illinois has suggested that Gandhi's views on nonviolence can be largely traced to his personal experiences and early encounters with bigotry on his journey to South Africa in 1893.[10]

As someone whose entire adult life was consumed with fighting against such injustices as racial discrimination in South Africa, British rule in India, and dehumanizing social practices within his own society, Gandhi sought to develop an approach to how moral persons could and should act in such struggles. He found the methods of both rational discussion and violence—the traditional methods that appealed to people in addressing injustice—unsatisfactory to various degrees and thus sought to discover an alternative and more powerful method.

In 1907, Gandhi, who was still in South Africa, read Henry David Thoreau. In seeking to conceptualize his philosophy, he borrowed the anglicized term *civil disobedience* from Thoreau, which was more often referred to as "passive resistance." But he was not satisfied with either

8 Huston Smith, *The World's Religions* (San Francisco: HarperCollins, 1991), 13.
9 J. Deotis Roberts, "Gandhi and King: On Conflict Resolution," *Shalom Papers: A Journal of Theology and Public Policy* 11, no. 2 (Spring 2000): 36.
10 Rajmohan Gandhi, "Gandhi's Unfulfilled Legacy: Prospects for Reconciliation in Racial/Ethnic Conflict," Cynthia Wedel Lecture, Church's Center for Theology and Public Policy, Wesley Theological Seminary, Washington, DC, April 27, 1995. In this lecture, Rajmohan Gandhi offers a view of Mohandas Gandhi's life and unfinished legacy from the perspective of a contemporary Indian scholar.

term. In his estimation, both were too narrowly conceived and appeared to be negative, passive, and weak. In his estimation, they could easily denigrate into hatred and would likely opt, finally, for violence. Thus civil disobedience and passive resistance became obsolete for Gandhi.

In a magazine called *Indian Opinion*, which he edited for a time in South Africa, Gandhi offered a small prize to be "awarded to the reader who invented the best designation for [Indians in South Africa's] struggle." One of his cousins, Maganlal Gandhi, produced a word that seemed almost right, *sadagraha*, which means "firmness in a good cause." Mohandas Gandhi corrected it to *satyagraha—satya* meaning "truth" and *graha* meaning "firmness, tenacity, holding on."[11]

The conception of satyagraha became fundamental to Gandhi's life and activity.[12] It is "truth-taking" or "the taking of vows of truthfulness." This "truth-force" is possible because it excludes the use of violence and because humans are capable of grasping the truth (but not in an absolute sense) and are not competent to punish. Theologically, truth in an absolute sense is God or the Ultimate Being. For Gandhi, *Sat* was "the only correct and fully significant name for God."[13]

Thurman and Mystic Activism

Alton B. Pollard asserts that Thurman appropriated "affirmation mysticism," in which encounters with God may lead to concrete social action.[14] According to Pollard, Thurman's was a form of mysticism—rooted in historic cenobitic monastic perspective—that sought to constructively engage in the process of community building. A designation of Thurman within the context of mystic activism focuses attention on

11 William Shannon, *Seeds of Peace: Contemplation and Non-violence* (New York: Crossroad, 1996), 154.

12 See Mahatma Gandhi, *Gandhi on Non-violence*, ed. Thomas Merton (New York: New Directions, 1965) for details on Gandhi's development of the conceptualization of satyagraha.

13 Shannon, *Seeds of Peace*, 153.

14 Pollard, *Mysticism*, 34.

the real potential of mysticism as a discomforting yet compelling call to action.[15]

Mystic activism, or social mysticism, is a praxis orientation to the world that relies—at least in part—on the political and intellectual arguments and dictates of society.[16] Thurman believed that transformed individuals are the first step in remaking the social order into a peaceful and just society. True community can only be established when transformed individuals act within and upon social structures and become involved in social mechanisms.

Luther E. Smith places Thurman's life within the context of the dual attributes of his mystical nature and prophetic witness. Smith writes, "Thurman's primary identity was that of a mystic, a mystic who recognized the necessity of social activism for enabling and responding to religious experience."[17] Smith further asserts that to study a prophet is to simultaneously study their people. The prophet's significance is the result of his relationship with his community.[18] Thurman wrote, "The social mystic sees that the world of things and men does not conform to the unity which he has experienced in his vision."[19]

Thurman's constant yearning was to move toward a clearer personal and communal comprehension of what he often referred to as "the irreducible essence" of life. Activist Jesse L. Jackson recounts how Thurman would often challenge him to move toward this irreducible essence. According to Jackson, Thurman insisted that if you ever developed a cultivated will, with spiritual discipline, the striving for community would persist. The irreducible essence, developed through the cultivated will with spiritual discipline, would result in spiritual and social transformation.[20]

15 Pollard, 1.
16 Pollard, 1.
17 Smith, *Howard Thurman*, 45–48.
18 Smith, 15–20.
19 Walter E. Fluker and Catherine Tumber, eds., *A Strange Freedom: The Best of Howard Thurman on Religious Experience and Public Life* (Boston: Beacon, 1998), 114.
20 Jessie L. Jackson interview by Madison Davis Lacey Jr. and Henry Hampton for *Eyes on the Prize II*, Washington University, St. Louis, MO, April 11, 1989, http://digital.wustl.edu/e/eii/eiiweb/jac5427.0519.072marc_record_interviewer_process.html.

Over the course of his life and ministry, Thurman lived into the divine moral and prophetic imperatives that the church and society share in seeking to eradicate racial hatred, economic oppression, and social disintegration and advanced the appropriation of the Christian love-ethic as foundational for constructively moving toward the realization of common ground and inclusive community. According to Anthony Neal, common ground for Thurman is the cause of any desire toward community in all living beings but specifically humans. Thurman refers to community as "realized potential." Without this level of development, human individuals are unable to actualize their highest potential.[21]

Pollard asserts that "social regeneration" is the type of mystical action in which Thurman engaged. Social regeneration discloses an ethical program working on three levels—synchronizing intraindividual (personal), interindividual (communal), and intergroup (societal) orderliness. In Thurman's case, social regeneration denotes a holistic process that is generally critical of church and society, but not in a fundamentally hostile or negating sense.[22]

The impetus for social regeneration lies not so much in social structures as in the transformation of individuals, who alone are capable of generating a force fully vibrant and sufficient to break through oppressive structures. Social regeneration is increasingly effected as more individuals experience the transforming "sense of wholeness" or ethical orderliness and the will to implement its verity in society. The aim of social regeneration is not to perpetuate conflict in society simply because or whenever there is no abiding evidence of hope but rather to facilitate and increase rapprochement between individuals and social groupings. This is the sine qua non for Thurman's advancement of the concept of "community."[23]

---

21 Anthony Neal, *Common Ground: A Comparison of the Ideas of Consciousness in the Writings of Howard Thurman and Huey Newton* (Trenton, NJ: Africa World, 2015), 69–70.

22 Pollard, *Mysticism*, 7.

23 Pollard, 7–8.

In Thurman's life and ministry, there is evidence that social regeneration can lead to social activism. The unconditional seriousness of the religious experience itself impels social corroboration, causing one to engage "the powers of this world" with a strident social dimension. The knowledge accrued in these encounters is relational and transactional in character, ushering in personally transformative systems of values and new or at the very least revitalized modes of interaction with others (community and society) and God. The impetus for social regeneration occurs when an individual's ultimate allegiances—race, creed, gender, nationality, and socioeconomic standing—are transvalued to a less defensive, penultimate status.[24]

Gandhi's Nonviolence and the Application of Satyagraha and Ahimsa

Mohandas Gandhi's philosophy was one of action. It was more than a philosophy for social engagement; it was a philosophy for social transformation. He came to believe that every person was of equal value and that oppressed people should struggle for their equality. According to Gandhi, persons must fight peacefully, and they must not hurt others while doing so. He strongly believed that unjust laws should not be obeyed but that people should not be violent in their attempts to change laws.

He warned against what he called the seven social sins, which, in his estimation, ultimately served to divide society into the powerful and the powerless. These social sins were identified as (1) politics without principle, (2) wealth without work, (3) commerce without morality, (4) pleasure without conscience, (5) education without character, (6) science without humanity, and (7) worship without sacrifice. Jim Wallis suggests that these social sins today are the accepted practices of the life of the nation (America).[25]

---

24 Pollard, 10.
25 Jim Wallis, *The Soul of Politics* (New York: New Press, 1994), xiii.

In his writings, teachings, and actions in South Africa, satyagraha became manifest as a technique for action. It is not dogmatic; it is neither static nor substantial. It is, rather, a dynamic and spiritual concept and a technique and process for action leading to personal and social transformation. In Gandhi's view, satyagraha is not intended to overwhelm one's opponent. It should not be used in an arbitrary way to rectify a situation. Satyagraha must be a last resort in an unbearable situation that merits the commitment of unlimited suffering.

Ahimsa (noninjury), the related concept used by Gandhi in the discussion of the meaning of nonviolent action, is borrowed from the Jains. Jainism, founded by Mahavira, is one of the oldest personally founded religions in India, and the Jains are known for their doctrine of the noninjury of all forms of life. Historically, Jains became merchants rather than farmers because they did not wish to destroy any form of sentient life. Even today, Jaina women wear veils over their noses and mouths to avoid breathing in any form of insect life.[26]

For Gandhi, ahimsa was the basic law of being. It can be used as the most effective principle for social action, since it is ingrained deeply in human nature and corresponds to humanity's innate desire for personal dignity, peace, justice, and freedom. Ahimsa is not preoccupied with seizing power as an end in itself; it is a way of transforming relationships in order to bring about a peaceful transfer of power.[27]

Gandhi was convinced of the power of nonviolence, with the principles of ahimsa and satyagraha as keys to resisting oppression and achieving the aims of peace. In 1926, he wrote, "Nonviolence is the greatest force humanity has been endowed with. Truth is the only goal we have through nonviolence."[28]

His conception of nonviolence, as expressed through ahimsa and satyagraha, began with the spiritual disciplines of prayer, solitude, and fasting. Nonviolence, the power of the powerless, he believed, is

---

26 Roberts, "Gandhi and King," 37.
27 Roberts, 37.
28 Mohandas K. Gandhi, "Nonviolence—the Greatest Force," *World Tomorrow*, October 1926.

the power of God, the power of Truth and love that goes beyond the physical world into the realm of the spiritual. This power can overcome death, as God revealed through Jesus's nonviolence, his crucifixion, and his subsequent resurrection in the resisting community.[29]

For Gandhi, ahimsa and satyagraha became manifest as principled techniques for action toward nonviolence, peacemaking, and community building that could lead to spiritual and social transformation. Satyagraha aimed to penetrate the barriers of prejudice, ill will, dogmatism, self-righteousness, and selfishness and to reach out to and activate the soul of the opponent. However degenerate, dogmatic, or violent an individual might appear to be, according to the satyagrahi, they had a soul and hence the capacity to feel for other human beings and, on some level, acknowledge their common humanity. Satyagraha was essentially "surgery of the soul," a way of activating "soul-force"— and "suffering love" was the best way to accomplish this.

Gandhi's Influence on Thurman

Beginning in the 1930s, many African American leaders went to India seeking Mohandas Gandhi's advice and seeking to study his nonviolent method, with Howard and Sue Bailey Thurman and Edward and Phenola Carroll being the first African Americans to meet personally with Gandhi in 1936.

In 1935, Thurman, then Howard University's dean of the Andrew Rankin Memorial Chapel and professor of religion, was asked to be a member of a delegation on a "Pilgrimage of Friendship" to India, Ceylon, and Burma. Thurman's participation was considered important because, "in a country divided by religious beliefs into 'Touchables' and 'Untouchables,' rich and poor, the testimony of representatives from another country's minority group might be far-reaching."[30]

---

29 John Dear, "The Experiments of Gandhi: Nonviolence in the Nuclear Age," *Fellowship* (January/February 1988): 98–119.

30 Yates, *Howard Thurman*, 95.

Members of the delegation lectured and discussed issues at forty-five academic centers in these three countries from October 1935 through the spring of 1936. Thurman was questioned continually about the compatibility of Christianity with Black people's struggle for human dignity in America. White Christians and churches had a history of being insensitive to Black people's worth and freedom. Thurman answered queries by distinguishing Christianity from the religion of Jesus. Despite this clarification, he admitted that "all answers had to be defensive because there was not a single instance known to me in which a local church had a completely integrated membership."[31]

Embarking on "a serious intellectual quest for a method to eliminate social evil," while on their trip to India, the Thurmans and Carrolls had asked for a chance to visit with Mohandas Gandhi. (Rev. Edward Carroll would eventually become one of the first African American bishops in the United Methodist Church, elected in 1972.) Gandhi had written welcoming them. Remarkably, he broke his fast for the duration of the delegation's visit, and they met for several hours in Bardoli, India. When the four Americans arrived, Gandhi went out of his way to greet them. He did not always do that with visitors. His secretary, Mahadev Desai, told Howard Thurman that he had never seen Gandhi greet visitors so warmly in his many years with him.

Their conversation was Gandhi's first opportunity to engage African Americans in a discussion concerning their respective struggles for freedom. Often an outspoken critic of traditional Christianity, Gandhi believed that Western interpretations of Christianity contributed to racial, economic, and gender discrimination and led to segregation of the world's people.

Their meeting was a seminal moment in each of their spiritual and intellectual journeys as parallels between the caste system of Hinduism and the segregationist exclusivity in the praxis of American Christianity became apparent.

---

31 Howard Thurman, *Footprints of a Dream: The Dawn of the Idea of the Church for the Fellowship of All Peoples: Letters between Alfred Fisk and Howard Thurman, 1943–1944* (San Francisco: Lawton & Alfred Kennedy, 1975), 24.

Thurman asked Gandhi to define nonviolence. Gandhi said he hoped it would be love in the Pauline sense—love as spelled out in Paul's second letter to the Corinthians—plus the struggle for justice. Thurman also asked Gandhi whether South African Blacks had joined his nonviolence movement. Gandhi replied, "No, they hadn't." He said he deliberately did not want to amalgamate those two struggles at that time. He added that this was due to South Africans' lack of understanding of the meaning and methods of nonviolence. But Gandhi's work there had an impact on influential leaders in South Africa such as Albert Luthuli who, like Martin Luther King Jr., was awarded the Nobel Peace Prize.[32]

Thurman later recalled that Gandhi asked persistent, pragmatic questions about American Negroes, the course of slavery, and how Blacks had survived it.[33] Gandhi inquired about the plight of Blacks in the United States with respect to issues such as economics, interracial marriage, and politics.

In the course of their discussion, Thurman recalled the following: "One of the things that puzzled him [Gandhi] was why the slaves [in America] did not become Moslems. 'Because,' said Gandhi, 'the Moslem religion is the only religion in the world in which no lines are drawn from within the religious fellowship. Once you are in, you are all the way in. This is not true in Christianity; it isn't true in Buddhism or Hinduism. If you had become Moslem, then even though you were a slave, in the faith you would be equal to your master.'"[34]

Gandhi asked his American visitors if they would sing a Negro spiritual for him. He was greatly moved as Sue Bailey Thurman sang two familiar Negro spirituals: "Were You There When They Crucified My Lord" and "We Are Climbing Jacob's Ladder." To all who heard them, these spirituals expressed the hopes and aspirations of the oppressed to climb higher and higher until freedom's goal has been reached.[35]

---

32 Thurman, 24.
33 Thurman, 24.
34 *With Head and Heart: The Autobiography of Howard Thurman* (New York: Harcourt Brace Jovanovich, 1979), 132.
35 Roberts, "Gandhi and King," 32.

After hearing these spirituals, Gandhi said to the four, "Well if it comes true it may be through the Negroes [in America] that the unadulterated message of nonviolence will be delivered to the world."[36] In other words, by this time in 1936, he was not sure that it would be India that would deliver a workable model of nonviolence to the world, and he gave expression to a prophetic intuition that African Americans would lead in demonstrating and modeling nonviolence on a global scale. The American civil rights movement of the 1950s and 1960s would confirm Gandhi's inclination.

An important contribution that Gandhi made to Thurman's work was offering a global perspective on the human condition. The anti-imperialist movement then surging through South Asia, exemplified by the implementation of ethical nonviolence and noncooperation on the part of the masses, provided the first critical international referent for Thurman's understanding of the relationship that exists between religion and the social world. Thurman's wartime essay "The Fascist Masquerade" offers a glimpse into this aspect of his development.[37] Later, other arenas of protest—colonial Africa, Nazi Germany, First Nations communities in Canada, and Native American communities in the United States—would further sensitize Thurman's thinking in this regard.

The trip to South Asia served as a catalyst for Thurman's understanding of the relationships among what he considered authentic religion, human suffering, and inclusive community. Here, he was confronted with the tension of political and social patterns of exclusion that rivaled racial discrimination in America. He discovered that the Hindu untouchable and the African American were similarly bound in their subordinate (social) status. Equally unsettling was the fact that religion and culture had conjoined to legitimate and encourage this sordid quarantine.[38]

---

36 Mohandas Gandhi, "Nonviolence," 124.
37 Pollard, *Mysticism*, 38. Pollard makes reference to Thurman's essay "The Fascist Masquerade," which appears as chapter 4 in *The Church and Organized Movements*, ed. Randolph C. Miller (New York: Harper & Brothers, 1946), 82–100.
38 Pollard, 23.

At the conclusion of the 1935–36 pilgrimage, looking down into Afghanistan at the Khyber Pass (between Afghanistan and West Pakistan), Thurman experienced a vision of a church that would be open to "seekers of all colors and creeds." He was compelled to see if "experiences of spiritual unity among peoples could be more compelling than the experiences which divide them." This vision would become the thrust of his spiritual and social witness for the rest of his life. Thurman wrote, "We saw clearly what we must do somehow when we returned to America. We knew that we must test whether a religious fellowship could be developed in America that was capable of cutting across all racial barriers, with a carryover into the common life, a fellowship that would alter the behavior patterns of those involved."[39]

Upon leaving India, Thurman realized that an influx of new ideas and new ways of seeing and being was necessary if Christianity and the religion of Jesus were to approach radical forms of inclusive community in America. As a result of his conversation with Gandhi, Thurman felt assured that nonviolence, as expressed in Gandhian principles and the practice of ahimsa and satyagraha, could transform whatever difficulties it confronted. The techniques might have to be refined—individuals would need to go through radical preparation to be faithful disciples of the method and large numbers of people might suffer and die—but the moral and spiritual imperatives for nonviolence would prevail over experiences of violence.[40]

In formulating his response to Gandhi's critique of Christianity and the race problem in America, Thurman began to integrate Gandhian principles of unity and nonviolent social change into his own Christian pacifism and mysticism upon returning to the United States.[41] He returned to the United States with "an enhanced interpretation of the meaning of nonviolence."[42] From Gandhi, "a man who [was] rooted in the basic mysticism of the [Hindu] Brahma," Thurman

---

39 Thurman, *Footprints of a Dream*, 95.
40 Gandhi, "Nonviolence," 105–6.
41 Fluker and Tumber, *Strange Freedom*, 7.
42 Pollard, *Mysticism*, 37.

learned the life-affirming concepts of ahimsa and satyagraha. He found
in Gandhi a kindred mind and spirit who refused to think in terms of a
disconnected Truth, God, or ultimate reality but focused his attention
on that which was preeminently practical and spiritual.[43]

Thurman returned to Howard University convinced that a religious
fellowship in America that would unite persons across social and
creedal divisions had to be conceived. At Rankin Chapel, he began to
experiment with the arts, meditation, and innovative liturgies to create worship experiences that affirmed the unity within the audiences
and that had religious, social, and philosophical diversity.[44] Thurman
discovered that common religious experiences had the potential to
transcend and diminish human separation and difference to transform
disintegrated, broken human relationships into authentic, inclusive
community.

Thurman and Gandhi: Toward a
Theo-praxis of Resistance and Peace

For Gandhi and Thurman, community is built not on presupposed
division but on the basic unity of humanity. As Gandhi saw it, the full,
consistent practice of nonviolence and peace demands a solid metaphysical and religious basis both in being and in God and is an expression of resistance in itself. This comes before subjective good intentions
and sincerity. For the Hindu, this metaphysical basis was provided by
the Vedantist doctrine of the Atman, the true transcendent self, which
alone is absolutely real and before which the empirical self of the individual must be effaced in the faithful practice of dharma.[45]

While Gandhi's influence on Thurman's emergent leanings toward
a resistance ethic of nonviolence and peacemaking was evident, Thurman's thought and praxis were rooted in his experiences of being

43 Pollard, 37.
44 Smith, *Howard Thurman*, 9.
45 Thomas Merton, "Blessed Are the Meek," in *Faith and Nonviolence: Christian Teaching and Christian Practice* (Notre Dame, IN: University of Notre Dame Press, 1958).

personally victimized by American racism. He was acutely aware that racism attacked human dignity and freedom. His mystical experiences, however, provided the assurance that he was a beloved child of God and that harmonious relatedness is the underlying structure of reality. Racism denied the truth about God's intent for creation. It put the welfare of the community in crisis. The prophetic questions for Thurman became, How could he help shape a transformational social reality that conformed with his religious beliefs? How could he speak to the crisis by restoring the community's (especially America's) sense of well-being?[46]

Clearly, Thurman's conception of Christian love was rooted in the example of the unconditional love of Christ. The practice of unconditional love is essential to breaking down social barriers such as racism. He suggested that nonviolent protests (e.g., boycotts, noncooperation, demonstrations, sit-ins) were key means of providing shock and transforming the social order. The development of a philosophy of nonviolent protest in the Black struggle is a foremost achievement of his social witness. Here, Thurman made a significant contribution to providing a peaceful method for change in American race relations.

Luther Smith also asserts that contrary to most public perceptions, it was Thurman's conception of community that served as a primary philosophical foundation for the American civil rights movement of the 1950s and 1960s. Thurman's concept of community tied the Black struggle for freedom to divine will and destiny. The Black struggle then became a holy struggle. In defining the ethic of nonviolence, Thurman gave the freedom movement a holy mechanism.[47]

In Thurman's mind, Jesus of Nazareth is the revelation of how personality creates community; Jesus personifies the transforming power of love. The conditions and circumstances of Jesus's life are significant in understanding Christianity and the meaning of Jesus in the world.[48] In 1948, Thurman delivered a series of lectures at Huston

46 Smith, *Howard Thurman*, 107.
47 Smith, 139.
48 Smith, 62.

College (now Huston-Tillotson College) in Austin, Texas, which in 1949 was published as *Jesus and the Disinherited*. The book offered a radical perspective on the mission, ministry, and teachings of Jesus, as compared with the general view of the majority culture at the time. Throughout, Thurman showed that Jesus's ministry in the world addressed the needs and aspirations of the disinherited. He pointed out that the concern of Jesus is still for the disinherited.[49]

In *Jesus and the Disinherited*, Thurman emphasized the social circumstances of Jesus, a poor and oppressed person, and then concluded that the religion of Jesus was a creative response that emerged from this social location to deal with transforming these conditions of oppression for developing an authentic community. How might impoverished ethnic and religious minorities respond to the material and spiritual assaults of imperial oppression? Jesus's example suggests a response of courage, truth-telling, and love.[50] According to Thurman, the ethical example of Jesus continues to have relevance for people who find themselves backed up against the wall.[51]

Alonzo Johnson points out that Jesus—as explicated and appropriated by Thurman—came to offer the good news of liberation to the disinherited.[52] Jesus came preaching a message of hope, one of peace with justice and righteousness, a radical hope that authentic community could and would be actualized. Amid the hopelessness, nihilism, despair, and injustice evident in the church and world today, Jesus offers the same hope.

Thurman asserted that Jesus was aware of the cultural context of his ministry. He knew that his teachings regarding God's justice, love, mercy, forgiveness, and peace would get him into trouble. Yet he

---

49 Olin Moyd, *Sacred Art: Preaching and Theology in the African American Tradition* (Valley Forge, PA: Judson, 1995), 22.

50 Greg Moses, *Revolution of Conscience: Martin Luther King, Jr., and the Philosophy of Nonviolence* (New York: Guilford, 1997), 151.

51 Howard Thurman, *Jesus and the Disinherited* (Richmond, IN: Friends United, 1969), 11.

52 Alonzo Johnson, *Good News for the Disinherited: Howard Thurman on Jesus of Nazareth and Human Liberation* (New York: University Press of America, 1997). Johnson provides a detailed treatment and explication of Thurman's Christology, with liberation as the defining motif of Christ's mission and ministry.

remained faithful to his mission and sought to perpetually live the God-inspired message that he had been given. There was no possibility of authentic and peaceful community without careful and constructive attention to the disinherited. Thurman asserted that the mistreatment of America's disinherited and acceptance of "the will to segregate" are betrayals of American and Christian ideals of community building.

Gandhi's experiments in Truth revealed that the mandate of the Sermon on the Mount—to love one's enemies—is of critical importance. In all of his public uses of nonviolence, he consistently expressed a desire for reconciliation and friendship with his opponent. He also always tried to stand in solidarity with the outcasts of society and to speak up for the rights of the marginalized as he begged his fellow Indians to banish untouchability from their hearts and lives.[53]

It is known that the Sermon on the Mount impressed Gandhi more than any other part of the Christian Scriptures. And although he never was convinced that it was necessary to abandon Hinduism for Christianity, he was able to defend the best that he had gleaned from the study of Christianity. He urged people to live more like Jesus Christ, practice the Christian faith without adulterating it or toning it down, and emphasize love and make it the driving force of life and action. It is not surprising that Gandhi asserted that his encounter with Christianity made him a better Hindu. His attention to some of the noblest principles of Christianity enriched his life as a religious person. Although he remained a Hindu, his understanding and expression of religious experience were more profound due to his engagement with Christianity.

Thurman concluded that love is the force that facilitates nonviolent change and inclusive community is the best expression of love. He considered the terms *reconciliation* and *love* to be synonymous.[54] He defined love as "the intelligent, kindly but stern expression of kinship of one individual for another, having as its purpose the maintenance

---

53 See Dear, "Experiments of Gandhi."
54 Howard Thurman, *Disciplines of the Spirit* (Richmond, IN: Friends United, 1987), 122.

and furtherance of life at its highest level."[55] Love responds to an individual's basic need of being cared for. It participates in the attempt to actualize potential and therefore completes the fragmented and unfulfilled personality. But on a larger scale, it brings together separated lives. It makes apparent the significance of relationships by stressing how interdependence is inherent in all of life. Love creates community.[56]

For Thurman, the hope of community is at the heart of Christ's work; in Christ, human beings are sons and daughters of God and brothers and sisters to one another. The church, the community of those who confess Christ as Lord, is an embodiment of unity and peace within history. For this reason, the church must help the world achieve peace while knowing that peace among human beings is possible only if there is real justice for all. Thurman asserted that community by its very nature includes persons of different races, sexes, ages, religions, cultures, viewpoints, lifestyles, and stages of development and serves to integrate them into a whole that is greater—more actualized and dynamic—than the sum of its parts. Forms of disintegration and disunity are, therefore, to be understood as antithetical to peace and community.

For both Gandhi and Thurman, the loving community of peace, justice, and equality can only be attained by loving and nonviolent means. Community cannot be built with the tools of hatred. Nonviolence responds in a caring way to the perpetrator of violence. It announces that the well-being of the individuals involved is of ultimate concern. It moves the level of confrontation to a higher spiritual plane. Instead of merely defeating one's offender physically or psychologically, one begins to create the climate for love to be a force, which has to be dealt with within the context of relationships and fellowship. Love and reconciliation offer new possibilities for peacemaking. Nonviolence permits love to enter conflict creatively and address the prevailing spiritual ills of separation, fear, and hatred and move toward peace with justice.

55 Howard Thurman, *Deep Is the Hunger: Meditations for Apostles of Sensitiveness* (New York: Harper & Brothers, 1951), 109.
56 Smith, *Howard Thurman*, 50.

In the final analysis, through their lives, leadership, and teaching, Gandhi and Thurman offer insights into how reconciliation and love can serve as means of overcoming forms of disintegration and moving toward peace and community. Both spoke to the divine and moral imperative that all people share in seeking to eradicate racial hatred and social disintegration and advanced nonviolence—as expressed through satyagraha and the Christian love-ethic—as a foundational necessity for constructively moving toward the realization of authentic community and peace. Both affirmed the divine intent is for the human family to live in community as interrelated members while the human dignity of all persons is affirmed and while peace with justice exists.

Bibliography

Bennett, Lerone, Jr. "Eulogy of Howard Thurman: Tributes to Genius." *African American Pulpit* (Winter 1981): 63–66.

Dash, Michael I. N., Jonathan Jackson, and Stephen C. Rasor. *Hidden Wholeness: An African American Spirituality for Individuals and Communities*. Cleveland: United Church, 1997.

Dear, John. "The Experiments of Gandhi: Nonviolence in the Nuclear Age." *Fellowship* (January/February 1988): 98–119.

Fluker, Walter E. "Dangerous Memories and Redemptive Possibilities: Reflections on the Life and Work of Howard Thurman." In *Black Leaders and Ideologies in the South: Resistance and Nonviolence*, edited by Preston King and Walter E. Fluker, 147–176. New York: Routledge, 2005.

Fluker, Walter E., and Catherine Tumber, eds. *A Strange Freedom: The Best of Howard Thurman on Religious Experience and Public Life*. Boston: Beacon, 1998.

Gandhi, Mahatma. *Gandhi on Non-violence*. Edited by Thomas Merton. New York: New Directions, 1965.

———. "Nonviolence—the Greatest Force." *World Tomorrow*, October 1926, 100–124.

Gandhi, Rajmohan. "Gandhi's Unfulfilled Legacy: Prospects for Reconciliation in Racial/Ethnic Conflict." Cynthia Wedel Lecture, Church's Center for Theology and Public Policy, Wesley Theological Seminary, Washington, DC, April 27, 1995.

Jackson, Jesse L. Interview by Madison Davis Lacey Jr. and Henry Hampton for *Eyes on the Prize II*. Washington University, St. Louis, MO, April 11, 1989. http://digital.wustl.edu/e/eii/eiiweb/jac5427.0519.072marc_record_interviewer_process.html.

Johnson, Alonzo. *Good News for the Disinherited: Howard Thurman on Jesus of Naza-reth and Human Liberation.* New York: University Press of America, 1997.

Merton, Thomas. "Blessed Are the Meek." In *Faith and Nonviolence: Christian Teach-ing and Christian Practice,* 14–29. Notre Dame, IN: University of Notre Dame Press, 1958.

Moses, Greg. *Revolution of Conscience: Martin Luther King, Jr., and the Philosophy of Nonviolence.* New York: Guilford, 1997.

Moyd, Olin. *Sacred Art: Preaching and Theology in the African American Tradition.* Valley Forge, PA: Judson, 1995.

Neal, Anthony. *Common Ground: A Comparison of the Ideas of Consciousness in the Writings of Howard Thurman and Huey Newton.* Trenton, NJ: Africa World, 2015.

Pollard, Alton. *Mysticism and Social Change: The Social Witness of Howard Thurman.* New York: Peter Lang, 1992.

Roberts, Deotis J. "Gandhi and King: On Conflict Resolution." *Shalom Papers: A Journal of Theology and Public Policy* 11, no. 2 (Spring 2000): 29–42.

Shannon, William. *Seeds of Peace: Contemplation and Non-violence.* New York: Cross-road, 1996.

Smith, Huston. *The World's Religions.* San Francisco: HarperCollins, 1991.

Smith, Luther E. *Howard Thurman: The Mystic as Prophet.* Richmond, IN: Friends United, 2007.

Thurman, Howard. *Deep Is the Hunger: Meditations for Apostles of Sensitiveness.* New York: Harper & Brothers, 1951.

———. *Disciplines of the Spirit.* Richmond, IN: Friends United, 1987.

———. *Footprints of a Dream: The Dawn of the Idea of the Church for the Fellowship of All Peoples: Letters between Alfred Fisk and Howard Thurman, 1943–1944.* San Fran-cisco: Lawton & Alfred Kennedy, 1975.

———. *For the Inward Journey.* Richmond, IN: Friends United, 1984.

———. *Jesus and the Disinherited.* Richmond, IN: Friends United, 1969.

———. *With Head and Heart: The Autobiography of Howard Thurman.* New York: Har-court Brace Jovanovich, 1979.

Wallis, Jim. *The Soul of Politics.* New York: New Press, 1994.

Yates, Elizabeth. *Howard Thurman: Portrait of a Practical Dreamer.* New York: John Day, 1964.

Index